RISE
TO SEEK HIM

The Joy of Effective Prayer

RON MEYERS

Soar
with
Eagles

A Publisher Driven by Vision and Purpose

Library of Congress Cataloging-in-Publication Data

Meyers, Ron, PhD
    Rise to Seek Him / Ron Meyers, PhD
        p. cm.
    ISBN-10: 0-9771403-6-9
    ISBN-13: 978-0-9771403-6-7

    1. Religion. 2. Self-improvement. 3. Theology. I. Title

Library of Congress Control Number 2007930271

"The names and characterizations in this book (with the exception of the author's wife, sons, and other authors referred to in the text) are drawn from the author's personal experience and rendered pseudonymously and as fictional composites. Any similarity between the names and characterizations of these individuals and real people is unintended and purely coincidental."

Scripture texts used in this work, unless otherwise indicated, are taken from the *New International Version*; copyright © 1978 by the New York International Bible Society.

First Edition

Published by
Soar with Eagles
2809 Laurel Crossing Circle, Rogers, AR 72758, USA
www.soarhigher.com

Interior design and illustration by Carrie Perrien Smith
Cover design by T.J. Pike
Edited by Jana Wegner and Michelle Crissup
Illustrations by Matthew McDaniel

Printed in the United States of America

Contents

Introduction

On June 14, 2002, my wife, Char, and I departed from Tulsa embarking on a six-month sabbatical/mission trip. It included four cities in South Africa and 74 cities or villages in nine different states in India. We conducted 50 seminars plus numerous other one-time speaking engagements during that period. Half of them dealt with marriage and family studies and the other half with pastoral and Christian leadership training. Even though I had been in professional Christian ministry 37 years at the time, those six months led to new patterns of ministry that are so much more fruitful than previous years that I do not want to go back to the old patterns.

I am compelled to share the experiment with you. I want to tell you how it has brought me into a new dimension of ministry. I am the same person I was before — I still wrestle with all the vices and challenges every Christian faces. Yet, because I am doing one thing differently, I am more fruitful; have more insight; and feel stronger in my spirit. I am amazed that I have more doors of ministry over which I personally have no control open to me, and my sense of partnership with God is keener than I ever imagined possible. Here is what has made the difference — I am praying more!

Much of what educators learn, we gain from books. Nevertheless, most of what I have learned during that sabbatical/mission trip and since, I learned from experience — not books. In *Habits of Highly Effective Christians,* I argued for the legitimacy of learning from experience. *Rise to Seek Him* assumes that legitimacy and carries the discussion forward with a pointed life illustration of how to learn by purposeful experimentation and intentional observation.

Briefly, here are some of the things I learned.

- **Learn from experiments.** Experiments, even in spiritual matters, are a legitimate way to learn. We will never know what God might do through us if we were to pray more unless we experiment. In experimenting with increased amounts of prayer, we are not testing God. Rather, we are attempting to learn about prayer.

- **Pray more.** We never deserve the answers to our prayers, and God is better at answering than we are at praying. Nevertheless, there is something of a *quid pro quo* element in prayer — God works when we pray. Likewise, there are things He does not do when we do not pray.

- **Change.** Change *is* possible later in life. We are not limited to past ministry patterns if we are willing to try something new. We may unknowingly plateau in our growth and development. If a major spiritual growth spurt, discovery, or new dimension in ministry has not occurred for a while in your life, do something different.

- **Ask.** He is "able to do immeasurably more than we can ask or imagine." If our lives or careers do not have more happening in them than only what we have asked for or imagined, we are not experiencing all God has for us. If He is not doing "immeasurably more" than we can ask or imagine, we are living beneath our privileges.

- **Pursue God.** The intercessor should be as disciplined, punctual, and diligent in the pursuit of God as any other professional who rises early in pursuit of his vocation.

- **Unlock the Word through prayer.** Nothing is as important to effective Christians — whether full-time ministers or non-professional Christian workers — as prayer and Bible reading or study. People who listen to preachers want to hear from God. Moreover, Christians called to other vocations need the presence and blessing of God on their work and ministries just as much as professional preachers do on theirs.

Too many times, we stop growing too soon. When we reach a mature age and make fewer mistakes, we should remember that our best years are yet ahead of us. Whether it is beginning to run marathons as I did at age 55, discovering ways to make prayer more effective and efficient at age 58, or committing to pray more, new discoveries can lead to new fruitfulness in life.

I have had major life-changing experiences concerning my walk with God at ages 6, 19, 35, and more recently when I was 58. Jesus said the Gardener wants fruitful branches to bear more fruit — he is willing to prune us so we can. God can help even older people learn new things. Personal development has little to do with age and much to do with eagerness or willingness to learn. After 37 years of public ministry, I was about to discover that all over again. You, too, could easily experience a remarkable change.

I am a full-time minister and write from my experience of prayer in my professional career. Yet the principles I learned and present in this book are equally applicable to any Christian who wants God to be more involved in his or her career or business. Full-time Christian ministers are not the only ones God uses greatly and neither are they the only ones who are eager to seek God with their whole hearts. It will not require much of a struggle for you to apply the same ideas to your situation. Prayer helps each one of us have greater success. Increased and better prayer will add much to what God accomplishes through your life.

$\overline{x}$

CHAPTER ONE

God's Surprise Agenda

*"Do not merely listen to the word,
and so deceive yourselves. Do what it says."*

James 1:22

I was a professor of Missions. After six years of teaching in the United States, I applied for and received a sabbatical leave — a break from classroom responsibilities in order to stay abreast of developments in my field.

Several students of mine in the School of Theology and Missions, a graduate school at Oral Roberts University (ORU), had returned to India after graduation. They had given me long-standing invitations to join them in ministry. I made plans to visit three of these students on my sabbatical.

To prepare, I designed questions that would allow me to determine how much of their American educations were applicable in India and what aspects had been the most helpful. My three student-friends are involved in indigenous Indian organizations in which future pastors are being trained for Christian ministry. The invitations to participate in their ministries provided ideal opportunities to research my areas of interest.

The Original Research Intent

One of the more important subjects taught in the Master of Arts in Missions curriculum is Contextualized Theology. In this course, international students are often eager to know what liberty they have to develop a theology that relates to important issues in their cultures better than American theology does. American students, on the other hand, are often surprised to learn that they need to tailor their theologies to address different issues in non-Western cultures.

During my sabbatical, I intended to research the usefulness of the principles I had taught in my Contextualized Theology class. I teach that we should strive for Christian truth that is applicable in the local contexts, so our theologies are both true to the Bible and relevant to the local culture. I wanted to know if I had succeeded.

As in any discipline, there are "arm-chair theorists" and practical field researchers. I wanted to be one of the latter. To grasp the important issues facing today's missionaries, this meant I should be involved in field work again — the ministry of training pastors in another cultural context.

I heartily accepted my Indian students' invitations. Through extensive e-mail exchanges from January to May of 2002, we planned schedules, curricula, lectures, pastors' conferences, and guest teaching commitments.

Happily, my wife Char, at the time a candidate for the Doctor of Education degree at Oral Roberts University, was eager to join me on the trip. She accepted invitations to use her newly acquired educational expertise in the area of Educational Leadership. She was also invited to teach Christian education subjects — her long-standing favorites.

We also responded to another long-standing invitation from Mount Carmel Ministry (MCM) of Johannesburg. They had asked me to return to South Africa for ministry among Bible College students and pastoral staff members. With Char as my traveling companion and ministry partner, it was easy to agree to add a two-month ministry visit in South Africa to the four-month sabbatical/mission trip planned for India.

Teaching on Prayer

On June 24, after being in South Africa for eight days, I began a five-week course on Pastoral Leadership. I presented a lecture on the subject of "The Pastor's Prayer Life." In my teaching that day, I challenged the participants to actually increase their own prayer times. Before they could effectively encourage their future congregations to pray, they needed to know how to pray themselves. As they learned to pray, they in turn could say to others, "This is how I pray. Follow my example."

This is much preferred to saying, "We should pray more." Teaching by example is more effective than saying we all ought to do something different than we are willing to do ourselves. Platitudes or "must-dos" are weak teaching instruments — they only produce guilt.

With this in mind and as an illustration of teaching by example, I told my students that I spent the first two hours of every day alone with God in prayer. I explained that this was enough time for me personally, and recommended they consider increasing their amount of prayer time according to how they felt God was leading them.

I shared that I use the Lord's Prayer as an outline. This use of the Lord's Prayer begins with praise, advances to inviting His Kingdom and will to earth, deals with daily provisions, forgiveness, and confrontation with evil spiritual forces and concludes with praise. Everything I need to pray about can be inserted in this comprehensive outline.

The Beginning of an Experiment in Prayer

About that same time, during my first week working with Mount Carmel Ministry, I had noticed a book called *God's Generals* by Roberts Liardon in the library of a pastoral staff member. I asked if I could borrow it and began reading this inspiring book. Chapter after chapter, I was impressed by how much time fruitful men and women of God with gifts of miracles and healing spent in prayer. It provided me with a greater challenge than many of the things I had read over the years *about* prayer.

By the second week of teaching Pastoral Leadership — just eight days after telling my class that I thought I was praying enough — I decided to conduct an experiment:

What would happen if a person with a teaching gift began to pray with the same intensity and commitment to intercession demonstrated by the men and women in *God's Generals?*

On July 9, 2002, I made the announcement to Char and the host pastor and his wife with whom we were staying — I would begin spending more time out on the hillside near their home where I was comfortable praying alone. I urged them not to worry about me. I was just conducting an experiment in prayer and would be out four hours each day instead of just two.

That very evening, I was told I had been invited to speak at a Sunday morning service at Grace Bible Church, the largest and most dynamic church in Soweto. Soweto, originally an acronym for Southwest Township, is well-known as the hotbed of racial unrest during the *apartheid* period. The Holy Spirit whispered to me that He was already at work and that this invitation was in response to my experiment in increased prayer. I had already heard of Pastor Mosa Sono and the very powerful work being done at Grace. In fact, when I was speaking previously at another smaller church in Soweto, I experienced a twinge of disappointment over not being scheduled at Grace Bible Church. O wretched ambition!

By the time I spoke at Grace, I had already preached the message of "The Power and Danger of Prayer" three times in South Africa. The sermon was well received, and I was becoming familiar with the right way to express each thought. However, I was in no way prepared for what happened at Grace.

Char ministered in music with an uplifting segment of worship music. Once she finished, I was introduced and I walked to the pulpit. Almost without looking at my sermon notes and certainly with no bondage to them, I began to teach the lessons in my message. Like most preachers, there have been times when I spoke with greater liberty. However, this time was intensely different. Never in my 37 years of public speaking and preaching had I delivered God's Word with such authority, precision, conciseness, and power.

Char, seated on the front row, immediately recognized the new freedom with which I spoke. She later told me she laughed in her spirit all the way through the sermon. It is true that the 2,000 plus attendees were responsive, but I knew that much more than human response had added energy to the message that day.

I might have been inclined to believe that the experience at Grace Bible Church was an isolated case. Perhaps it was the result of the mature zeal that this congregation has for God and His Word. I do not claim to always speak with the same power evident that morning; but I can say that the increased authority and anointing has continued since doubling the time I spend in daily prayer.

Does God anoint according to the amount of time spent in prayer? Are quid pro quo exchanges with God possible? Does God work as a **payment of** or in **exchange for** our prayer; or does His sovereignty have more control than my puny efforts?

I can't answer all those questions yet, but I do know that the experiment — doubling my prayer time in order to see what would happen if someone with the teaching gift were to be more serious about prayer — began right away to produce something new in me.

The Legitimacy of Experimentation in Spiritual Matters

God invites us to reason with him.

> "'Come now, let us reason together,' says the Lord" (Isaiah 1:18).

> Job 33:14 says, "For God does speak — now one way, now another — though man may not perceive it."

> Proverbs 25:2 says, "It is the glory of God to conceal a matter; to search out a matter is the glory of kings."

It seems like God invites experimentation and discovery by concealing some of his treasured ideas. Experiments, motivated by an honest inquiring mind, are one way God communicates with us.

A prayer experiment is a solid way to discover how to increase your effectiveness in the special gifts that God gave you. Anyone can experiment with prayer. Spending hours in prayer each day has long been largely limited to the Christian ministries of deliverance, miracles, healing, and evangelism. Nevertheless, to have an effective teaching ministry, a teacher also needs the strong touch of the Spirit of God. No longer do I wistfully observe that miracle workers and healing evangelists seem to have a more dramatic or interesting ministry. My own experiment with increased prayer gives evidence that a teacher too can exercise powerful influence with his gifts. I suspect this is also true for you regardless of what gifts God has given you.

Sometimes words seem trite or meaningless. At other times or with other speakers, words are authoritative and convincing. What is the difference? Because of my experiment, it seems evident that words have added weight, value, and persuasive power over listeners when the Holy Spirit bears witness to them in answer to serious prayer. I had prayed my two hours a day, fasted regularly, and spent hours with God over the previous 37 years of ministry. However, I had never experienced the consistent and continuing touch of the Spirit of God on my teaching, lectures, preaching, and study of God's Word as I have since July 9, 2002.

God does not reject a person who wants to increase in fruitfulness. Don't you want to be even more fruitful regardless of the degree of fruitfulness you are experiencing currently when using your gifts?

You, too, can conduct your own experiment with increased time spent in prayer to see what greater things God might do through you in the exercise of your gifts. Conduct the test and see if more time in prayer produces more fruit or not. Prayer releases, enhances, facilitates, and expands the use of anyone's gifts. Prayer does not make us become someone we are not, but rather brings out new fullness in the use of natural and spiritual gifts — existing or dormant. Prayer may not change your unique combination of gifts, but it will more fully release the gifts you have.

When we see the conditions under which God blesses and compare them with the circumstances under which His blessings are not so evident, should we not attempt to learn to duplicate the state of affairs under which He blesses? We certainly must!

> When we see the conditions under which God blesses and compare them with the circumstances under which His blessings are not so evident, should we not attempt to learn to duplicate the state of affairs under which He blesses? We certainly must!

Should I Share My Experiences?

I do not know if other ministers who spend hours in prayer talk about it or not — there are specific scriptural instructions not to brag about how much we pray. I'm inclined not say anything about my personal prayer life. However, I have a strong need to share this discovery with other pastors, missionaries, and Christians. I want them to know increasing prayer time will allow them to experience greater authority in teaching, preaching, and counseling. It will allow them to receive greater wisdom in pursuit of any God-given career.

For my experiment to benefit others, I *must* share it. To me, as a trainer of Christian leaders, sharing is the way I can challenge others in my efforts to lead by example just as Paul did by sharing his experiences and then inviting others to follow him.

The Biblical Basis of Teaching by Example

Jesus taught by example. "I have set for you an example that you should do as I have done" (John 13:15). He also taught us to, "… let your light shine before others, that they may see your good deeds and glorify your Father in heaven (Matthew 5:16). The Bible teaches us to watch for good examples and imitate them. "Remember your leaders … consider the outcome of their way of life and imitate their faith" (Hebrews 13:7). The New Testament tells us that we are to learn from the examples in the Old Testament. "These things happened to them as examples …" (1 Corinthians 10:11).

Paul repeatedly encouraged his readers to imitate his example. His motive in asking his disciples to follow his example was not pride. Instead, he was using an effective and trusted teaching method — teaching by example. "Follow my example, as I follow the example of Christ (1 Corinthians 11:1). "Therefore I urge you to imitate me" (1 Corinthians 4:16). "Join with others in following my example, brothers, and take note of those who live according to the pattern we gave you" (Philippians 3:17). "… our gospel came to you not simply with words … you became imitators of us and of the Lord … you became a model to all the believers in Macedonia and Achaia. (1 Thessalonians 1:5-7). He said he did some things deliberately "… in order to offer ourselves as a model for you to imitate (2 Thessalonians 3:9). Paul also taught others, in turn, to teach by example. "Set an example for the believers in speech, in conduct, in love, in faith, and in purity (1 Timothy 4:12). "In everything, set them an example by doing what is good (Titus 2:7).

It is no coincidence that the apostle who invited his readers to follow his example numerous times is also the only New Testament writer to write extensively about his own life experiences, hardships, prayers, faithfulness, and attitudes in actual ministry. This was planned. He writes about his own life and encourages us to follow his example. It's an effective way to invite others to do it too. The problem with teaching by example, however, is that you have to be good at whatever you are teaching to teach by example. This automatically reduces the number of effective teachers, but then again, who would want to learn to do something from someone who was not very good at doing it?

Only Jesus is an example to follow on all points. The rest of us have only limited promising strengths that we can draw on as we challenge others to follow our example. Also, we all have weaknesses. Learn to share those pitfalls with others while at the same time prayerfully working to overcome them. The best we humans can do is selective modeling by inviting duplication of only the good things in our lives. There are things about me I hope you will not copy, but for the sake of challenging you, I am willing, as Paul did, to invite you to imitate me on this point. If an ordinary person like me can more than double his effectiveness and influence for Jesus by doubling his prayer time, you can too.

If an ordinary person like me can more than double his effectiveness and influence for Jesus by doubling his prayer time, you can too.

In this book, I submit to you, "This is what I do. Follow my example." If we want to increase our effectiveness in service to our Lord, then our purpose is to pray more, strive to be more humble, and be a more obedient tool for the answer if God chooses to use us. I invite you to join me in praying more. God will show you how much.

Hunger for God

Since I am now spending more time seeking God, it amazes me to find so many Scriptures that encourage me to continue the pursuit. It is as though God was waiting all the time for me to begin to pursue Him more earnestly — more tenaciously. The challenge was there all along.

Spending four hours daily at anything requires a great deal of organization and prioritization. A day still has only 24 hours — this forces me to schedule my priorities carefully. I decided to eliminate some activities (such as the longer training runs and marathons) so that I can do more of what is really important. The following verses help me to know that I am on a good path. They encourage me to continue in prayer, and they mirror my own passion for God. These verses are now a part of the décor on the walls of our garage where I regularly go to pray alone.

- "… seek first His kingdom and His righteousness …" Matthew 6:33.

- "Come near to God and He will come near to you." James 4:8.

- "Love the Lord your God will all your heart … soul … strength … mind." Luke 10:27.

- "He rewards those who earnestly seek Him." Hebrews 11:6.

- "Do not be afraid … I am your shield, your very great reward." Genesis 15:1.

God's Surprise Agenda

I thought the centerpiece of my learning experience on the sabbatical/mission trip would be the Contextualized Theology curriculum and its usefulness in non-Western nations. Indeed, I did see how effective they had been. However, God had a higher agenda — He wanted me to learn of the increased fruitfulness possible with increased time spent with Him. This lesson will certainly apply in any cross-cultural ministry or any career situation. One lesson God wanted this professor to relearn on his sabbatical was the power of prayer — and the increase of power that is possible through even more prayer.

> If prayer was really the most important thing I did, I needed to do it more than anything else I did.

I am told that in industry, manufacturers should discover what product they produce most profitably and focus on finding better ways to produce more of that product. In successful businesses, smart businessmen identify what works best for them and concentrate on that. I have long said and felt that prayer was the most important thing I do in any given day. So, when I realized my amount of time spent in prayer did not match my belief, I knew I needed to change either my belief or behavior. If prayer was really the most important thing I did, I needed to do it more than anything else I did.

Being 58 and at that stage of my career, I thought I knew what ministry fruitfulness was, but I discovered it was possible for an older person to still make a new breakthrough. I learned that I could pray more, become more fruitful, teach with more authority, and that there were increased quantities and qualities of service opportunities available.

What increased fruitfulness awaits you and your career?

CHAPTER TWO

The Power and Danger of Prayer

"So he gave them what they asked for,
but sent a wasting disease upon them."

Psalm 106:15

You probably have never read — nor have I — a message
or lesson referring to the danger of prayer. Yet, something
even as wonderful as prayer can have negative consequences
if used unwisely.

We incorrectly assume that God automatically cancels wrong
prayers. Well-intentioned Christians believe that whatever they
receive as an answer to prayer must be God's will for them.

What you are about to read can revolutionize the way you feel
about prayer. Without question, God has used this lesson more
than any other lesson I have shared.

The Meat was Great, but the Plague was Horrible

Chapter 11 of the book of Numbers records the story of Israel's
request for meat in the wilderness. The entire chapter tells the
story, but Numbers 11:33 says, "But while the meat was still
between their teeth, and before it could be consumed, the anger
of the Lord burned against the people, and he struck them with a
severe plague."

What went wrong? With the meat still between their teeth, why did God strike them with a severe plague? Were they not only eating what God Himself had provided?

While the historical record in Numbers leaves these questions unanswered, Psalm 106:13-15 provides some answers. This is a good illustration of how the Bible interprets the Bible — a clearer passage helps us understand an obscure passage.

In these most sobering verses, three noteworthy things are found. The Israelites: (1) did not wait for God's counsel, (2) were motivated by their own craving, and (3) received the answer to their prayer, but it was not good for them.

> "But they soon forgot what he had done and did not wait for his counsel. In the desert, they gave in to their craving; in the wasteland, they put God to the test. So he gave them what they asked for, but sent a wasting disease upon them" (Psalm 106:13-15).

Psalm 106 makes it clear that sometimes God gives us what we want even though it is not good for us. It is far safer to pray in sincere submission that God would answer only if it is His will. We cannot assume God will automatically cancel wrong requests; we are not safe to pray carelessly.

In the wilderness, the Israelites did not pray for meat with a submissive attitude. They were motivated by their own cravings. They willfully sought and obtained an answer to prayer that was not good for them. Israel's mistaken prayer and its tragic consequences warn us to be careful when we pray.

We all know people who are living with the mistakes of their past. In some cases, they are living with the consequences of their own wrong praying. Some have, in answer to prayer, married a wrong spouse, pursued the wrong college major, worked in an incorrect vocation, bought houses they should not, attended churches they should not, or have mistakenly done any number of other things. In many cases, we have not analyzed our situations carefully enough to realize we are living with the consequences of our own wrong praying.

Many mistakes could have been avoided by praying right. Our answers are supposedly justified by the knowledge that we received what we asked God for. We reason, therefore, it must have been God's will. Such careless reasoning, however, is not consistent with Scripture.

Praying, and then sincerely adding the safety clause — if it is your will — is safer than careless praying. Nevertheless, there is an even more efficient way to pray.

Your Partnership with God in Prayer

Prayer, correctly understood, is an opportunity for you to partner with God in bringing His Kingdom and His will to earth. Prayer is your participation in a continual cycle where God and you cooperate. Ideally, prayer begins in God's heart as seen in Step 1 in Figure 2-1. Through the Holy Spirit, He lets you know what or how you should pray. When you pray that kind of prayer, God and you cooperate to fulfill his purposes. Through the name of Jesus — literally through Jesus in whose name we pray — the prayer goes back to the Father who, upon hearing your prayer (originally His idea), says, "I like it." God grants the request by working through His Holy Spirit in the affairs of men. He often (but not always) answers through the same person who prayed the prayer.

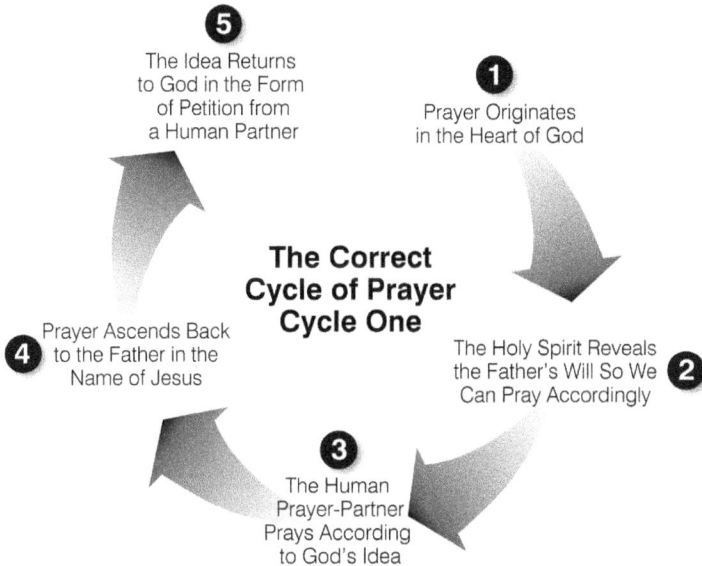

5 The Idea Returns to God in the Form of Petition from a Human Partner

1 Prayer Originates in the Heart of God

The Correct Cycle of Prayer Cycle One

4 Prayer Ascends Back to the Father in the Name of Jesus

2 The Holy Spirit Reveals the Father's Will So We Can Pray Accordingly

3 The Human Prayer-Partner Prays According to God's Idea

Figure 2-1. The first cycle of the correct cycle of prayer.

Let us visualize this by assuming God is at the top of the circle of events and we are at the bottom. *God initiates the idea* and reveals it to us by the Holy Spirit so we can pray according to His idea. As the idea from *God* becomes a prayer in our mouths, it moves from *us* back up to *God*. As we pray in Jesus' name, the prayer moves back to where it started at the top of the circle. The first cycle is then complete — from God to us and back to God.

The second cycle (Figure 2-2) begins as the *answer* proceeds from God and around the circle down to us. *We* receive the answer to the prayer *God* placed in our hearts. However, the second cycle does not end with us because *praise, glory, and thanks* for the good answer ascend back to the Father.

The prayer began with God and the cycle is only complete when God's idea re-crosses His desk twice — the second time as *your* request and then finally when it arrives *as praise from you,* God's human prayer-partner. Having fully gone around twice, it ends where it began — with God. This is a wonderful cycle. One of our goals as God's partners should be to repeat this process often. The more we do, the more fully the Kingdom of God comes to earth and the will of God is done on earth as it is in heaven. It is not about you; it is about Him, both beginning and ending with Him. We are just the human partner praying ideas that come *from* God which — when fulfilled — bring glory *to* God.

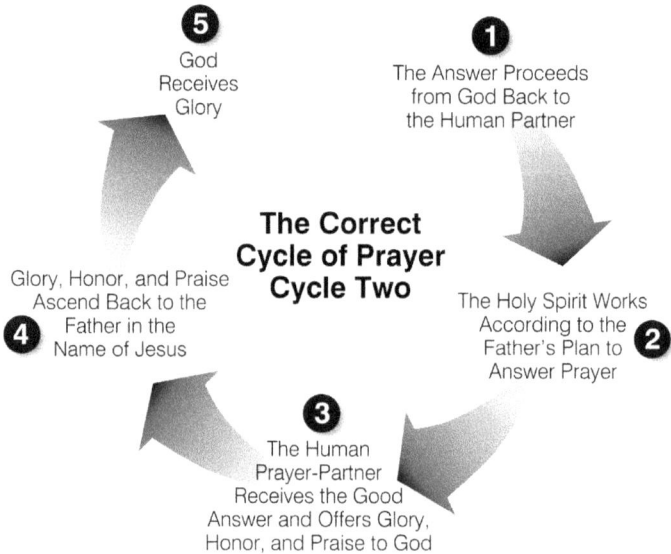

5 God Receives Glory

1 The Answer Proceeds from God Back to the Human Partner

The Correct Cycle of Prayer Cycle Two

Glory, Honor, and Praise Ascend Back to the **4** Father in the Name of Jesus

The Holy Spirit Works According to the Father's Plan to **2** Answer Prayer

3 The Human Prayer-Partner Receives the Good Answer and Offers Glory, Honor, and Praise to God

Figure 2-2. The second cycle of the correct cycle of prayer.

The problem is that sometimes prayer begins in *our* hearts, not God's. *We* have an idea of what *we* would like to do. Some of these well-intended ideas concern what we want to do even for

God. While good things can come from the hearts of good people, humans, nevertheless, are not as smart as God is.

If we are only praying our ideas — not God's — without concern for negative consequences, our prayers cannot possibly be as rich or unconditionally good as God's can. Prayers, based on our ideas, are simply not as good or far-reaching as those that begin with God.

God said, "As the heavens are higher than the earth, so are my ways higher than your ways and my thoughts than your thoughts" (Isaiah 55:9). In addition, Paul writes that He "is able to do immeasurably more than all we ask or imagine" (Ephesians 3:20). A prayer originating in *our* hearts — not *God's* — can be illustrated by starting the prayer process at the bottom — in our hearts — rather than at the top in God's heart where the best ideas originate. When the cycle goes from our heart to God and back to us as seen in Figure 2-3, the answer merely ends with us where it started, but little or no glory, honor, or praise goes to the Father. The prayer, though answered, neither brought great glory to the Father nor fulfilled His plan. Our ideas may even be good, but God's prayer ideas are still far superior.

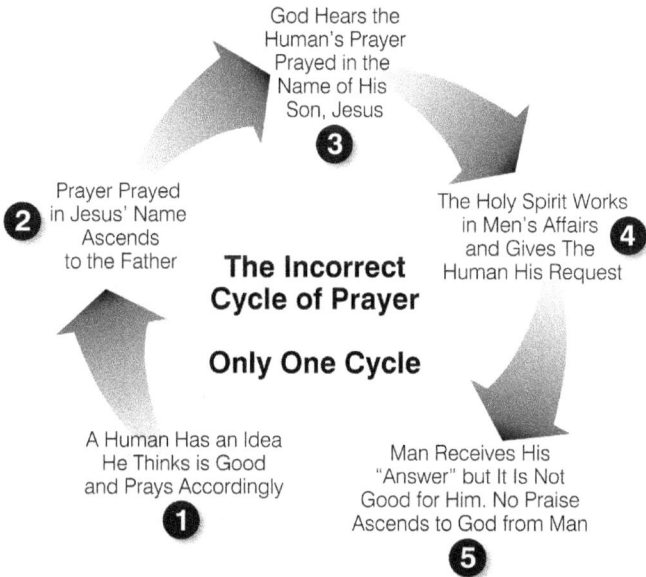

God Hears the Human's Prayer Prayed in the Name of His Son, Jesus
3

Prayer Prayed in Jesus' Name Ascends to the Father
2

The Holy Spirit Works in Men's Affairs and Gives The Human His Request
4

The Incorrect Cycle of Prayer

Only One Cycle

A Human Has an Idea He Thinks is Good and Prays Accordingly
1

Man Receives His "Answer" but It Is Not Good for Him. No Praise Ascends to God from Man
5

Figure 2-3. The incorrect cycle of prayer.

Israel's prayer in the wilderness illustrates no partnership or, at best, poor partnership with God in prayer. It certainly was not a part of any cycle of partnership with God for God's glory. Yet, there is another often misunderstood and even more pointed illustration in the Bible — someone who asked for and received something that was not good for him or his kingdom.

One day, my wife, Char, told me she thought she saw a message in the story of Hezekiah that is different from the usual one emphasizing the power of Hezekiah's prayer for healing. I followed her hunch. After rereading the text, I was forced by the story line to agree with her. Therefore, I include the story of Hezekiah in my list of biblical evidences of the need for caution in prayer. Hezekiah's case in Israel's history, recorded in II Kings 20, bears witness to this central truth: We should find out what God wants to do and pray accordingly; otherwise, we suffer the consequences of our own error.

A King's Prayers, Both Good and Selfish, are Answered!

This second example is both subtle and compelling. In his earlier years, Hezekiah was faithful to God and succeeded spiritually, administratively, politically, and militarily. Sennacherib, King of Assyria, sent a threatening letter to Hezekiah (II Kings 19:15-19) insulting God. Hezekiah promptly took the letter to the temple and spread it out before God.

His intercession is a wonderful prayer concerning God's reputation and Israel's precarious military situation. Hezekiah's lofty and noble petition reveals that he was concerned primarily for the honor of God among the nations. There is no indication of selfishness in this earlier prayer for his concern was rightly and entirely for God's glory.

> "O Lord, God of Israel, enthroned between the cherubim, you alone are God over all the kingdoms of the earth. You have made heaven and earth. Give ear, O Lord, and hear; open your eyes, O Lord, and see; listen to the words Sennacherib has sent to insult the living God. It is true, O Lord, that the Assyrian kings have laid waste these nations and their lands. They have thrown their gods into the fire and destroyed them, for they were not gods but only wood and stone, fashioned by men's hands. Now, O Lord our God, deliver us from his hand, so that all kingdoms on earth may know that you alone, O Lord, are God" (II Kings 19:15-19).

This glorious, God-centered prayer illustrates highly effective cooperation with God in prayer. It brought great glory to God when the answer came to earth — God's Kingdom came and His will was done.

Subsequent to God's wonderful answer to that prayer with a great and miraculous deliverance from Sennacherib, Hezekiah became ill. The prophet Isaiah informed him to put his things in order and prepare to die (II Kings 20:1). God was evidently finished using Hezekiah.

You may have heard lessons from this text to the effect that if you will pray as Hezekiah prayed, you too will receive your healing. I agree that if you pray as Hezekiah prayed you, too, might receive your healing. However, I will also argue that it may be neither God's will nor good for you. Reasoning from the results of Hezekiah's prayer, it is easy to see that Hezekiah's prayer was similar to the prayers of Israel in the wilderness. It was not the prayer he should have prayed, and the results were not good for Hezekiah or Israel.

My analysis of Hezekiah's prayer prayed toward the end of his years contradicts the interpretations of some well-known preachers. The records of Hezekiah's behavior reveal that his attitude during the last 15 years of his life was remarkably different from his attitude during his godly, former years. What he *said* in his prayer of thanksgiving when he was healed (Isaiah 38:9-20) seems to indicate he was humble and grateful to God. Yet, how he *behaved* in subsequent years, indicate that he was prideful (Isaiah 39 and II Kings 20). How he *behaved* is more of an indication of his attitude than what he *said* — actions speak louder than words.

Furthermore, in II Chronicles 32:31, the history record states, "… God left him to test him and to know everything that was in his heart." Evidently, his pride and self-sufficiency led him to pray according to his own desires rather than seek or submit to God's plan. Notice this in the passages and paragraphs that follow.

> "In those days, Hezekiah became ill and was at the point of death. The prophet Isaiah, son of Amoz, went to him and said, 'This is what the Lord says: Put your house in order, because you are going to die; you will not recover.' Hezekiah turned his face to the wall and prayed to the Lord, 'Remember, O Lord, how I have walked before you faithfully and with whole-hearted devotion and have done what is good in your eyes.' And Hezekiah wept bitterly.

Before Isaiah had left the middle court, the word of the Lord came to him: 'Go back and tell Hezekiah, the leader of my people, 'This is what the Lord, the God of your father David, says: I have heard your prayer and seen your tears; I will heal you. On the third day from now, you will go up to the temple of the Lord. I will add fifteen years to your life'" (II Kings 20:1-6a).

The first indication that something is amiss in this prayer is that Hezekiah prayed the opposite of God's will that Isaiah revealed to him. In this prayer, there is no mention made of God's glory or reputation among the nations. This contrasts with the earlier prayer in which Hezekiah, fearing the Assyrian army, was very eager for God to glorify Himself "… so that all kingdoms on earth may know that you alone, O Lord, are God" (II Kings 19:19).

Another warning sign about this prayer is Hezekiah's reference to his own former good works as though good works were the basis for God answering our prayers. Hezekiah was bragging. His prayer was both misguided and incorrectly motivated. Whenever we refer to our good works as though they earn the answer to our prayer, it should be a warning to us. Perhaps, subconsciously, we think our petition should be answered because *we* are good. In such cases, our focus is wrong; God answers because *He* is good.

A third indication of error is in the bitterness with which he wept and prayed. Parents know that not all crying of their children is in submission. Sometimes crying can express defiance or anger. "Weeping bitterly, with his face against the wall," is a different picture than the godly prayer warrior who, just a little earlier, had spread the Assyrian's letter out before the Lord in the temple.

These may be new ideas to you, but please give them a fair reading.

Weeping with bitter resentment toward circumstances or an authority figure is different from a submissive cry of petition, sorrow, or loss. Hezekiah's weeping is no sure sign of any sincerity. He wept bitterly, not in humble or submissive petition, but in annoyance and insubordination. Nevertheless, God granted Hezekiah's prayer and gave him 15 more years of life.

Even though the above three arguments are credible, the most convincing indication that Hezekiah was resisting God and praying amiss is shown by the tragic results to his kingdom as a consequence of his 15-year life extension. Some time later, visitors arrived from Babylon to congratulate Hezekiah on his recovery.

> "At that time, Merodach-Baladan, son of Baladan, king of Babylon, sent Hezekiah letters and a gift because he had heard of Hezekiah's illness. Hezekiah received the messengers and showed them all that was in his storehouses — the silver, the gold, the spices, and the fine oil — his armory and everything found among his treasures. There was nothing in his palace or in all his kingdom that Hezekiah did not show them" (II Kings 20:12-13).

We talk about things that are important to us. What Hezekiah talked about and showed to his Babylonian visitors indicates to us today the object of his trust and attention. He took them to the armory, showing them the swords, spears, bows, arrows, and other implements of war. He took them to the treasury and showed them the spices, silver, and gold. At this later stage in his life, it seems he trusted military and economic strength, not God. Let's read on.

"Then Isaiah the prophet went to King Hezekiah and asked, 'What did those men say, and where did they come from?' From a distant land,' Hezekiah replied. 'They came from Babylon.' The prophet asked, 'What did they see in your palace?' 'They saw everything in my palace,' Hezekiah said. 'There is nothing among my treasures that I did not show them'" (II Kings 20:14, 15).

The state visit of the messengers from Babylon would have been a good opportunity for Hezekiah to take his foreign guests to the temple in Jerusalem and say, "This is where I brought the threatening letter of Sennacherib and laid it out before our mighty God. This is the temple where the Creator — God, Jehovah, El Shaddai, Yahweh, our great God — dwells and receives the prayers and praises of His people. Come with me to see the temple of the great God of all the earth." He could have pointed out that the God that was worshipped in that temple was the very same one who had delivered Israel and healed him, but he did not.

At the earlier and humbler stage in Hezekiah's life, when the Assyrians laid siege to Jerusalem, Hezekiah did not go to the armory or treasury; he went to the temple. At this later stage in his life, he instead took his guests to the armory and treasury, not to the temple. The contrast between the former and the latter Hezekiah is quite clear.

There appears to be no mention made of Israel's real Protector, just boastings of armaments and treasures. At this later stage when the congratulations and accolades were coming his way, he didn't go to the temple to give God praise. Instead, he went to the armory and treasury to brag.

My main emphasis here is to stress the importance of finding God's will and praying accordingly, but there is another lesson too. How many times do we run to God in prayer when we have a problem? Then, after He has helped us, we brag about something else other than our true Deliverer?

There's more. The most revealing exchange between Hezekiah and Isaiah is yet to come.

"Then Isaiah said to Hezekiah, 'Hear the word of the Lord: the time will surely come when everything in your palace, and all that your fathers have stored up until this day, will be carried off to Babylon. Nothing will be left, says the Lord. And some of your descendants, your own flesh and blood, that will be born to you, will be taken away, and they will become eunuchs in the palace of the king of Babylon.' 'The word of the Lord you have spoken is good,' Hezekiah replied. For he thought, 'Will there not be peace and security in my lifetime?'" (II Kings 20:16-18).

Isaiah did not wait long to confront the King. When Hezekiah admitted to Isaiah that he showed the treasures and armaments to the Babylonians, Isaiah delivered a very sad message: those treasures and some of Hezekiah's own offspring and Israel's citizens would be carried off to Babylon as slaves.

This terrible message should have sobered Hezekiah and made him realize that he had just made a horrible spiritual and political mistake. Amazingly, Hezekiah revealed his selfishness, pride, and arrogance, caring not for the future suffering of Israel, but only for his own safety. He said that Isaiah's message was good because the suffering would take place *after* his life had passed in peace and security. The narrative does not spell out this interpretation, but why else would the writer point out what Hezekiah thought in his heart? "'The word of the Lord you have spoken is good,' Hezekiah replied. For he thought, 'Will there not be peace and security in my lifetime?'" (II Kings 20:18).

After Hezekiah's 15 years were complete, he died. However, the problems Israel experienced because of Hezekiah's prayer and the 15-year life extension did not end with Hezekiah's passing.

> "Hezekiah rested with his fathers. And Manasseh, his son, succeeded him as king. Manasseh was twelve years old when he became king, and he reigned in Jerusalem fifty-five years. His mother's name was Hephzibah. He did evil in the eyes of the Lord, following the detestable practices of the nations the Lord had driven out before the Israelites" (II Kings 20:21 and 21:1-2).

How many years after Hezekiah's healing did he die and Manasseh begin to reign? — 15. How old was Manasseh when he began to reign? — 12. Then, how many years passed between the healing of Hezekiah and the birth of Manasseh? — 3. Had Hezekiah died when God said he was to die, Manasseh would not have been born. Presumably, there would have been another of David's descendants who could have preserved David's line.

II Kings 21:16 says, "Manasseh also shed so much innocent blood that he filled Jerusalem from end to end ..." It is possible Isaiah, the faithful prophet who tried to influence Manasseh's father towards righteousness, was among those killed by Manasseh. One tradition says that Isaiah was sawed in two and another says that Manasseh had Isaiah killed. Some believe when Hebrews 11:37 states, "... they were sawed in two ..." it implies that Manasseh killed Isaiah.

It is sad to note that Manasseh led Israel with ungodly influence for 55 years only to be followed by two more years of ungodly leadership by Manasseh's son, Amon. "Amon was 22 years old when he became king, and he reigned in Jerusalem two years ... He did evil in the eyes of the Lord, as his father Manasseh had done" (II Kings 21:19a and 21).

However, had Hezekiah accepted God's Word and died according to His plan; no innocent blood would have been shed. Hezekiah is a sad illustration of the danger of prayer when it is not submitted to the good use for which the privilege of prayer is given to human beings. It was not until the reign of Josiah, Hezekiah's great-grandson, that Israel finally had a godly king once again.

> **Hezekiah is a sad illustration of the danger of prayer when it is not submitted to the good use for which the privilege of prayer is given to human beings.**

On the other hand, Scripture provides us with several equally graphic and beautiful examples of godly persons who sought God's will and prayed accordingly. It is much more enjoyable to reflect on positive illustrations about how prayer is supposed to work — bringing the good results God intends.

The Advantage of Consulting the Lord

David had been Israel's king only a short time when the Philistine army came against Israel. David was the commander-in-chief, a successful military man, a war hero, and a crafty fighter. No one would have thought he was presumptuous had he simply gone out to fight with the Philistines. However, David "inquired of the Lord" (II Samuel 5:19). Only after clear direction from God did he go into battle against the enemy. Israel won a great victory, and God's people benefited because their king cared enough about doing things right that he first inquired of the Lord.

Again, the Philistines came up against Israel. Coasting on the momentum of his former victory and the direction of the Lord to go against the Philistines, David could have understandably gone, once again, against them in battle and not been presumptuous. Even with all that in his favor, David still did not go into battle without inquiring of the Lord a second time. This time, God said not to make a frontal attack, but rather "circle around behind them" (II Samuel 5:23). With instructions to wait for God's signal to attack, David and his men circled behind the Philistine army and waited.

When the wind blew — the signal God had given David — the army rose up out of hiding, surprised the enemy from behind, and won another great victory. What a wonderful picture of strength under control — a winning army waiting for God's signal in the wind! What a fascinating illustration of partnership between God and man! When we learn to do that, God's kingdom comes to people, God's will is done on earth, and God works for His glory and man's good. God only needs a human co-worker who will wait on Him, receive His direction, and let God work through him. How many victories do we miss because we are unwilling to find out what God wants to do and pray accordingly?

> How many victories do we miss because we are unwilling to find out what God wants to do and pray accordingly?

A Strange Thing to Pray

Elijah's experience in prayer is even more pointed. In his day, there was a great moral and spiritual decline. Ahab was Israel's ungodly king. His Phoenician queen, Jezebel, was the daughter of a Sidonian monarch and an avid worshipper of Phoenician gods. Largely through her influence, Ahab energetically served and worshiped several Phoenician gods. Asherah was the mother goddess and wife of El. Four hundred of her prophets ate at Jezebel's table at state expense. Asherah had 70 children including Baal. Ahab created an altar for Baal in a temple he built for him in Samaria. He also erected an Asherah pole that may have actually been an image of her.

According to another tradition, Baal was a Cannanite god and Asherah was his wife. Baal was both the fertility god and the god of rain and thunder. Four hundred fifty of his prophets ate at Jezebel's table. Clearly, worship of the true God was in a state of decline, but God had an idea about how to arrest Israel's attention.

If a drought occurred, Baal, the god of rain and thunder, would be the one the people would pray to. In order to defame him, God planned a lengthy famine — an interruption of the natural rainfall in the land flowing with milk and honey. God shared his idea with a human partner — an intercessor.

> "Now Elijah the Tishbite, from Tishbe in Gilead, said to Ahab, 'As the Lord, the God of Israel, lives, whom I serve, there will be neither dew nor rain in the next few years except at my word.' The word of the Lord came to Elijah: 'Leave here, turn eastward, and hide in the Kerith Ravine, east of the Jordan. You will drink from the brook, and I have ordered the ravens to feed you there. So he did what the Lord had told him" (I Kings 17:1-5a).

I particularly like that last sentence. Elijah did what the Lord told him to do.

Despite the fact that people usually pray that it will rain, according to James 5:16c-18, it is clear that Elijah actually prayed that it would *not* rain. What kind of a prophet prays that it would not rain? The answer is a prophet who knows the mind of God and prays accordingly.

> "The prayer of a righteous man is powerful and effective. Elijah was a man just like us. He prayed earnestly that it would not rain, and it did not rain on the land for three and a half years. Again he prayed, and the heavens gave rain, and the earth produced its crops" (James 5:16c-18).

He prayed according to God's ideas, not man's.

If that was not strange enough, note that Elijah later changed his prayer 180 degrees. After praying for three and a half years that it would not rain, he prayed that it would rain. What kind of prophet changes the direction of his prayer to begin to intercede for God to do exactly the opposite of what he just prayed? The answer is a prophet who knows that what God wanted to accomplish in phase one was complete, and now it was time to move to the next phase.

We often do what God tells us to do — too long.

During a classroom discussion one day, a student of mine completely amazed me with this profound thought: "We often do what God tells us to do — too long." Ever since then, I realized that what God directs me to do one day or in one phase of my life might change. When God shows us what to pray or do, sometimes we pray or do it too long. We must learn to stay current.

The sensitive human partner will move through the stages of the unfolding plan, smoothly transitioning from phase to phase with accuracy in both direction and timing. Elijah was such a partner. He knew what God was up to and prayed accordingly. Because God had a willing partner who would pray correctly through each stage, God's kingdom came, God's will was done, Israel saw the power of God, Baal and Asherah were defamed, their prophets were slain, and God was glorified. God just needed a man who would pray according to His plan, not the ordinary kinds of prayers that humans often pray.

The New Testament commentary in James gives us the insight we need to understand that both God and Elijah were actively involved in a wonderful divine-human joint venture. If you will first learn to find the will of God and then pray, you may discover you are praying differently than other people.

Knowing what to pray about and how to pray is of greater consequence than exerting force and spinning wheels. Purpose is more critical than activity and direction is more important than speed.

If you pray God's thoughts and prayers, you might be out of sync with people, but wouldn't you rather be in sync with God? If God is speaking, and He often does if we will listen, I would rather be God's faithful partner than appear proper in man's eyes.

What kind of bold and creative plans might God have for the difficulties we face in our nations, communities, churches, and families if we learned to first consult Him and then pray? It is the challenge of every generation to discover what God is doing and do it with Him. This is just as true in our generation as it was for past generations.

If you want to increase the effectiveness and efficiency of your prayer life, pay careful attention to how you pray. Effectiveness and efficiency in prayer are both important. Effectiveness has to do with getting the job done. Efficiency has to do with getting the job done with the least amount of wasted effort. Since human resources are limited, life is short, and the need is great, we cannot ignore the issue of an efficient prayer life. Learning to pray according to God's plan increases efficiency, effectiveness, and fruitfulness in prayer.

In order to receive answers to prayer, it is sometimes necessary to get on our face before God, fast, intercede, travail, experience the burden of prayer, persevere, and show disciplined consistency and fervency. After all, Jesus taught us to seek and keep on seeking, knock and keep on knocking, and ask and keep on asking.

To receive the right answers to the right requests requires us to rethink our prayer *content*. It is an extremely important prerequisite to achieve before we focus on the issue of *fervency*. In prayer, the ability to discern the mind of God and pray accordingly is most certainly more important than fervency — unless, of course, fervency is used in prayer to know God's will in the matter at hand before we pray. However, we don't have to choose between fervency and accuracy; both are possible. Nevertheless, the emphasis in this chapter is on accuracy.

Knowing what to pray about and how to pray is of greater consequence than exerting force and spinning wheels. Purpose is more critical than activity and direction is more important than speed.

CHAPTER THREE
The Roller Coaster Ride

*"If you remain in me and my words remain in you,
ask whatever you wish, and it will be given you."*

John 15:7

Gradually, it became apparent that the agenda the Lord had prepared for my sabbatical missions trip was practical instead of scholarly. The discipline of four hours of prayer per day was producing a change. In only a few days, I realized that it was not difficult to pray that long. In addition, freedom in teaching and preaching became a comfortable, enjoyable, and repeated experience.

Slowly in my mind, the idea became real that the change might be life-long. Moreover, I had to ask myself, "Do I continue the new prayer pattern upon returning to Oral Roberts University?" I began to consider continuing the experiment for the 2003 spring semester to see if what I had experienced in South Africa and India would continue in my home setting. Looking at it from a scientific perspective, continuing the experiment back in the U.S. would simply be a matter of testing the hypothesis in another more familiar environment.

The new results I was experiencing in ministry were the reason I considered continuing the experiment. Insight, character development, opened doors, and a new intimacy with God were all part of that wonderful combination. Nevertheless, there were accompanying difficulties — it wasn't all positive. This chapter's title is an attempt to express the great joy of answered prayer along with the struggles we often experience in becoming more fruitful. This chapter will address both spiritually rewarding "highs" and some "low," difficult experiences. The new highs, lows, twists, and turns were much like a roller coaster ride; the joys of the highs were wonderful, but the pressure of the difficulties was also greater than before.

God's training program in prayer and ministry life is not organized like an orderly teaching outline. Rather, it is a combination of a variety of lessons that have differing themes. His agenda includes a series of pleasant and hard experiences, encouraging results, horrible reverses, glorious victories, and unspeakable surprise adversities.

The ups, downs, twists, turns, jerks, and excitement of a roller coaster perhaps best illustrate the experiences God uses to stretch us. Each experience has its own lesson even though the "lessons" may not *seem* related. However, the combination of all of them in succession is a growing process. As we recognize this process and cooperate with it instead of resisting it, it works better.

Lofty Ideas about Kneeling Low

My discoveries through my extended prayer experience were confirmed often by what I read. I read wherever I go, but the reading plan while abroad is often simply to read what is available on my hosts' bookshelves. I explore the libraries of the people I visit. When I find a book that interests me, I ask to borrow it. When I do this, either God or "coincidences" are in charge of my reading schedule as I travel.

The first book I read was *God's Generals*, the book that sparked the big question for me: *What would happen if a teacher prayed at length, seriously, and regularly?* The second book that had an impact on me was *Foxe's Book of Martyrs*. It is worth its weight in gold. It enriches readers with the absolute devotion, commitment, and zeal demonstrated by Christians of previous generations. Simply stated, old books can help you break out of the narrow confines and experiences of your own generation as this one did for me.

After our two months in South Africa, we arrived in India. Our first of eight assignments there was Beersheba Theological College in Pathankot in Northwest India, not far from the disputed India-Pakistani border. While visiting a foreign teacher at the college, I noticed a large volume entitled *E. M. Bounds on Prayer.* It contained all seven of his books on prayer: *Purpose in Prayer, The Necessity of Prayer, The Possibilities of Prayer, Essentials of Prayer, Obtaining Answers to Prayer, Power through Prayer,* and *The Weapon of Prayer.* I borrowed it and read the whole volume while traveling through India.

In addition to learning that prayer is more important than intellectual abilities to a minister, Bounds brought to my attention these themes on prayer.

- Pray more and better.

- Ask for anything in prayer.

- Expect to get answers from prayer.

- Be persistent in prayer.

- Put your heart into praying.

These lofty ideas about humble prayer are just one way a fruitful prayer life is like a roller coaster. The ideas are profound and exciting, but the struggle to practice them alone in the prayer closet brings one low. The way up is down.

A Life of Prayer Influences Many

After returning to the United States, I read *Rees Howells Intercessor* by Norman Grubb. This amazing book confirmed much of what I was discovering. It also challenged me to continue my pursuit in my newfound source of increased vigor, faith, and confidence in God. I found, however, that Rees Howells' *life* spoke to me more by *the way he prayed* than other authors did by what they *said* about prayer. In Grubb's portrayal of Howells, Howells' *life* spoke. If what he did and how he prayed had so much to "say" to me in biographical anecdotes, I could not help but reconsider the influence of biographies. As I read about how Howells trudged through the mountains praying, spending hours alone with God, I was encouraged to continue to pursue God with vigor.

> I found, however, that Rees Howells' *life* spoke to me more by *the way he prayed* than other authors did by what they *said* about prayer.

Yet, what would have been available to his readers if Howells had candidly written his inner feelings about his experiences? How did he feel when he got tired and had to sit down? Did he too go to sleep as I do if I sit down? What happened when his mind wandered? What mechanisms did he use to keep focused? What might have been the influence on his readers had Howells himself shared those kinds of *auto*biographical anecdotes? In order to encourage each other to pray, do we need to be more transparent with each other about how we handle these issues? I am encouraged to continue to try to be transparent.

One of Howells' more impressive accomplishments through prayer occurred toward the end of his career during World War II. I was amazed by the influence of his prayers in the unwritten history of World War II. He and his students in England spent hours in prayer that affected momentous events in Eastern Europe, Northern Africa, and the results of the entire war. His story of prayer gives insight into events and outcomes in foxholes and deserts thousands of miles away. Like Howells, we too can make our private places of prayer into "centers" for world evangelism, spiritual ministry, and international influence.

I am encouraged by Howells' example as, in my garage, I "travel" from continent to continent and nation to nation lifting them and their governments, peoples, churches, Christians, pastors, families, and missionaries during prayer. God has high purposes for the low valleys that people are experiencing in far away places. The idea that there are no distance barriers for prayer took on a deeper meaning.

Spiritual Growth and "Success"

Success for the child of God is not measured as the world measures it. For God's children, the degree of their success is the degree to which they have done the will of God. This line of thought is more fully developed in another book I wrote, *Habits of Highly Effective Christians*. If spiritual growth occurs and the will of God is done, even what some might call a "failure" would be a testimony of God's answer to prayer. According to God, maintaining righteous attitudes and behaviors in difficult situations is considered a success while some would call it a "failure." In addition, fulfilling what God wants to do in those circumstances also illustrates true success. Prayer helps each of us align our definitions of success with God's definition.

Whether we experience what people call "success" or "failure," the more important eternal issue is how God sees us. Do we respond with grace and humility or with bitterness and pride? Wrong attitudes and/or behaviors in an apparent *success* would make the supposed *success* actually *unsuccessful* in God's eyes.

Scripture illustrates this well. For example, was Joseph more successful than Isaiah because Joseph was elevated to the position of Prime Minister of Egypt (Genesis 41:41) while Isaiah was sawed in two by the evil king Manasseh (if the tradition regarding Isaiah's death is true)?

Was Manasseh successful because he was a king? Was Amos unsuccessful because he was a mere shepherd from Tekoa? King Manasseh shed a lot of innocent blood and ruled Israel with a grievously evil influence, while Amos, merely tending sheep, spoke God's Word obediently to his generation. Who was more successful to God?

Would the three Hebrews (Shadrach, Meshach, and Abednego) have been unsuccessful if they had burnt to ashes? I think not. Were they "successful" because they were delivered from the fiery furnace? No. They were already successful because of their courage, uncompromising faith, and trust in God whether or not they were delivered — not *because* they were delivered.

The pursuit of and love for God's will is success; resisting God's will is failure.

Paradoxically, there are "successful failures" — successes by God's standards, though they appear as failures by man's standards. Wouldn't you rather experience a successful failure in God's eyes than a failure in God's eyes even though man might call it a success? Power in prayer does not mean *we* control things; true success occurs when God's will is done and we rest on that.

The time has come for us to prefer "success in the eternal scheme of things" (success in God's eyes) and to question the *success* of what people usually think of as success. Seeing how prayer and life issues blend together can help us work harder to achieve the success *God* wants for us.

High Purposes in Low Valleys

I'll use an illustration of one of our sons. Our Air Force son has amazed us over the years with his long string of professional successes. His long climb up the ladder of accomplishment has also been accompanied by godly responses and humble trust. He was accepted into the Air Force Academy, assumed leadership positions as a cadet, and graduated with military honors. Later, he received a pilot training slot and finished at the top of his class. That achievement enabled him to choose his fighter plane.

After successfully completing training for the F15E, he earned the positions of wing pilot; two-ship flight lead; four-ship flight lead; instructor pilot; evaluator pilot; and chief evaluator pilot for all the F15E fighter planes at Elmendorf Base where he was assigned. As a captain selected for advanced officers' leadership training, it was clear to Joel that God had promoted him far beyond the merits of his own abilities. Next, Joel earned the rank of major by being in the top 15 percent of his peer group. He is positioned to eventually become a lieutenant colonel and receive an advanced commander position if he chooses to remain in the Air Force.

As a result of his success, he was selected to attend fighter weapons school. This program educates the top one percent of the fighter pilots in the Air Force — the "top guns." It is the pinnacle — a high-water mark of any pilot's career by military standards. This rigorous and intense combat training — the toughest in the Air Force — entails leading the planning, briefing, execution, and debriefing of combat flight tactics and training.

Joel had experienced God's favor and enablement for years. However, through a remarkable series of problems and in the midst of circumstances beyond his control, he saw God orchestrating events. Unexpectedly, things were going poorly and he wasn't performing as well. For the first time in Joel's military career, he didn't even finish. What was God doing?

The experience was more spiritual than practical for Joel — he grew spiritually. Throughout the experience, the questions, unfairness, difficulties, prayer, Scripture, God-given dreams to guide him, guidance, confirmations, and affirmations all became the ingredients of Joel's spiritual training. Joel successfully completed a spiritual character development course with infinitely greater eternal consequences than the human course. God sought not to develop a fighter pilot, but a man.

Somewhere in the midst of the drama surrounding Joel, I awoke at 1:20 a.m. and went to the garage to pray for an hour. The entire time, I sensed the Holy Spirit was prompting me to pray for Joel. I did not understand the issues involved for I am just a civilian — a praying dad. However, I felt something was wrong, and God was leading me to intercede for our son. I knew that whatever was happening had a spiritual dimension, and God wanted to be involved. By 2:20 a.m., the burden of prayer lifted, and I returned to bed and slept the rest of the night.

The next day, I learned that at precisely the time I was praying for Joel, he was at the end of an exhausting debriefing session. During the session's closing minutes, officers supervising and evaluating his performance were making important decisions relating to Joel's career.

In the days that followed, he began to view it as a successful "failure." Joel did not finish the program and returned to his home base to continue his career as a flight instructor. Through the entire experience, Joel maintained a godly stance. His evaluators even stated that he had a good attitude. He climbed the ladder of success effectively and received the opportunity to have a "successful failure" — a more important achievement in God's sight.

For me, the hour alone in my garage praying for Joel gave me peace during those difficult days. I knew God was at work accomplishing His purpose — developing character while a soldier, pilot, and officer grew. Meanwhile, an intercessor alone in his prayer closet learned again of the power of prayer. The fingerprints of God were on Joel's entire experience.

Some months later, a brand new opportunity developed for Joel. He was offered and accepted the position of flight commander for a Korean pilot training program. This opportunity would not have been likely if he was busy being a top gun. As Char and I observe the interpersonal skills and character development affected by his career path, we conclude once again that God knows more about success than we do.

Here is the obvious lesson regarding prayer: the next time you are distressed as I was by circumstances over which you seem to have no control, you can influence even distant events through prayer. Nothing is impossible when you are on God's side. Prayer works at a distance and changes things — including people. Not only was Rees Howells able to influence situations in other parts of the world through prayer; other ordinary men and women just like you and I can do it again today.

A less obvious lesson is that God is more concerned about how we respond in our apparent failures than about our apparent successes. Do we want God's affirmation or man's applause?

However, another important yet often-overlooked lesson from this experience happens quietly *every* time we pray. Every experience in and answer to prayer and every miracle reveal something about God and our relationship to Him through prayer. He is constantly teaching us about prayer. He is willing to allow our experiences in prayer and miracles to stimulate our own faith, even as we also challenge others to work with Him in accomplishing things and growing through prayer. He is developing prayer warriors and seeking intercessors. He is teaching us about prayer even when we do not receive answers — or at least the answer we expected. He likes it when we are attentive to his lessons and are willing to learn through His instruction how to pray better.

The Hourglass Principle

An hourglass has two large compartments separated by a narrow passage. The sand in the upper compartment must squeeze through the narrow neck to reach the waiting, empty lower section. The narrower the neck, the slower the flow of sand and the longer it takes for the upper compartment to empty and the lower to become full — the wider the neck, the more rapid the flow. Now let's apply the lesson of the hourglass to prayer.

In the top half of the hourglass, there are infinite qualities available to the intercessor such as breadth, depth, height, and richness in God's abundant power and wisdom. Infinity is beyond our imagination, so open your mind and acknowledge that God's fine qualities are incomprehensible. It will become quite clear to you too that there is no limit to God's ability to accomplish His mighty works in our behalf. He is, after all, "able to do immeasurably more than all we ask or imagine" (Ephesians 3:20). His ability to answer prayer is infinite. However, the hourglass has two more parts: the lower compartment and the neck.

In the bottom half of the hourglass, the difficulties you, your career or ministry, and your family experience in life are proof of the magnitude of human need. Multiply that by the world's population compounded by human immorality and the needs of the human race — it is beyond comprehension. Each individual, Christian or not, has enormous potential for wrong thoughts and behavior. Additionally, many do not have the refining and correcting ministry of the Holy Spirit at work in their character. By their own uninformed, foolish choices and even deliberate decisions, they give themselves to godless living. We live in a world of sin, sorrow, consequences of poor decisions, outcomes of hateful actions, debauchery, suffering, sickness, perversion, filth, and discord. The lower half of the hourglass is the vast expanse of human need.

My point is not that man is evil as much as it is that humanity has a great need for God's help. No one knows the exact population of the world, its suffering, or the weight of human unhappiness, suffering, and sin. Nor does one person carry that total weight. Nevertheless, the needs are apparent and require our attention. God's infinite good qualities in the top half of the hourglass are able to meet man's vast needs in the bottom half, but He needs intercessors.

Intercessors are positioned between two huge entities — one full of solutions, blessings, and answers and the other filled with desperate problems. Intercessors form the small passage through which the vast mercies of God flow to meet the great needs of the human race. Intercessors are the narrow neck of the hourglass.

God's infinite good qualities in the top half of the hourglass are able to meet man's vast needs in the bottom half, but He needs intercessors.

Here is the challenge: the neck of the hourglass is very narrow and restrictive. How can intercessors increase the size of the passageway between God's adequate blessings above and the vastness of human need below? How can we enlarge the neck? How can we increase the speed of the "sand" of God's immeasurable blessings into the immense bottom half of the hourglass where those wonderful granules are so welcome and needed?

With the hourglass image in mind, think of the powerful, unseen ministry you could have in your place of private prayer. Think of how God might use you. Think of how much good you could do just by being a conduit and how many blessings you could bring by developing your own ministry of prayer.

Personal Growth through Delays in Answers to Prayer

In the beginning of Chapter 7 of *Essentials of Prayer*, Bounds quotes W.E. Biederwolf.

- "… If Hannah's prayer for a son had been answered at the time she set for herself, the nation might never have known the mighty man of God it found in Samuel. Hannah wanted only a son, but God wanted more. He wanted a prophet, and a savior, and a ruler for His people. Someone said that 'God had to get a woman before he could get a man.' This woman He got in Hannah. Precisely by those weeks and months and years there came a woman with a vision like God's, with tempered soul and gentle spirit and a seasoned will, prepared to be the kind of mother for the kind of a man God knew the nation needed."

I pondered the experience of Hannah and how the delay produced a better woman who raised a better man. It caused me to think more positively about delays in answers to prayers. If God is so eager to answer prayer, wouldn't there have to be a good reason for Him to delay?

What if the delay is caused by something on our end, not God's? What if we were more willing to examine ourselves — how we may need to learn, become, do, or not do something — in order to be the person God wants us to be just so He could answer our prayers?

God is ready to bless and He is blessing all He can! Problems of our own making often hinder Him. I pondered this fact when, even after months of diligent efforts, I had been unable to find a publisher for an earlier book I had written. What was I doing to block God's answer? What if the reason was that God wanted me first to deal with my arrogance, pride, and stubbornness? Is God's delay in answering prayer the way He opens us to the possibility that *we* — not the situation — need to change? Is God trying to develop more broken intercessors? Are Christian character development and refinement, accompanied by self-examination and introspection, His reasons for delayed answer to prayer? In a later chapter, we will look more at becoming a "broken" intercessor.

Let's consider perseverance. Isn't it fair to state that the development of tenacity in prayer is also part of character development? With this in mind, take a new look at the story of Jesus' treatment of the Canaanite woman in the regions of Tyre and Sidon recorded in Matthew 15:21-28. Why was our compassionate Savior so hard, resistant, and unmoved by this woman's prayers? I also pondered the story of the unjust judge recorded in Luke 18:1-8. I realized that this parable and the character development exercise He used with the Canaanite woman both had the same emphasis — perseverance. In Chapter Seven, you will read the results of my ponderings as I realized that the Holy Spirit was giving insight into the way God uses delays to develop character and persistence in prayer.

Greater Revelation, Inspiration, and Illumination in Prayer

In my prayer experiment, I noticed a marked difference in the ease, liberty, and effectiveness in delivery of God's Word. I have also observed God giving me new insight in the preparation of those messages. In the second week of our ministry at Beersheba Theological College, I felt led during my routine morning prayer to prepare a teaching based on Peter's walk on the water recorded in Matthew 14:28-32. The Holy Spirit's ministry of revelation during prayer produced the 12 principles in that lesson. I recall praying for revelation, inspiration, and illumination. I felt the Lord was urging me to pray for those three things. Like you, I make it a serious matter to pray what God wants me to pray, not just my own agenda.

I have found many wonderful insights into the depths of the wisdom and richness of God's Word through the writings of godly commentators. Commentaries are books that are tools of ministry for preachers in Western nations. In them, Bible scholars make numerous helpful comments on the meaning and application of Scripture. However, in the developing world, commentaries are scarce, and one of the things I teach is how to prepare and deliver expository sermons without using commentaries.

While preparing a lesson based on Peter's walk on the water, I experienced the Holy Spirit's ministry in a way I never had in 37 years of ministry. It was academically sound and intellectually informative and interesting. In addition, this sermon was a unique, personal creation because each thought evolved through prayer. Before that day was over, I had written the manuscript and preached the sermon at the evening service. Compared with other sermons prepared with the use of good commentaries, the one the Holy Spirit gave me was in no way inferior.

Unfortunately, some ministers preach sermons that they have hastily prepared. The lack of depth in those sermons makes those preachers look like they never developed the discipline or have grown lazy in the rigors of sermon preparation. Perhaps some rely too much on the Holy Spirit.

I teach pastors to read, research, dig, and study the Bible so that their sermons are strong in content. In addition, I teach them to pray fervently so that they can deliver the sermon in liberty and power. Because of my experience at Beersheba Theological College, I now have a new appreciation for the ministry of the Holy Spirit that can reveal spiritual truths to the teacher/preacher who is willing to take prayer seriously. I can now, with greater confidence, teach pastors who do not even have commentaries how to pray, work hard, prepare, and still deliver rich, convincing, and content-laden sermons. The persistent prayer warrior will insist on receiving rich truth from the text, and he will not be content with the shallow and unimportant. There is a wealth of spiritual truth in the Bible, but it has to be mined through prayer and study.

The Mixture of Joys and Difficulties

The roller coaster ride includes some wonderful statistics. Actually, these are great days to be involved in world missions. Foreign missions in developing nations place you on the front lines of the most exciting happenings in the world. In any given generation, the most significant happenings in the world are connected to what God is doing.

Consider what God is doing in our generation. Every day, 23,000 sub-Sahara Africans and 25,000 to 30,000 Chinese convert to Christianity. Every week, 469 new churches (67 per day) are founded in Africa south of the Sahara. Thousands of Christian missionaries from south India are serving fruitfully as crosscultural missionaries in northern India. I was privileged to be involved firsthand in teaching pastors and missionaries in each of the host organizations with which we served in India. For a missionary-minded person, it gave me a high level of excitement and joy throughout the entire six months of the trip.

However, there is also a down side — bodily weakness and human frailty. The physical difficulties experienced in pursuing foreign mission opportunities are no small factor. They should be considered in any honest assessment of ministry (including this record of an experiment with increased prayer). The living and traveling circumstances that we experienced tested our strength and challenged our commitment.

For example, during the six months of that trip, I experienced two serious cases of diarrhea, a sore throat, bronchitis, and a deep scrape on my bald head from the doorway of a train car. Additionally, the almost-constant blaring of Hindu and Moslem prayer chants over loudspeakers late into the night and again at 5:00 every morning significantly contributed to extended sleeplessness. The heat and ambitious, hungry mosquitoes, the spicy-hot flavor of Indian dishes, and the absence of toilet tissue created even more inconvenience. When the physical body wears down, its resistance to disease is reduced. Combine all that and you can imagine that it is even more difficult to maintain a positive attitude in crosscultural interpersonal relationships.

The mixture of the exciting times of ministry on the front lines with the suffering and inconvenience of living in undeveloped places is another aspect of riding on the roller coaster. Times of extreme satisfaction in being a part of what God is doing are highs. Times of physical pain, extreme fatigue, and sleeplessness are lows. The stakes are higher and the challenges are greater. In the routine of ministry-as-usual back in the homeland, we had become accustomed to a comparatively steady mixture of challenges and victories. On the front lines of world missions, the highs are higher and the lows are lower — the victories are wonderful; the pain is real. Unlike the analogy of the roller coaster, however, the highs and lows often take place simultaneously. The following two stories demonstrate this.

The Highs and Lows of Northeast India

We arrived in Siliguri, India about noon after a 30-hour train trip. Twice, I had passed the hours in prayer sitting in the doorway between our coach and the one ahead of ours because our air-conditioned sleeper was too cold for my sore throat and cough. I enjoyed my hours of prayer with the warm Indian wind in my face, countryside sights in my eyes, and zealous expectation for what God was going to do in northeast India in my heart. I felt ready for ministry in Siliguri. On the train, we had snacked on crackers, fruit, and nuts for two days, so the hotel meal upon arrival was welcome and filling. The pastors' conference began the next day.

That next evening at the pastors' conference, I was about two-thirds of the way through the message when I realized I had to take a quick break. I turned to my interpreter and told him I was going to the toilet and would be right back. When I returned, I was able to finish the sermon, and it was well received. However, that was the beginning of 24 hours of severe diarrhea.

All night long, I was up multiple times each hour. The pain, discomfort, weakness, and sense of hopelessness and despair were intense. Early in the morning, I warned Char to be ready to speak for the first session and to be prepared to deliver the second session, too. I assured her that she would do just fine, but in my heart, I was disappointed to be unable to do what I went there to do. Using her own materials, Char made three presentations. She did so well that had the Lord not enabled me to make my presentation that evening, I would have been out of a job!

During that time, I spent miserable hours traveling from the bed to the toilet and trying to get liquids into my system. Our host provided some oral, granular hydration salts, and I managed to get some apples, bananas, rice, and milk to stay in my system. Char and the interpreter lovingly cared for me when they were not teaching. I was naturally appreciative for their help, but what energy and power of concentration I could muster was spent praying that God would bless the sessions in my absence and that I would soon recover. By the time of the evening session, I felt strong enough to make the presentation, and it was well received by grateful, godly, and eager learners.

In 24 hours, I had felt the weakness of my physical body on the one hand and the glorious strength of the presence of God and warm appreciation for the message on the other. I experienced disappointment, despair, weakness, sickness, and pain in my body. Simultaneously, I felt satisfaction, victory, fruitfulness, and joy in the spiritual ministry dimension. There is a price to pay for the joy of ministry.

Another Roller Coaster in East India

By the time we reached Ongole (in the state of Andra Pradesh the next week), my sore throat and cough were much better. However, six weeks of perspiring in India's heat had taken its toll on my chest and stomach area. The painful heat rash that produced hundreds of painful red spots caused me terrible physical pain. In addition, it was a psychologically painful reminder of what had happened two years ago when a similar heat rash had developed into a massive hair follicle infection. It had taken an injection of steroids and an extended use of antibiotics to heal the multitude of nickel-sized, quarter-inch thick, infected, and swollen sores on my chest. The menace of this heat rash was the same as the early stages of the previous one. Thinking I might be in for a repeat of the former difficulty greatly compounded my misery.

By the end of September, the drought and hot summer weather of Andra Pradesh is usually over and a cooler rainy season has begun — not so that year. I was taking three or four baths each day, washing the afflicted area on my chest and stomach with medicated soap or shampoo. I soon had dreadful heat rash all over my back, stomach, and chest.

On one trip to a village, we stopped the car for someone to buy bananas. The torture of the heat rash was increased by the heat of the sun on the motionless jeep. It was unbearable. I fled for the shade of a fruit stand canopy on the side of the road. When we were ready to go, I reentered the "oven on wheels" and we moved on.

Upon arrival at the countryside church, my hosts arranged a bath area in a nearby house for me to use. After the bath with medicated soap, I applied medicated powder to my chest and stomach. One of the young men was kind enough to apply it to my back. I was bathed, powdered, and ready for the day's seminar sessions — so I thought.

Returning to the church, we learned that the meeting would be delayed. The men had gone to appeal to the village governmental authorities to stop an aggressive farmer from occupying and planting crops on a Christian burial site in the area. In front of the church, a canopy about 12 feet wide and 30 feet long had been erected to provide lunchtime shade.

Finding no shady place to pray, I slowly paced back and forth in the hot air under this canopy. When I say, "shady place," I mean simply not as blistering hot as the sunny places. I pleaded with God that just as he had with the three Hebrew men recorded in the book of Daniel, he would deliver me from my fiery furnace. I pleaded with him to intervene for the conference while we waited for the return of the burial site defenders. In enough time to bake a loaf of yeast bread in a more conventional oven than the one I was in, we began the conference.

It was a joy to share inspirational and liberating truth about marriage and family. Such a seminar for these villagers is unheard of! As the day's sessions proceeded, Char and I were able to present a full complement of teachings. Our topics included "Grow in Character as your Marriage Grows," "How to Raise Confident Children," and "How to Raise Obedient Children." For well-intended but inadequately informed village pastors, this information was helpful. It not only helped them nurture their own families, but also equipped them with new information as Christian models and leaders. Their feedback repeatedly reflected their appreciation.

By 5:00 p.m., we had completed a victorious day and had individual prayer with each participant. We returned to Ongole exhausted. It was such a privilege to share wonderful Christian ideas that make a positive difference in marriages and parenting.

Such is life on the roller coaster of missions life. For all the challenges we experienced on the trip to get there, the joy and thrill of spending time with these villagers was worth the trip. We must decide if the joys of effective and fruitful ministry are worth the price we must pay. My value system says to me that it is.

Keeping Perspective

Over the years, we have learned to ask if a project has worth — not if it is easy. There are times when a project of worth is accomplished with relative ease, but often the enemy opposes good projects. This principle holds true for Christians in a wide variety of careers. Some opportunities for fruitful, spiritual ministry are rare precisely because they are so difficult. Not everyone is willing to pay the price.

On the other hand, from an entirely different perspective, perhaps God allows difficulties to keep fruitful Christians prayerful and humble. If that were the case, I would rather

The resilient and determined among us will press through in such cases.

submit to the process than become lifted up in pride and rendered unfit to serve. The enemy intends to steal, kill, and destroy. He does not want Christians of any kind to succeed or anyone to benefit, be saved, or grow. He does not want pastors or Christians to become equipped for more effective Christian living.

The next time your wonderful career opportunity is simultaneously accompanied by adversity, bear in mind that a sovereign Lord lovingly balances the mixture — bitter and sweet, sorrow and joy, and cross and crown — so that we are sufficiently emboldened and encouraged while remaining prayerful and dependent. The resilient and determined among us will press through in such cases.

The careers of full-time Christians are not boring. There is plenty of adventure, discovery, and challenge for the most courageous, daring, and zealous among us. Gospel work or serving God in any workplace is not for weaklings. In the next chapter, you will read about Peter doing the impossible and be challenged to follow his example. That daring and adventurous man never held back from any opportunity to serve his Master. If you seek a full and rich career, consider world missions. However, if God leads you to remain in your own home culture, do not hold back from venturing forth on miraculous and fruitful paths.

If a full-time Christian makes serious efforts in prayer and trusts God for miracles, miracles will happen. They may be the kind of miracles a teacher needs such as revelation, wisdom, and insight. On the other hand, they might be a more readily recognized miracle such as physical healings. Depending upon your profession, miracles of diplomacy, administration, connecting an impossible pipefitting, or the miraculous protection of your child all could reveal God's involvement in your life. In any case, if miracles — large or small — are not happening, we are not praying enough. If we are praying enough, God is working, and there will be miracles.

The very moment that those miracles occur, a very subtle temptation arises. The Holy Spirit works so naturally in partnership with humans that we think we were clever enough to have conceived the ideas, insights, or solutions that we experienced. Experiencing miracles of revelation, for example, may produce pride — we may think *we* thought of it. The partnership between God and man in ministry is a beautiful fusing of the divine and the human. God needs human bodies and minds through which He can work — vessels where He is "made flesh" once again on earth. Nevertheless, sometimes we are deceived and think it is *our* skill at work.

When this happens, our choices are simple: when miracles take place, we experience increased ego-related temptations. When miracles are not taking place, we are not praying enough for God's supernatural involvement in our lives. It's either one or the other. With heavy intercession, miracles and their temptations occur. With limited or no prayer, neither miracles nor their related tests occur. The roller coaster ride of the miraculous highs and the occasional ego-deflating lows that drive us to our knees both accompany God-seekers.

On this fruitful yet difficult ministry path, the excitement of the supernatural is tempered by the humility with which we respond to those difficulties. This is God's way. Without aggressively seeking God in prayer, the steady but mundane human performance avoids these extremes and is safer. A ship in harbor is safe and sound, but is that the purpose of a ship? Take your choice: one route is more comfortable and well traveled while the other is less traveled, more dangerous, and far more fruitful.

CHAPTER FOUR

How to Do the Impossible

> *"'Lord, if it is you,' Peter replied,*
> *'tell me to come to you on the water.'"*
>
> *Matthew 14:28*

Miracles can and should happen repeatedly in our lives. Miracles — grand or modest, answers to prayer, blessings, or God's intervention and involvement in our lives — ought to occur regularly. Furthermore, it is *our* responsibility to recognize them. Just because God cleverly slips miracles into the fabric of our everyday life so that they *appear* as coincidences does not mean they happen by accident.

Some of the miracles we need are God's clever responses to impossible situations. Take the story of the storm when Jesus walked on the water to the disciples. The story of what happened next between Jesus and Peter reveals wonderful ideas about handling impossible conditions. Peter did the impossible — he walked on the water. We, too, can do the impossible when we recognize these principles. Additionally, this story helps distinguish between faith and presumption. It illustrates how prayer can lead to faith and how we can test our ideas so we avoid presumption.

Of all the messages I have presented, this one is more the result of sitting at the feet of Jesus, the Master Teacher, than any other; it is not the result of book research. I do not think I have ever heard anyone teach any of these ideas. Therefore, I take full responsibility if any part of this sounds too imaginative.

However, the applications of these ideas have been a stabilizing force in my own life since July of 2002 as I do things I had never dreamed possible for me. What God showed me in Patankot of Northwest India through the following verses is extremely important to anyone who wants to do more for God. Here is the story from Matthew 14:28-32:

> "'Lord, if it is you,' Peter replied, 'tell me to come to you on the water.' 'Come,' he said. Then Peter got down out of the boat, walked on the water, and came toward Jesus. But when he saw the wind, he was afraid and beginning to sink, cried out, 'Lord save me!' Immediately Jesus reached out his hand and caught him. 'You of little faith,' he said, 'Why did you doubt?' And when they climbed into the boat, the wind died down. Then those who were in the boat worshiped him, saying, 'Truly you are the Son of God.'"

This amazing story illustrates 12 significant principles of overcoming impossible conditions with miracles. I believe you and I both can increase our faith throughout the rest of this chapter as we re-live this experience with Peter. First, let me explain how God used these verses in my life.

Experience Reinforced after Learning the Theory

February 9, 2006 was the first day of an unexpected and strange series of events. That morning, I woke up with horrible pain in my left elbow. Unable to bear the agony, I sought medical treatment for what I learned was bursitis in my elbow. After the doctor aspirated the fluid from the elbow, infection set in. As that day came to a close, I had developed a debilitating case of cellulitis in my whole arm in addition to excruciating bursitis. Coincidentally, within a day or two, Char developed serious infections in the roots of two upper teeth dangerously near her brain. This caused her face to swell like a basketball with her eyes becoming just narrow slits.

Also on February 9, something even more significant happened that left our future completely suspended in mid-air. After eight months of talks, correspondence, meetings, board decisions, and discussions of job definitions, we had both been invited to take up new full-time missionary appointments with a Christian organization that has churches in 140 nations. They had invited me to coordinate the professional development of their missionary personnel and continuing education for the national pastors in those nations. Char was to have her own professional role. She would have taught missionary appointees and served as a consultant to the Bible colleges and institutes in those 140 nations. These exciting and challenging opportunities merged our academic work with full-time missions involvement. The organization repeatedly assured us the invitation was real. We were excited about our new opportunities, and I resigned my positions as Professor of Missions at Oral Roberts University (ORU) and as Associate Pastor for English Ministries at the Tulsa Chinese Christian Church.

The very same day I had my painful attack of bursitis, February 9, we got word that the new missions opportunities had been withdrawn. So as Char and I struggled with horrible physical pain, we also tried to process what appeared to be a major career reversal. When the notice came, we were stunned beyond description. Fine people whom we respect made decisions that enormously impacted us. Suddenly we were thrown into an impossible situation and an opportunity for God to do something immeasurably more than we could imagine. We no longer were gainfully employed and had no idea what the future held. Our boat had capsized and we weren't even thinking yet about trying to walk on water.

However, within a few days as we took our situation to the Lord, God began to point us in a new direction. Upon inquiry, we received an invitation to work with a networking organization in Africa that would enable us to focus on training Christian leaders throughout that great continent in seminars and lecture series similar to the ones we had already done. It looked like a good possibility, but we still needed God's confirmation. If we were to move in that direction, we would have to "walk on water" in a number of ways. In Chapter Fourteen, you will read the rest of the story about our plans for a new ministry in Africa!

The following pages reveal scriptural principles that helped us as we left the boat and began to walk on the water as Peter did. In the drama and difficulties of transition that played out in the following months, the lessons of this Scripture passage were an enormous help to us. We learned, through experience, that the lessons of Peter walking on the water put our feet on the solid ground of the Word of God even when we were walking on the water. Now, let's look at the 12 lessons.

Lesson 1: Those Who Do the Impossible Recognize the Lordship of Jesus

Peter said, "Lord, if it is you, tell me to come to you on the water." Peter called Jesus "Lord," but, more importantly, Peter really *recognized* and *submitted to* Jesus as Lord. This is shown more by what Peter did or didn't do than by merely calling Jesus "Lord." Peter passed the test on both points. From the boat, he called Jesus "Lord." Then, by waiting until Jesus told him to step out onto the water, Peter demonstrated by his behavior that Jesus really was his Lord — his authority.

We may call Jesus "Lord," but if we are avoiding or not doing what He asks, He is not our Lord. Waiting until we have the Lord's approval on a possible action is as much an act of obedience as to take action after we have His approval. In either case, our obedient action speaks more loudly than just calling Him "Lord."

> Our obedient action speaks more loudly than just calling Him "Lord."

My dean offered to reverse the faculty search process set in motion by my resignation if I could assure him that I would remain a length of time at ORU. I recall ever so clearly asking God about our Africa ministry opportunity, "Lord if this is you, tell me to come to you on the water." I certainly did not want to leave the security of the ORU boat and walk on water in Africa unless I knew it was of the Lord. Better men than I have had difficulties with ministry in Africa. Here are the important questions: Have we submitted our ideas to Him for His approval? Do we know it is God's will?

Lesson 2: Those Who Do the Impossible Are Willing To Take Initiative

The two simple words, "Peter replied," are the focus of this thought. Jesus identified himself to all the disciples in the boat, not just Peter. They all had equal information; Jesus had walked on the water to meet all of them as they struggled with the wind that was against them.

Yet Peter, unlike the other disciples, had an idea and took the initiative to ask if he could walk out to Jesus. We know that Jesus approved of Peter's proposal since He told Peter to come; it was a good idea. Jesus evidently had a plan to use this in Peter's and others' lives.

God likes creativity. We are made in His image with power to come up with our own ideas of what we might do for God. It is good to be an active participant in a ministry partnership with God using our God-given creativity. It says to God that we recognize the gift of creativity that He so richly gave us, and we want to use it always and only for His glory. It is not presumptuous to brainstorm, consider data, think, strategize, propose ministry ideas, and submit them to the Lord for his approval.

God often dictates our activities, but that does not mean we should stop initiating. Responding obediently when God directs is an important part of a partnership with God. However, that is different from the consideration before us. The important issue in this principle is whether we are willing to be creative or not.

This lesson is liberating because it allows us to initiate ideas. Later, we may discover that it was God working through our resourcefulness that gave us the idea. Nevertheless, we ought to feel free to be an active participant by initiating ideas. Philippians 2:13 says, "It is God who works in you to will and to act in order to fulfill his good purpose." Jesus said, "If you remain in me and my words remain in you, ask whatever you wish, and it will be done for you" (John 15:7). God actually working in us — giving us His desires and ideas, and enabling us to do them — is an exciting aspect of our partnership with Him. This goes right along with Peter's creativity. Here is, at least this time in reported conversations between Jesus and Peter, an instance where Peter was thinking God's thoughts along with Him.

> It is not presumptuous to brainstorm, consider data, think, strategize, propose ministry ideas, and submit them to the Lord for his approval.

If Peter can take the initiative, submit his idea to his Lord, and be right once; perhaps we can too. It's not wrong to try. We won't always be right, just as Peter wasn't always right, but we must try or we will never know. Submissive human initiation is one means of cooperation with God. Let the creative juices flow. Put your heart into your work — and learn how to avoid presumption.

Lesson 3: Those Who Do the Impossible Should Not be Presumptuous

It is presumptuous to act on our own initiative without the Lord's approval. That is why it is always important to submit our ideas to Him. Peter waited for Jesus' instruction. Jesus responded to Peter by saying, "Come." Peter did not act on his proposal until Jesus indicated his approval. Waiting for Jesus' response further demonstrates Peter's submission to the lordship of Jesus. Even in the midst of all the excitement of initiating a new, creative, bold, and daring idea, Peter walked to Jesus on the water but only in complete compliance to His Lord.

Have you ever been so excited by something you were praying about that your faith carried you away into presumption? Did you suffer loss? Do you know anyone else who has suffered damage because they mistook presumption for faith? I know of a couple who tried to buy a house that was beyond their income. Because of faith, they thought God would supply their need, but they lost the house.

We all know of ministries and businesses that have overextended themselves in an effort to exercise faith. Good and sincere Christians make honest mistakes like these. We don't know all their circumstances, but we can learn from the facts without assuming the unknowns. We observe to learn, not to criticize. Is there any way to protect ourselves? Peter's model provides a safety mechanism.

Jesus said if we were going to build, we should count the cost ahead of time. The same one who told us to have faith also taught us to measure our obstacles against our resources. This is one way to avoid presumption with our finances when trying to exercise faith.

> "Suppose one of you wants to build a tower. Will he not first sit down and estimate the cost to see if he has enough money to complete it? For if he lays the foundation and is not able to finish it, everyone who sees it will ridicule him, saying, 'This fellow began to build and was not able to finish'" (Luke 14: 28-30).

Surely, Jesus intended this principle to apply to more than the relatively few people who build towers. Let us exercise faith in building ministries and businesses while also exercising the caution Jesus Himself taught. Such caution is not due to a lack of faith but to the presence of wisdom. Scripture maintains a good balance between faith and reason; we are to exercise faith but balance it with good judgment. God may lead us in faith beyond our resources, but we should be sure it is God and not just our imagination.

From another angle, presumption can also lead us to *not* do something we *should* do. Do you know people who have possibly experienced early deaths because they were determined to work their way through their fatal sicknesses by "faith," declining the windows of opportunity the doctors gave them to receive medical treatment? We will never know in this life if they could have been cured through medicine. However, the important point is whether their faith was in response to a directive from God or whether it was actually presumption.

Proverbs has an obscure verse that is rich in reason and poignant in its warning against presumptuously *not* doing what we should do to help our situation. According to this verse, it is presumptuous not to do all that is humanly possible to accomplish a task and then blame God if things go awry. Proverbs 18:9 states, "One who is slack in his work is brother to one who destroys." One destroys by slacking — taking too little or no action or not completing what could have been accomplished. The other destroys by actively destroying what has already been accomplished.

The difference between one who slacks off and one who destroys is that one is careless and the other is evil. However, they are both errors placed in the same category by Solomon. Both errors result in destruction. Presumption can be expressed by acting without God's authorization or *not* acting responsibly when we should be doing something and instead expecting God to intervene for us.

If we do not do all that is in our power to accomplish a task and carelessly trust *God* to do what *we* could have done, we are inappropriately testing God. The Scripture says we should not test God in this way. "Do not put the Lord your God to the test" (Matthew 4:7). "God helps those who help themselves" is not Scripture, but it does contain an element of truth consistent with the Bible. In the case of Peter walking on the water, he was right to first ask for Jesus' permission and *then* act only after receiving it. Following Peter's example, carefully confirming that Jesus — not our imagination — is telling us to walk on water, we can balance boldness and caution, accomplish much for the Lord, and still be saved from presumption.

We find another type of presumption and a contrast to Peter's submission in the overconfidence of the seven sons of Sceva in Acts 19:13-16:

> "Some Jews who went around driving out evil spirits tried to invoke the name of the Lord Jesus over those who were demon-possessed. They would say, 'In the name of Jesus, whom Paul preaches, I command you to come out.' Seven sons of Sceva, a Jewish chief priest, were doing this. One day, the evil spirit answered them, 'Jesus I know, and I know about Paul, but who are you?' Then the man who had the evil spirit jumped on them and overpowered them all. He gave them such a beating that they ran out of the house naked and bleeding."

We know for many reasons that the sons of Sceva were brazenly presumptuous, especially since they were not even believers. However, their example provides another illustration of contrast to Peter's miracle. In their presumption, they experienced involvement with the very powerful evil spirit world, but it did not do them any good! It left them beaten and bleeding. Their experience can be a warning to us to be careful in dealing with enemy spiritual forces.

Faith fiascos are due to neither God's nonchalance nor weakness. They are not proof of God's failure but of man's presumption.

Our presumptuous efforts on God's behalf often leave evidence of men's failures, not God's. Faith fiascos are due to neither God's nonchalance nor weakness. They are not proof of God's failure but of man's presumption. God can protect us from them if we let Him. The unfinished projects are not productive; they are counterproductive, and often discredit God's reputation. Yet, who can travel the globe and help every scoffer understand that many Christian "failures" are due to misguided zeal (presumption)?

Of the many miracles recorded in the gospels, it is curious that this is the only one Jesus performed that lacked an apparent useful purpose. Later, while teaching in the synagogue in Capernaum on the other side of the sea (John 6), Jesus declined to provide a miraculous sign for the crowd of Jews who asked for one. Jesus does not perform needless miracles or signs just because asked. He usually performs useful miracles. Yet on this occasion, Jesus came surprisingly close to performing a miracle that had little or no apparent usefulness.

Peter did not really need to go walking on the water because Jesus was on his way to the boat and would arrive soon enough. So why did Jesus tell Peter to come? The miracle itself was not one of healing, provision, deliverance, or forgiveness. Though I see no apparent reason or need, I dare say *Jesus* had a reason. Perhaps later, Peter or even ourselves would look back on this event and learn from it.

Could the reason for this miracle have been the lessons we would learn from the conversation between Jesus and Peter throughout this narrative? Could it be that God desires for us to learn how to experience miracles — including avoiding loss through presumption? Perhaps this time, He performed a miracle for instruction rather than for the usefulness of the miracle itself. Promotion of faith and the belief in miracles may be one reason God performs miracles.

Jesus' miracle of causing Peter to walk on the water is possibly the most interesting and entertaining miracle in the Gospels. It seems to be an exceptional miracle. For this reason, we must be even more careful not to standardize this miracle and presumptuously expect miracles that merely entertain. We must not use God as though He were merely a source of magical power; that would be to misuse Him. He has personality, opinions, thoughts, plans, and feelings. Let us have bold faith, but avoid anything resembling trivia. We are dealing with the Almighty God. Just because Jesus performed this exciting miracle this time does not mean we can expect any kind of interesting miracle any time we want.

Lesson 4: Those Who Do the Impossible Are Willing To Leave the Safety of the Boat

My 10 years as missions professor at Oral Roberts University were wonderful. My life was full, and I was blessed. To me, ORU had a great working and spiritual atmosphere. I had a wonderful dean under whom to serve and stellar colleagues with whom to share ideas. My students, both international and American, were mature and dedicated ministry candidates. Moreover, for the first time in my life, I experienced a degree of financial security.

Years before I had obediently followed God's calling to go abroad as a missionary. Then equally obediently, I became a trainer of missionaries at ORU in the United States. You may ask, "With all of those advantages, why would you leave such a position at age 62? Wasn't it enough that you traveled to Europe, Africa, Asia, or the Pacific Islands each year?" I admit that I felt quite secure in my ORU surroundings. How did I discover my sense of security in a human institution? What else can we learn from Peter's experience?

Boats are safe; water-walking is not. The boat illustrates the safety of normalcy. Boats are the usual way to travel on the water. Peter was willing to leave the safety of the normal, usual routine. He was willing to go alone on a new venture. This adds an interesting dynamic to Peter's action within the passage, "Peter got down out of the boat."

You can enjoy not only physical safety by staying with the normal flow of life in boats, but also psychological safety by remaining with the people there. Whatever your cultural context, the two thoughts of physical safety in the boat and psychological safety in the crowd within the boat are both easy to grasp. You do not stand out in the crowd when you are doing what the crowd is doing nor are you so likely to do the impossible!

Peter had the courage to leave both the physical safety of the boat itself and the psychological safety of the group in the boat. God may call on you to do that some day. Or, God may honor your initiative if you volunteer to try something new and daring for Him. Are you willing to ask Him? Are you willing to leave physical and psychological safety? Think of the heroes of the Bible who braved both physical dangers and misunderstandings. Peter is a good illustration of this point, but many other Bible characters showed us the same courage.

To Char and me, the opportunity was worth leaving Tulsa to do — to take the teachings and the teaching experiences gained at such a well-known evangelical seminary to the pastors of Africa. It is our great joy to serve those who do evangelism and church planting in Africa. We smile at the prospect of conducting conferences that can enable pastors to provide discipleship and nurture those coming to Christ throughout sub-Sahara Africa today. Their invitation to us was just like Jesus saying, "Come" to Peter. Our response to what God is doing in Africa was to ask Him if we can join Him in the great work that He is doing there. We know that many good, faithful people remain at their posts year after year and for them it right to do. However, we continue to thank Him for the challenge and opportunity before us and trust that He will enable us to "walk on water."

There were several times during those first months out of the "ORU boat" that we took comfort in Peter's courage. We had to walk by faith when our stable income was no more. Furthermore, our "commute" to work was about to increase from a mile and a half to the thousands of miles necessary to travel to conduct pastors' conferences. Just as Peter, after leaving the security of the boat, walked where he had never walked before, so are we. And so will you when you, at Jesus' approval, leave your boat.

Lesson 5: Those Who Do the Impossible Follow Through With Their Intentions

There is nobility in initiating a bold plan, but there is greater nobility in executing it. I am very grateful that Peter showed us how to follow through when he got down out of the boat and walked on the water.

Intention is an interesting word. It suggests that an action has been decided but not executed. For some, an intention is as good as an action because they have already established the habit of doing what they think — executing intentions.

In Matthew 21:28-31, Jesus tells the story of two sons. It illustrates the difference between intention and execution of intention.

> "'What do you think? There was a man who had two sons. He went to the first and said, 'Son, go and work today in the vineyard.' 'I will not,' he answered, but later he changed his mind and went. Then the father went to the other son and said the same thing. He answered, 'I will, sir,' but he did not go. Which of the two did what his father wanted? 'The first,' they answered."

That lesson shows the necessity of obedience and following through on intentions. Peter's follow-through demonstrates the importance of moving forward after initiation and prayer, exercising the faith needed to execute, and completing the proposal. The objective of this book is to learn how to rise up from mediocrity and seek Him so that the supernatural occurs.

We earnestly desire to change things through prayer. We learn from Peter that if our prayers are to produce miracles, they too should be matched by faith and action when God gives us permission to proceed.

In order to follow through with intentions, you have to put your "decider" in neutral and your "actor" on automatic pilot. I have learned to do that in running marathons. The middle of a 42-kilometer endurance race — with pain moving from one part of my body to another — is not the time to decide whether to run a marathon! During the race, one must persevere based on a previous decision. Peter initiated a proposal, received permission, and followed through on his decision in spite of the psychological and physical dangers.

Lesson 6: Those Who Do the Impossible Move toward Jesus

When Peter stepped out of the boat and began walking on water, Matthew tells us he "*came* toward Jesus" (italics mine). The original Greek text also uses the word for "came," not "went." If I had been writing this story, I would have said *went*. However, on reflection, Matthew correctly understands who is the center of this story; it is Jesus, not Peter. Peter "*came* toward Jesus." The best of stories always have Jesus at the center and all action moves toward Him. If the choice of each word in Scripture is deliberate and hints of theological truth, Matthew has it right. The action *comes* toward Jesus who is at the center regardless of the writer's location on the sideline. Jesus had told him "come" and Jesus was Peter's goal or destination. Peter wanted to reach and experience Jesus in a supernatural way. This is an important spiritual lesson for us.

Whenever we seek to do something for God in the supernatural realm, we should move toward Jesus. A genuinely theocentric worldview has powerful potential. As revealed in Jesus Christ, God is the great Center around which all activities revolve; the Goal toward which we strive; the Fountain from which all blessings flow; the One toward whom all glory is reflected, and the One whom we rise to seek. When He is no longer the central character in our story — or our ministry, project, service, or enterprise is focused on pleasure or gain or even good human accomplishment — our story loses the center around which all plots, drama, and colorful story lines should revolve. Matthew makes a great statement when he says Peter "came toward Jesus."

Lesson 7: Those Who Do the Impossible Will Have Their Faith Tested

The Bible says you cannot see the wind. "The wind blows wherever it pleases. You hear its sound, but you cannot tell where it comes from or where it is going" (John 3:8). We all know you can't see the wind. So why would Matthew write, "But when he saw the wind, he was afraid." We do not "see the wind;" we see its effects. When we see the leaves moving in the trees, we say we see the wind blowing in the trees. Actually, we are only seeing the leaves move in the trees. Peter saw the waves, the rain, the spray, or Jesus' robe blowing in the wind; he didn't *see* the *wind*. What are the lessons here? Did Matthew deliberately say Peter saw the wind? I see three possible spiritual lessons in the wind.

The first lesson is that the swift movement of uncontrollable events around us makes doing the impossible *seem* more difficult. We become fearful like Peter. Take the movement of the waves into consideration and assume the waves made it more difficult to exercise faith. Following this line of thought, water in motion under the influence of wind requires greater faith to walk on than calm water. It does not require unusual amounts of human imagination to agree that uncontrollable water might be a greater test of faith than controlled waters. When we experience rapid movement or commotion in the waters of our miracles, the motion or uncontrollable development of events around us can make us afraid. It made Peter afraid.

> You can safely assume that the same power enabling you to walk on the water will also help you with the troublesome waves.

Here is a truth both profound and easy to miss: we wouldn't even be on that water to begin with if it weren't for a miracle! Somehow, the swirling of waves, in addition to the fact that we are already on water doing the impossible, makes us afraid. However, if you are already walking on water (doing the extraordinary), just remember the miraculous nature of what you are already doing. You can safely assume that the same power enabling you to walk on the water will also help you with the troublesome waves. In these cases, the rapid developments around us — the waves — provide us with even more reason to keep our eyes firmly focused on Jesus who made the impossible possible in the first place.

The second lesson is that visible problems often stem from invisible causes. The waves were the obvious or visible problem; the wind was the real cause behind the visible cause. Our storms have visible, apparent aspects and invisible, real causes. When Matthew said Peter saw the wind, could he be hinting that in our "storms" we need to think beyond the material phenomena and *see* the deeper, invisible, spiritual causes behind them?

The invisible spirit world affects the material world. When we learn this, then we are ready to learn how to solve material problems with spiritual tools. We can assume there is always a spiritual reality working invisibly behind visible problems. Spiritual solutions are necessary in solving these physical problems. Such problems in the physical realm must be solved with spiritual solutions. Either the solution comes to us as God gives us wisdom, or He conveniently intervenes while working on His own in response to our prayer. Therefore, there are no problems that are not spiritual. Every problem has a spiritual component. Problems can and should be a matter of prayer. And when satisfactorily resolved, they produce testimonies of God's grace and victory manifested among us.

Thirdly, we may be tempted to think that seeing the wind portrays the reason for Peter's doubt. I question this. There had to be something other than the wind that caused Peter to doubt. If the wind was the real reason for Peter's doubt, wouldn't that mean that without the wind Peter could have walked on calm water? Are we, therefore, to believe it was the wind that made this water walk difficult? The wind was blowing so Peter doubted and began to sink! Clearly, that is not the case. Peter could not walk on any water, calm or with waves. His problem was not the wind; his problem was that he took his eyes and faith off Jesus.

The invisible spirit world affects the material world. When we learn this, then we are ready to learn how to solve material problems with spiritual tools.

The text says, "… when he saw the wind, he was afraid and beginning to sink," (Matthew 14:30). Peter got distracted by the wind and waves from looking at Jesus. The problem was not that he saw the waves, but that he focused more on them than he did on Jesus. We should be aware of our situations at hand. It is not wrong to look at, face, and try to responsibly handle issues that we encounter in our work for the Lord. However, our *focus* should not be on them. When we walk on water, we had better remember to keep our eyes on Jesus.

Lesson 8: Those Who Do the Impossible Call on the Lord

Peter succeeded more than he failed in this story. He called Jesus "Lord," initiated an idea, submitted it to Jesus' timing, followed through with his intention, and walked on the water! Already that is great success! He experienced failure when he became afraid and took his eyes off Jesus. Yet even in this one failure among all his successes, he was right to acknowledge his failure and call quickly on Jesus. Peter did that. Matthew wrote, "… beginning to sink, he cried out, 'Lord, save me.'" This was the right thing to do.

Peter could have swum to Jesus from the boat, but that would not have been considered a success in this case. Peter was on a spiritual mission. He had asked to walk on the water. However, he was not thinking about how to reach someone on the water in which he himself was swimming. Furthermore, by the time he had to call out to Jesus for help, he had already been walking on the water and was thinking in terms of walking, not swimming. Swimming — using normal human means of traveling in the water when you are out of the boat — was not in his paradigm for success at the time. Given that water walking was his goal, purpose, and focus, he did the right thing: He called on the Lord.

Swimming may have been the prideful, independent, self-reliant, or the face-saving thing to do, but Peter was not concerned about that. Peter was more interested in getting it right than covering a failure. He called on the Lord. So let's add another success to Peter's account.

Calling on the Lord is the right thing to do when we fail. Calling on the Lord can change a failure into a successful learning opportunity — a successful failure. Even in a failure, a successful recovery is possible. Instead of lamenting the failure, why not celebrate the great recovery?

We too, when trying to walk in the supernatural, will often encounter waves with an unfriendly spiritual power behind them. Even if our faith falters as Peter's did, we dare not trust the "arm of flesh" — our own or others'. That would be falling and failing. Instead when we fall, we want to turn our temporary failure into a success. Look at the following two passages:

> **Falling and failing:** "See how the evildoers lie fallen — thrown down, not able to rise" (Psalm 36:12).

> **Falling and succeeding:** "If the Lord delights in a man's way, he makes his steps firm; though he stumble, he will not fall, for the Lord upholds him with his hand" (Psalm 37:23-24).

When we stumble, and we all do, we can call on the Lord so we do not utterly fall.

Lesson 9: Those Who Do the Impossible Experience Jesus' Faithfulness

As we have just mentioned, among all his successes, Peter had one failure. Jesus, in short order and at the appropriate time, taught him something about that failure. However, a more urgent matter was at hand — first save the sinking man.

"Immediately, Jesus reached out his hand and caught him."
Jesus quickly helped Peter. There is a seminar worth of truth in
this for us.

When we work with God's people — whether they are seasoned
believers or little lambs — there are lessons they need to learn
and eventually they must be taught. However, we often need to
precede the instructions with some mercy and some help. Jesus'
treatment of Peter illustrates the times when helping is more
appropriate than tutoring. First, we must learn to save the
sinking man and help the person as Jesus did. Once he is
rescued, he will be ready to receive instruction. In time, we can
teach him what he should have done, correct his errors, and
show him how he can do it better in the future.

In my field of missions, we call this the "starting point and
process." In Kingdom work, we deal with spiritual
transformation (change, growth, and progress). We must begin
where people are and let them grow gradually over the long
process. This is the way Jesus worked with Peter on the Sea of
Galilee, and it is the way God works with us. People around us
will make mistakes; they will sink into the water. We don't have
a choice in that matter — they will fail just as surely as we
ourselves have failed at times.

We do have a choice, however, as to whether we will judge and
lecture them or help, nourish, and care for them before we teach
them what they did wrong. I like Jesus' example. In spite of
Peter's lapse of faith, Jesus helped him and then taught him. Can
we learn from this not to criticize anyone who has weak faith?
They need our help more than our criticism. Many times, they
can discover for themselves what they did wrong. At first, they
just need some help with the consequences of their failures.

Lesson 10: Those Who Do the Impossible Learn Something from Jesus

Do you ever feel like God is more firm in His dealings with you
than He is in His dealings with others around you? He seems to
allow them to get away with things the Holy Spirit would never
let you do. Join the company of Peter, the leading disciple. Peter
had more faith, courage, boldness, and creativity than the other
disciples did. He excelled. He tried something new. He dared to
attempt the impossible. Yet, Jesus rebuked Peter — the most
bold disciple with apparently the most faith — when he said,

"You of little faith," and "Why did you doubt?" Why did Jesus criticize Peter and not the others? There is a noble reason for the more *difficult* treatment some of us receive and remembering it will give us added confidence.

We do not read that Jesus criticized the other 11 disciples for remaining in the boat. No mention is made of any remark that He may have made regarding their inactivity. They evidently sat in the comfort and safety of the boat without hearing one word of correction from Jesus. Jesus did not ask them, "Why didn't you try? Why are you sitting there safely in the boat?" Why did Jesus single out Peter for correction?

Skilled mentors often use this tactic when they teach others. If we are developing others, we do not invest time to comment on those from whom we expect less. Our critique of our more able followers is our compliment to them because we believe they can do even better. We critique those with more potential. So did Jesus. So does God.

When you know how God further develops successful people, you realize the rebuke was a compliment.

Jesus was essentially happy with Peter's progress. He did not discourage Peter from starting. He saved Peter when Peter needed saving. Throughout the dialogue, Jesus had a positive attitude toward Peter and wanted to develop him even further. Peter came so close to reaching Jesus that Jesus pointed out what he should have done to be completely successful. If Jesus is developing you and is happy with your progress, He often indicates it with opportunities for even further improvement.

Jesus accepts the little steps of faith we can make. He encourages us to try. When we fail, he tells us the truth — what we should have done to succeed. In rebuking Peter, Jesus may have been implying, "You almost made it. You could have done it. You walked on the water, Peter." Jesus prunes fruitful disciples so they will become more fruitful. Fruitful Peter got pruned! Pruning is ultimately a compliment. Ouch! Yes, the critique hurts, but we have to keep God's goal in mind. When you know how God further develops successful people, you realize the rebuke was a compliment.

Lesson 11: Those Who Do the Impossible Gain an Opportunity to See God in New Ways

When Jesus and Peter arrived safely at the boat, the disciples responded to the miracle with the proper reaction. "Then those who were in the boat worshiped Him, saying, 'Truly you are the Son of God.'" They worshipped Jesus, recognizing the significance of the multiple miracles of Jesus walking on the water, enabling Peter also to walk on the water, and calming the sea. The parallel record of this story in Mark 6 tells us the sea grew calm as Jesus climbed into the boat. The miracles of God show us that He is awesome. Those who do not experience miracles do not have the same appreciation for God's power and glory experienced by those who do. If we want to see God's glory, we may have to walk on water and take some risks. Miracles contribute to our awareness of Jesus' authority, honor, majesty, and glory.

Somewhere between inactivity and presumption is the ideal of courage coupled with submissive and obedient faith in God to do the impossible.

Miracles help us in practical ways, but in the grand scheme of things (the eternal realm), they help us see the true God. In this case, the disciples acknowledged that Jesus was the Son of God. Later, after seeing Jesus' scars as evidence of the miracle of the resurrection, Thomas would further acknowledge that Jesus was God and declare, "My Lord and my God" (John 20:28). For now, the disciples were making progress in acknowledging Jesus as God's Son. There are many Scriptures indicating that God is willing to let us make incremental progress. Nevertheless, the emphasis is on exercising faith, taking risks, and seeing the glory of God in new ways. Earlier, we learned to avoid presumption, but most of our emphasis has been on taking the initiative. Somewhere between inactivity and presumption is the ideal of courage coupled with submissive and obedient faith in God to do the impossible. Remember, those that do the impossible gain opportunities to know God in new and special ways.

Lesson 12: Those Who Do the Impossible Know *God* Does the Impossible

Nowhere in this story does Matthew tell us whether it was Jesus' faith or power (not Peter's own faith) that produced this miracle. We cannot know for certain whose faith was operating — Jesus', Peter's, or both. In any case, for Jesus to either encourage or enable Peter (the human) to walk on water is a greater miracle than for Jesus (who is deity) Himself to walk on water.

When Peter walks on the water, the miracle is closer to me. I can identify more readily with Peter than with Jesus in this case. I, too, am encouraged to walk on the water. If Peter can, perhaps I could, too. I like finding places in Scripture with which I can identify and look for doable targets and achievable goals. It is more likely for me to arrive where Peter did than to become as perfect as Jesus was. It is God who does the impossible, not ordinary people. Nevertheless, when He does it through a man like Peter and even me, it is obviously all the more personal — and glorious.

I cannot express how many times this story has encouraged me since leaving the security of teaching at ORU. That was a wonderful opportunity for the 10 years I was there. However, as the Israelites of old traveled through the wilderness, we must be willing to move when the glory cloud moves. What boat are you in? What new and challenging opportunity is waiting for you? Let's continue to make progress in increments accepting greater challenges and initiating greater projects as our capacity expands.

In God's thoughts, accomplishment is a greater value than convenience; fruitfulness is more important than comfort. To some of us, the challenge of the waves is more attractive than the security of the boat. God still says "come" to anyone willing to "walk on water."

Yet, the 12 principles we look at in this chapter contain cautionary ideas. It may seem more like a lesson on how to be cautious than how to experience miracles. There is a reason: boldness balanced by caution leads to real accomplishment! It is not the attempt to walk on water that glorifies God; instead, it is in the actual walking on water that His glory is shown. It is not enough to try; we must perform. If we try but fail in God's eyes, how does that glorify God? If we leave the boat and accomplish something, the accomplishment glorifies God. The reason for the practical checks and balances discussed in this chapter is that God wants you to actually achieve something, not just try. When God wants you to do something, it is your accomplishment — not your attempt at achievement — that will bless others and praise God.

CHAPTER FIVE

On the Edge of the Experiment

"I tell you the truth, my Father will give you
whatever you ask in my name."

John 16:23

As the weeks of my prayer experiment passed, repeated indications of a significant difference in the quality of my teaching ministry became apparent. Freedom in ministry and delivery, authority beyond my own, and continued new insights during preparation all indicated this.

As with any experiment, provided all the evidence points in the same direction, the greater the number and variety of situations in which a thesis is tested, the stronger the conclusion. God was about to offer another setting in which to test my idea.

A Challenging Request That Tested My Experiment

All preachers have favorite subjects on which they can speak with greater authority and persuasiveness. When the speaker selects the subject — and each audience is made up of different people — the speaker can use his most inspirational materials multiple times. Of course, the Lord can use us when we preach our strongest messages, but a different kind of test occurs when we are assigned materials that we would not have selected.

Our host in Ongole of Andra Pradesh requested that we teach out of the books of 1 and 2 Timothy in a two-day pastors' leadership conference. Pastoral Epistles was one of Char's subjects when we had taught in a Korean Bible College. For me, it required new preparation. Therefore, in the first days of ministering in Ongole of Andra Pradesh, the opportunity arose for me to measure the effects of increased hours of intercession in a new way. I wondered, "Will the liberty, authority, and inspiration be maintained even with assigned topics requiring new preparation?"

Small group Bible studies, rather than large audiences, are easier to address. They are less formal and create easier communication by providing increased participation, better eye contact, and closer proximity. Naturally, I had some concerns about how my materials would translate into the local language of the 300 pastors. However, my greater concern was that the curriculum seemed neither motivational nor inspirational. Look at the books of 1 and 2 Timothy yourself. The subjects include important yet un-inspirational topics such as authorship, lists of duties, qualifications of elders, and qualifications of widows eligible for assistance.

Having enjoyed my travels in Africa and India delivering exciting and inspiring materials, I tried to urge our host to change the 1 and 2 Timothy assignment in favor of the more expository messages prepared especially for pastors. I felt these would be a blessing to his pastors as well. My host was not unkind in any way, but he still wanted the Timothy Bible study.

Then a realization came — this presentation of 1 and 2 Timothy would put my experiment in prayer to a new test! Before leaving Chennai, I printed the lesson plans for the two-day pastors' conference featuring Timothy. Char and I read and divided the presentation while on the train bound for Ongole. She would take the first and third quarters, teaching the two morning sessions, and I would take the second and last quarters, presenting later in the day. Additionally, I was asked to address the leadership of the host organization, India Christian Mission, all day before the pastors' conference. These extra sessions offered many human and physical challenges; nevertheless, it also provided another good way to test the power of prayer in ministry effectiveness.

India's climate is divided into hot and very hot. We arrived near the end of the very hot season. By the time we reached Ongole, we had been struggling for five weeks with the extreme heat and the sudden physical adjustment from South Africa's winter to

India's summer. I had already had two severe bouts of diarrhea, heat exhaustion, and periods of sleeplessness. Meanwhile, the heat rash on my chest and stomach was becoming more painful, irritating, and a cause for disquiet. Concerns about the considerable pain and extensive medical treatment that might be necessary were beginning to affect me. Not only was I faced with the challenge of trying to make the study interesting, if not inspirational, I was not well physically.

In addition, I was asked to give the morning session's greeting in addition to the above-mentioned commitments. Now, my morning routine of prayer and preparation would be interrupted. Meanwhile, the need to appear pleasant and upbeat before speaking would require all the fruit of the Spirit that I could muster. My experiment measuring the effects of increased prayer on a teacher's ministry was about to be severely tested.

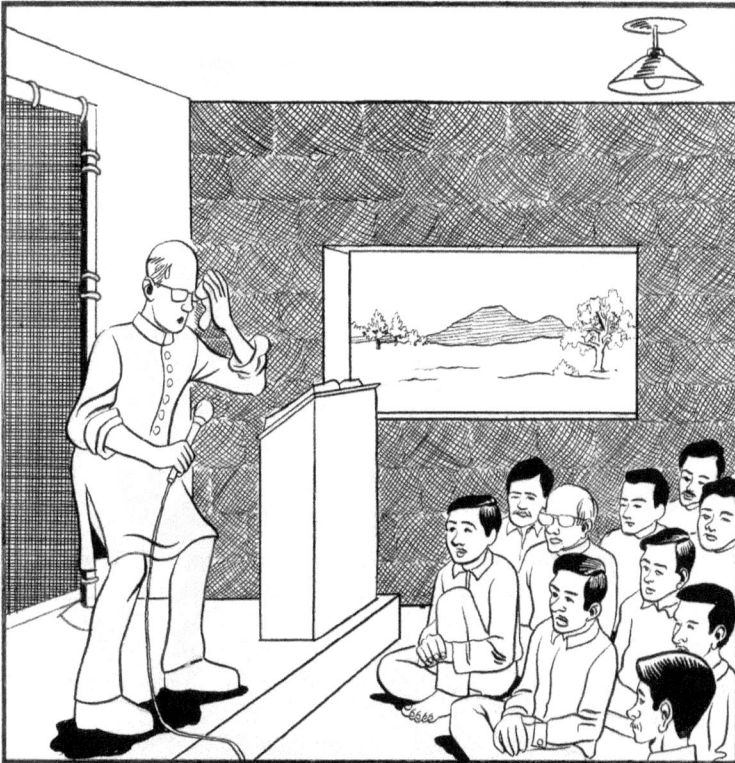

Before my evening engagement, Char and I prayed together asking God to be merciful, heal the heat rash, relieve the pain, help me teach well, and bring me successfully through. With a heavy sprinkling of medicated powder and a fresh shirt, I was out the door.

Three hundred very lively worshippers singing, jumping, dancing, clapping, and rejoicing enthusiastically in the hot hall knew nothing of my personal physical and mental agony — they were ready for the guest speaker. Char's presentation had gone well, and I was hoping for the same. As I danced before the Lord on the front row of that congregation of pastors, a strong sense of inadequacy pervaded my spirit. In desperation, I pleaded with the Lord to compensate for my weaknesses. He graciously heard my prayer. Details are unnecessary about how the Holy Spirit enabled me to take the factual material before me and present it in a lively and engaging manner. You, too, may have experienced God's help in ministering His Word, so you know what a miracle it can be. I can only say that what could have been a fiasco became, with His help, an inspirational presentation.

Near the end of my presentation, however, I was explaining the three types of widows that Paul discusses in I Timothy 5:3-8 and 5:16. Since caring for widows is more obligatory than inspirational, I wondered how I could make this material motivational. Verses 3 and 5 describe the widow who is really in need; verses 4, 8, and 16 describe widows with families whose families should take care of them; and verse 5 explains about the widow who lives for pleasure.

I was nearing the presentation's end, and I wanted to prepare the listeners for Char's lesson the next morning on how widows without families must meet certain criteria to qualify for assistance from the church. I asked myself, "How do you make *that* inspirational?" I felt the dear pastors certainly deserved something a little more inspiring to end their day than an analysis of widow types.

How the Lord Came Through

Almost as rapidly as the thoughts occurred to me, I told my audience it would be easy to get lost in all the details of qualifications and disqualifications for widows who expected to be assisted by the church. Yet, there was an underlying important message in this entire discussion — God cared about widows! Remember, India is the land of *sati,* where, for centuries, a widow was often forcibly burned alive with her husband's corpse at his cremation. That terrible treatment of widows 200 years ago had broken the heart of the famous missionary to India, William Carey. After years of his vigorous campaigning to oppose it, *sati* was finally outlawed.

In a culture that lacks the Christian emphasis on tenderness, compassion, mercy, care, and gentleness, this seemed to be just the opportunity to reiterate God's character. It is because God Himself is a compassionate, kind, gentle, and merciful person that reaches out to help others — not harshly judge them — that He needs pastors to reflect that same character. No wonder 1 Timothy's pastors' qualifications are spiritual — clearly, pastors must be gentle. A gentle pastor with a plan to meet the needs of all widows best represents a gentle God.

God is not some strange-looking being with multiple arms and beast-like fierceness as depicted by the statues and pictures of Hindu gods; He is compassionate, kind, loving, and gracious. Our "weapons" of spiritual warfare are not carnal; they are spiritual. They are "weapons" of mercy, kindness, compassion, tenderness, and goodness that can conquer the hardest, cruelest enemy.

God's gentle character is revealed in His instruction for responsibly taking care of helpless widows. Even though Hindu scriptures did not require widows to be burned, Hindu scriptures allowed them to be burned alive. The Christian's Scriptures gave instructions for how to care for widows. Some contrast!

You may not think that this is impressive, but to a stodgy professor who usually teaches only after careful preparation, it is.

I could not have thought of such a fitting conclusion to that day's teaching! Additionally, my Western theology certainly never prepared me to deal with such an important issue in the Indian context. Though I felt bound by the subject material assigned by my host, the Holy Spirit answered prayer and spontaneously provided revelation, illumination, and inspiration that immeasurably surpassed anything I could have asked or imagined. In addition, the Indian pastors seemed to appreciate that the Bible addressed human concerns pertinent to India.

For more than three months, I had been praying daily for a list of things such as revelation, illumination, and inspiration that I thought should accompany the ministry of a praying teacher. Recently, I had added truth, perception, and perspective to that list. "Perspective" was in the list because I had begun to seek the objectivity to see things from new vantage points.

Referring to God's character as the basis for His requirement that pastors be gentle and care for widows was a new idea to me.

Amazingly, this new insight came at just the right moment. You may not think that this is impressive but to a stodgy professor who usually teaches only after careful preparation, it is. To receive inspiring revelations from the Lord applicable for a specific cultural setting and deliver them with sensitivity and authority is a wonderful experience.

Pray That the Holy Spirit Will Reveal Truth and Expose Errors

Just because the Bible says something will happen does not mean we should just be passive. If we are a partner of God's, we should pray that His will is done. Some of the last words of the Bible (Revelation 22:20) are a prayer that the predictions *would happen*. Partners care. Partners are involved.

Consider what Daniel did. Realizing Jeremiah had prophesied 70 years of captivity and that those years were nearing their close, he sought God "… in prayer and petition, in fasting" (Daniel 9:3) concerning His plan for Israel's ongoing history. Just because the return of the Jews to their homeland had been prophesied, Daniel did not just watch to see what would happen; he prayed that God's prophesies would actually occur.

What about the Holy Spirit's teaching ministry today? The Holy Spirit, our Teacher, in answer to prayer used mundane qualifications for widows to reveal a particularly applicable Christian truth in a Hindu context. What other scriptural secrets might He use to expose errors or limitations in other ideologies? The Holy Spirit has come into the world, according to Jesus, to reveal truth. What would happen if we *prayed* that the Holy Spirit would reveal God's truth exposing the weaknesses of Animism, atheism, Buddhism, Communism, Confucianism, hedonism, Islam, Jainism, Judaism, materialism, secularism, and Shintoism? What other thought systems and evil imaginations might a minister, inspired by the Holy Spirit, be able to delicately and effectively address? If the Holy Spirit can do it in a Hindu context, He can do it in others.

What if we prayed that the Holy Spirit would reveal the exact truth pertinent for each situation? What if we actively and earnestly prayed that unique, relevant truths be released through each one of us such as, "Lord, reveal the exact and most applicable truth that exposes the errors believed by the dear people I am about to address?" What would happen?

In the business, political, educational, industrial, law-enforcement, news, transportation, or housekeeping worlds, there are thousands of complicated issues. If God can use a 1 Timothy discussion of the qualifications of widows to reveal God's tender character to a group of pastors, couldn't He also show you what to do on your job, in your neighborhood, or at your place of employment? God has solutions to every kind of career or community-related problem.

If God showed John Calvin, a theologian, reformer, and pastor, how to design a sewage system for Geneva, Switzerland where he lived, couldn't He show you how to solve the problems on your job? If God showed the political diplomat Daniel solutions to difficulties in his generation, couldn't He show you how to solve your neighborhood, career, or family-related problems? When we ask Him for wisdom,

> God has solutions to every kind of career or community-related problem.

God, the Generous Giver and Non-Faultfinder, gives to all. Test and see what God can and will do through you in response to your increased prayer for specific aspects of His Kingdom to come. Conduct your own experiment to learn how to become a more active partner with God.

A Surprise Door and Unusual Leading

On October 4, 2002, we arrived back in Ongole after a full, hot day ministering to a countryside gathering of church leaders. Immediately upon arrival, I headed for a cool shower; however, I was interrupted by a phone call from my host asking me to teach that evening in Ongole. I accepted the surprise invitation thinking that perhaps God was answering my prayer for increased fruitfulness. Then I faced the matter of not knowing what God wanted me to say.

After prayer, I decided to share some thoughts on horizontal versus vertical leadership. Vertical management places the responsibility and authority for direction and new ideas on the personnel at the top. Horizontal management spreads out both authority and responsibility so that more people feel ownership and share new, helpful ideas. It allows for more participation and creativity regardless of the group's ministry objectives. I share this type of knowledge from time to time and feel comfortable with the ideas and materials.

The session seemed to go okay, but there was not time for feedback. I often wonder about the audience receptiveness to a presentation. Was it helpful? Did I connect? Horizontal leadership has many teamwork-related benefits for church workers and organizations. It is consistent with Bible teachings, releases creativity, and promotes unity. Nevertheless, I am an outsider in India. Did I help them from their perspective? I wondered about this for the next several days as I continued praying and experiencing the new things God did in creatively answering my prayers.

Breaking Out of the Shell

In the second week in Andra Pradesh, I noticed another change in my prayer patterns. I began to pray that I, the "chick," would be able to break out of whatever "shell" was hindering me from being all I could or should be for God in the latter years of my life. Our Tulsa pastor gave the following advice, "If you are content with things the way they are, keep doing the things you are doing; but if you want to be something different, do something different." As a part of my continued prayer experiment, I was willing to pray for a release from the "shell" or whatever other barrier restricted me. Strange as it may seem, as I wrestled in prayer, I pushed, kicked, and pleaded with God to help me break free from self- or Satan-imposed restrictions.

> As I wrestled in prayer, I pushed, kicked, and pleaded with God to help me break free from self- or Satan-imposed restrictions.

The increased touch of the divine on my preaching and teaching was causing me to realize that God had more for me than I had thought. If I were to continue to function at this new level for the rest of my life, there would be more for me in my future than I had experienced in my past. Perhaps it was because of the intensity and reality of that spiritual struggle to "break out" that I was able to notice some changes in the days immediately following that unique time of prayer.

Breaking Hard Shells with Softness

I am quite fascinated with the notion that if you want to be something you've never *been* before, you must be willing to *do* something you've never done before. Since I was now praying more, my faith increased, and I became expectant that something new would happen. Also, I became more sensitive to new ideas and new possibilities.

Therefore, I considered it significant to suddenly feel prompted one morning to write a gentle and friendly letter to the people with whom we had worked in Korea. It had been 17 years since we had worked together. My relationship with them had not always been peaceful and over the years since leaving Korea, I had never even thought of writing them a personal letter. I had sent greetings through other people, but never a written letter. I felt this idea was from God. So later that same day, I typed an e-mail-ready letter to send to them the next time we went to the Internet café. When God spoke to Abraham and later Elijah, they both obeyed right away, and I wanted to follow their examples.

If you want to _be_ something you've never _been_ before, you must be willing to _do_ something you've never _done_ before.

Within a day or two after that, I found another emphasis shift in my prayer content. Up until then, my prayer times included my list of concerns with authority in teaching and preaching. Now a new, additional theme emerged — a list of character issues including humility, brokenness, yieldedness, and a contrite heart. These attitude issues definitely influence the effectiveness of a teaching ministry. Simply put, the more gracious the messenger, the more attractive the message. Being eager to "break out of the shell" and to do something different to produce something different, I added these tender and personal character issues to the former prayer list. I wanted a teacher's experiment in prayer to be successful. In order for that to occur, I had to give it my best shot, crucify the flesh, and become more gracious.

By October 23, four months into the prayer experiment, I was fully convinced that my prayers regarding character issues (the Lord's pruning) were directly related to my earlier prayers for a deeper and an improved influence among more people. Just as humility equals promotion — or the way up is down — the way to break out of the shell is to become more broken. The personal letter that I wrote the Koreans proved that theory. Additionally, I found myself eager to write more friendly letters to others who had hurt me many years earlier. I sensed I was becoming more tender.

The Word of God says to pray for those who despitefully use us. For 16 years, according to that principle, I had prayed for those who had misunderstood me during our years in Korea. However, I had never contacted them in a warm, personal way. I had simply prayed daily for them. Now that I was spending more time in prayer — seriously and intensely pursuing God with tenacity at deeper levels — I felt inspired to contact them. I happily expressed that I had gladly forgiven them and hoped they, too, had forgiven me. God uses soft instruments. From a man's limited understanding, the infinitely superior and mysterious ways of a complex God are only expressed through a multitude of "paradoxes." Scripture and theology have many such paradoxes. Breaking hard shells with soft spirits seems to be one. Jesus, for example, "resolutely set out for Jerusalem" (Luke 9:51) to accomplish the will of the Father in the greatest struggle ever faced. Yet the way He dealt with the adversary and conquered sin and death on Calvary was to *yield*. "… He was led like a lamb to the slaughter, and as a sheep before her shearers is silent, so he did not open his mouth" (Isaiah 53:7). Jesus resolutely set Himself to *yield*!

I intensely wanted to break out of a shell, so I strenuously labored and pleaded with God only to discover that one way He empowers is to soften. We break through to new opportunities by becoming more kindhearted.

An Encouraging Sign from Heaven

Two days after writing the personal letter to the Koreans, God gave me a hint of encouragement, a divinely appointed meeting in a restaurant in Ongole. It had been many days since I had shared the message about horizontal leadership, and still I didn't know how it had affected my Indian brothers.

That afternoon, Char and I had worked on correspondence at a local

We break through to new opportunities by becoming more kindhearted.

Internet café. Next, we went to a restaurant for a rare meal out together alone. There, in a divinely orchestrated meeting, we met Sangram, the cousin of our host. Sangram eagerly told us of the favorable impact that the horizontal leadership message had on the pastors in attendance and on the India Evangelical Relief Fund — the group he worked with. Fourteen staff members, including seven that had heard my presentation, had joined the CEO for a regular meeting the following Saturday morning. For the first time in the India Evangelical Relief Fund's history, the meeting was spirited and many pastors participated enthusiastically. The workers were inspired to participate with interest and vigor. It was, he said, because of my talk on horizontal administrative structure!

As a foreign visitor, it was a thrill to be unexpectedly affirmed for teaching management principles to preachers in the Indian culture. To know that I had connected with them by teaching something they needed and wanted was a surprising, affirming, and rewarding signal from heaven. I was becoming more tender and broken and, at the same time, more useful. *Money cannot buy the satisfaction this brings.*

Prayer for Fruitfulness Doesn't Have To Be About Us

When I began this prayer experiment, I prayed for revelation, wisdom, and illumination as a teacher. Also, my prayers included the inspiration necessary to be a better, more effective, and supernaturally equipped teacher.

Table 5-1: Helpful things for a teacher to seek through prayer

Opportunities	Teaching Abilities	Communication Skills	Character
Breakthrough	Wisdom	Verbal Skills	Submission
Barrier Removal	Insight	Persuasive Powers	Brokenness
Release	Understanding		Yieldedness
Open Doors	Knowledge	Logical Sequencing	Contrition
Deeper and Better Influence On More People	Truth	Conviction	Sensitivity
	Information	Rhetorical Skills	Tenderness
Increased Fruitfulness	Perspective	Reasoning Ability	Purity of Heart
	Perception		Humility
Ability To "Scale a Wall" Psalm 18:29	Discernment	Concise Speech	
	Guidance	Succinct Sentences	
Breaking of the "Shell" So the "Chick" Can Face the Challenges Outside the Shell	Direction		
	Leading		
	Revelation		
	Illumination		
	Inspiration		

By October in India, it became apparent that though these prayers were *for* me, they were *not just about* me. My list now included an increased number of items related to *opportunities, teaching abilities, communication skills, and character*. Never before in my life had I so systematically prayed for these things.

Asking for God's help with the areas listed in Table 5.1 in my work is necessary to increase the influence of my teaching career. Increased influence is equal to praying for increased fruitfulness. It is a desire that Jesus Himself has for us unless selfish ambition is our motivator. Prepare your own list of abilities and characteristics you need to develop in order to be more influential with the use of your gifts in your career. God wants you to be more fruitful; praying to that end is a way you can partner with Him in His desires for your increase.

God prunes us so we will have increased fruitfulness, which brings Him glory. A desire for increased influence for His glory is therefore a good motivator for serious prayer, while egotistical ambitions are not. Our efforts in spending a considerable amount of time praying for a breakthrough are not for ourselves but for Him. Settling this issue is helpful if we want to pray for increased effectiveness without it seeming to be for ourselves. Whatever career obedient children of God are in, with increased prayer, God can and will make them more successful if they are willing to be pruned and give God glory. My experiment has convinced me of this. If I can be more fruitful, anyone can.

> Our efforts in spending a considerable amount of time praying for a breakthrough are not for ourselves but for Him.

CHAPTER SIX

Better Than Silver and Gold

*"Silver or gold I do not have, but what I have I give you.
In the name of Jesus Christ of Nazareth, walk."*

Acts 3:6

For six consecutive weeks with one day off per week, we traveled to different villages each day. Interestingly, we began noticing an expectation pattern by the Indian villagers. When lining up for prayer after meetings or bringing their children to us for prayer, we realized that they thought of us as special, holy people with direct access to God. At first, we thought it was wonderful that they wanted prayer, but later sensed that they were too dependant on *our* prayers and unaware of their *own* access to the Father. We wanted to provide more than just a prayer that might temporarily address a momentary need.

Peter and John, in ministering physical healing to the lame man at the gate in Acts 3, gave the man more than what was asked of them. To follow their model, instead of just praying for the needs of the villagers, we began to *teach* them not only how to pray for themselves, but also how to pray for others. One of our first lessons was teaching a 10-year-old boy how to pray for himself as well as other people as he stood before a crowd of villagers Every set of eyes were riveted on the young lad who was learning to pray. We created that scene to teach people that every Christian has access to the Father, not just exclusive persons. God has no grandchildren.

We used the following story from Acts to further encourage everyone to learn to become intercessors:

> One day Peter and John were going up to the temple at the time of prayer — at three in the afternoon. Now a man who was crippled from birth was being carried to the temple gate called Beautiful where he was put every day to beg from those going into the temple courts. When he saw Peter and John about to enter, he asked them for money. Peter looked straight at him, as did John. Then Peter said, 'Look at us!' So the man gave them his attention, expecting to get something from them. Then Peter said, 'Silver or gold I do not have, but what I have I give you. In the name of Jesus Christ of Nazareth, walk. Taking him by the right hand, he helped him up, and instantly the man's feet and ankles became strong. He jumped to his feet and began to walk. Then he went with them into the temple courts, walking and jumping, and praising God. When all the people saw him walking and praising God, they recognized him as the same man who used to sit begging at the temple gate called Beautiful, and they were filled with wonder and amazement at what had happened to him (Acts 3:1-10).

This true and interesting story has seven hidden spiritual lessons that are beneficial to all Christians. Each of the following seven lessons comes directly from this story.

Lesson 1: Prayer Reaches Another Realm of Power and Wisdom

Peter and John went "up" to pray (Acts 3:1). Since the temple was on a hill in Jerusalem, the disciples physically went "up" to the temple. However, there is a more symbolic meaning. Whenever we go to pray, we go "up" to a higher dominion when we call upon God. In prayer, we focus on God, His power, His ability to help, and His willingness to hear us. When we pray with our spirits, we turn from the natural, physical, and material realm in which we live and go "up" to the spiritual and supernatural realm.

When we pray with our spirits, we turn from the natural, physical, and material realm in which we live and go "up" to the spiritual and supernatural realm.

More than we realize, we live with the consequences of another realm — the spiritual one. Those who try to solve material world problems with mere material solutions experience a distinct disadvantage. However, it is unnecessary to solve life's problems with just our own strength. Solving earthly problems on our own without allowing ourselves the benefits of prayer is equivalent to saying, "God, I don't need your help." We may say or think we are relying on God, but unless we are seriously praying to Him about our issues and focusing on His solutions, our behavior indicates self-reliance in its unhealthy sense.

When we temporarily go "up" to God in prayer, we do not permanently leave or ignore day-to-day responsibilities; rather we take our problems to the only One who can really understand the whole picture. Leaving the material world with its problems and going "up" to God in prayer is not ignoring problems; it is the best way to handle them. It does not mean we are being irresponsible; instead, we are being more responsible. This is amazing! Our bodies can remain in the material realm with its problems and yet, in the spirit, we are in touch with another kingdom with its supernatural and powerful solutions. We are in touch with God. That is why we go "up" to him when we pray.

> Leaving the material world with its problems and going "up" to God in prayer is not ignoring problems; it is the best way to handle them. It does not mean we are being irresponsible; instead, we are being more responsible.

Lesson 2: Prayer Should Be Systematic

A second lesson we learn from this event is that prayer should be systematic. They went to the temple "at the time of prayer" (Acts 3:1). Spending time with God in prayer is the most important thing we do. If we believe that, we will regularly do it at length and with consistency. We schedule the things that we value; *if prayer is our priority, we will schedule it to make sure it happens.*

Scheduling *our* priorities is more important than prioritizing our schedule. Take charge of your schedule and schedule prayer! Set aside a regular prayer time to commune with God for whatever length you feel you need.

Praying is the most important thing I do. To make sure my practice matches this belief, I design my daily schedule so that I spend more time in prayer than I do in any other activity.

The New Testament says a lot more about praying than it does about preaching, service to others, or work. If we fail to recognize the difference between what is important and what is urgent, then we will be controlled by all the urgencies in our life, and we will not have time to pray. Prayer is important. When we schedule this as a priority in our daily life, we find that we have fewer crises requiring urgent attention — all because of adequate prayer time. We will pray more, but only if we schedule it rather than pray only when we feel like it or when we think we have time for it. The priority we place on praying and the amount of time we spend with God in prayer tells us how much we really value it.

Because Peter and John were men of regular prayer, when they said to the lame man, "Silver or gold I do not have, but what I have I give you. In the name of Jesus Christ of Nazareth, walk" (Acts 3:6), the man walked. If they were not men who talked with God in prayer, they would not have said that. If they were not men of prayer, they would not have had the faith to say that. If they were not men of prayer, nothing would have happened even if they had said that.

Lesson 3: God Needed Peter and John

Scripture only indirectly implies this third lesson. The Bible story says that the lame man was placed "… where he was put every day to beg …" (Acts 3:2). Although Jesus often went to this same temple in Jerusalem during his 33 years of human life — especially during his three and a half years of public ministry — and healed men, he did not heal this man. It is possible that Jesus had walked right past this very man since He had entered the temple numerous times. Here are a couple of questions that comes to mind: "Why hadn't Jesus healed this man?" Jesus evidently did not heal all the sick in Jerusalem. "Why didn't the Healer heal everyone?"

Sometimes we learn something from Scripture by what it implies. We have to *think* more carefully to pick up these subtle messages from the narratives of Scripture. When we do, we are rewarded. The Bible does not say that Jesus walked past this man time after time. There are many possible explanations as to why Jesus did not heal the man. Perhaps Jesus arrived at the temple before or after he was there for the day. Nevertheless, Jesus could have, but chose not to heal him. Apparently, Jesus intentionally saved this opportunity for Peter and John.

What can we learn from this lesson that has any particular value to us today? In your situation, no matter how many soul-winners, church-planters, pastors, evangelists, missionaries, and other people of faith and power there are already serving in your own community or around the world, there is still a place for you and your work. No matter how many other Christians there may be in your work place or community, Jesus still has a need for you. Jesus reserved this miracle for Peter and John, and He has saved miracles for you too.

Make yourself available to God to be a tool in His hands. Ask God to show you the person in need or the situation He has saved for you. Discover the opportunities to serve God and His people by praying to become a tool in His hands. Watch for situations where He wants you to use the tools He has given you. Be a person of prayer; find the needs near you, and discover your own miracle by seeing miracles happening through you!

Lesson 4: Humanity is Lame Until They Know Jesus

Luke tells us that the man was brought or helped to the temple and then was miraculously healed so he could walk and leap. "… a man crippled from birth was being carried …" (Acts 3:2). Just as He did back then in our story, God still miraculously heals physically crippled people today. It is one of the important lessons of this story. Even after Jesus ascended into heaven, many of us have felt or witnessed His healing power. Amazingly, His work lives on through believers today that know how to pray effectively in Jesus' name. Additionally, we may see other lessons. This once physically crippled man may symbolize crippled humanity — those who do not know how to walk in the ways of the Lord — and provide us with insight into how we are to perceive, pray for, and minister to it.

Luke's original emphasis teaches of God's power to heal bodies and perform miracles through believers who know and minister in the name of Jesus. However, the lame man, as we use him in this chapter, illustrates the crippling effects of bad habits — another possible lesson from this passage. This symbolism is consistent with Bible teachings that humankind is crippled by various vices (even though this is not Luke's original meaning).

> We need to go to the "crippled" in our communities and teach them how to "walk" in Jesus' name.

The lesson I am teaching comes from spiritualizing the story. Spiritualizing is the process of drawing a spiritual lesson from something we see as a symbol in something else. Such spiritualizing of symbols is allowed. When spiritualizing, we should, however, first recognize the intended meaning and then draw an abstract symbolism. To maintain the integrity of Scripture, the intended meaning is that "God heals bodies." Spiritualizing this passage — or finding the abstract symbolism — is to ask ourselves, "How is mankind crippled?"

Some people are "crippled" by drinking problems. They spend money on beer and wine and then make foolish decisions while they are drunk. Others are "crippled" by the use of tobacco. First, they waste money on tobacco products or drugs, and then they waste even more money treating their medical problems caused by these poisons in their bodies. Some people are "crippled" by extramarital affairs or being involved with prostitution. They are afraid that everyone will discover their secrets so they tell a series of lies and live a life of complete falsehood. Some are "crippled" by pornography. Since the brain cannot erase images, every image we see will remain permanently "visible" in our brains. To have sensual images in one's mind is crippling. Some people are bound by those sensual images, which causes them to be unable to "walk" right. Still, other people are "crippled" by idolatry, or materialism and don't recognize the value of living a simpler life made internally rich by worshipping God

These poor habits may not be your personal problems, but they may cripple people that you encounter. We need to go to the "crippled" in our communities and teach them how to "walk" in Jesus' name. We must try to understand their crippling behavior and help them stand up straight; it is not our job to criticize people of their bad habits. The Holy Spirit can convict anyone personally involved with any of these vices; we do not need to accuse them. We can help "crippled" people without being critical.

Lesson 5: One of His Two Problems Was His Own Choice

Peter and John met the lame man at the gate to the temple (Acts 3:2). Our fifth lesson stems from the lame man's two problems: he was lame and he begged. It was unfortunate that this man was lame. However, begging was a different kind of problem; it was a personal choice. You can be lame or handicapped, without begging for a living. The Bible portrays begging as a difficult situation of need — a circumstance to change if possible. Nevertheless, the Bible

Some, including ourselves, might not even recognize our own beggar mentality. We may need the Holy Spirit's help to see this flaw in ourselves.

encourages work, not begging. The Bible says that if we do not work, we should not eat. Some religions place value on begging, but the work ethic of the Bible is one of its unique strengths.

During my travels, I have observed people whose religion encourages begging by strongly emphasizing that the gods reward those who support beggars. In those religions, the "value" given to those who promote begging when they give to beggars, actually stifles a sense of responsibility, accountability, and the need for personal progress and growth in the beggar.

To the contrary, our Scriptures teach us not to be fatalistic, but rather able (or enabled) to do something about our adverse circumstances. Paul said, "I can do everything through him who gives me strength" (Philippians 4:13). Jesus takes away our dependence on begging.

This lesson applies to the American society too, no matter how tactfully we beg through a "testimony" or "prayer request." Some, including ourselves, might not even recognize our own beggar mentality. We may need the Holy Spirit's help to see this flaw in ourselves.

We all have handicaps of some kind, but handicaps do not justify a beggar mentality. We may not be as strong, intelligent, educated, handsome, or well connected with important people as we wish. Nevertheless, it does not mean we have to become beggars. Anyone who knows God through Jesus Christ has the best "connection" with the highest, most influential person anyone ever knew. Through prayer, we can overcome any disadvantage just by using Jesus' name.

Separate your handicap from your handicap-complex. Be self-motivated and creative with personal dignity as you experience God's help in overcoming your handicaps.

I have a paraplegic friend in Korea who is confined to a wheelchair. He purchased parts, assembled them, and then sold the finished electronic product. He then hired another paraplegic, and eventually rented a room to start his own business — a small factory that employs a number of paraplegics. Although he was physically handicapped, he chose a better life for himself than just begging for a living. When I visited his factory one afternoon, I played wheelchair basketball with his workers in a room adjacent to the assembly room. They did not feel sorry for themselves; they had good jobs, healthy laughter, and a powerful sense of competition during our very active game!

One of my professors in graduate school, Dr. Tom Brewster, was paralyzed from his neck down when he broke his neck in a swimming accident. He was only 18 years old at the time of the accident. Although he was in a wheelchair, he graduated from college, earned a PhD in Linguistics, and taught Language Acquisition to hundreds of Christian missionaries who now serve all over the world. He was lame, but he did not beg.

Receiving needed assistance, however, is different from having a beggar complex. Occasionally, we need help from others, but no one likes to be completely dependent on others. A beggar mentality that uses others is not good; it is negative. It is different from having a healthy dose of personal responsibility and a desire to help others. Separate your handicap from your handicap-complex. Be self-motivated and creative with personal dignity as you experience God's help in overcoming your handicaps.

Lesson 6: Look Straight at People

Our sixth observation from the story of the lame man is that going to prayer helps us better see the needs of others. Then we can even more effectively pray for them. The story mentions that "Peter looked straight at him" (Acts 3:4). I see a message in the idea of looking straight. Peter and John focused on the man.

It is possible to see people, but not really *see* people. To some of us, people are scenery to look at: "Hmm! Look at those clothes," or "Look at that man's beard." Others are a curiosity to research: "I wonder why he is doing that?" "What makes him think that way?" "What treatment do I need to administer to correct his sickness?" To some people, other persons are competition that they need to impress or conquer: "How can I show that I can do it better than he?" "How can I show that woman I am better than she is?" Sometimes people are customers, or even suckers, that other people use to their own advantage: "What can I sell her?" "How can I seize this opportunity?"

What would happen if we asked God to help us see people correctly? By this, I mean look "straight" at people in a symbolic sense. Peter and John looked with their eyes straight at a real lame man. If we look "straight" (correctly, spiritually, and accurately) at other people, then we, too, can minister more effectively to their needs. What would happen if we always saw people from a spiritual perspective? Can we learn to see other people as persons for whom Jesus died and become more sensitive to their needs? What would it do to our service for God if we could see every person as a valuable person whom God loves? Consider these six questions as an exercise in sensitivity:

- What if we remembered that every person we see has feelings just like ourselves?

- What if we realized the feeling of loneliness another feels is just as real to him or her as our feeling of loneliness is to us?

- What if we knew the anxiety another feels is just as painful to him or her as ours is to us?

- What if we became aware that the fear another person feels is just as intense and uncomfortable to him or her as ours is to us?

- What about using the discomfort of our own anger as a reminder of how uncomfortable another may feel when he or she is angry?

- What if we became intensely aware that the feelings of helplessness of the person we are facing are just as real to him or her as our feelings of despair are when we ourselves do not know what to do?

This line of thought compels us to be less prone to judge others and more likely to pray for them. What if we prayed for everyone because we saw him or her this way? What changes would happen in our family, neighborhood, workplace, church, community, or nation if we all saw people correctly — if we all looked "straight" at people like Peter and John looked straight at the crippled man?

Lesson 7: Pray for What People Need, Not Necessarily What They Ask For

The seventh and final lesson of this story — and the reason that this story has such a wonderful ending — is that Peter and John did *not* give the lame man what he asked for. Instead, they said to the lame man, "Silver or gold I do not have, but what I have I give you …" (Acts 3:6). If they had given the lame man what he had asked for, he would have needed more the next day, and in the future. What people want and what they really need are often different. This man thought he needed money. He was there to beg for money. He failed to realize that God was able, willing, and ready to meet his deeper need. The lame man was so preoccupied with the need he "felt" that he lost sight of his real need.

The apostles did not give him what he requested but responded to the more basic need *they* perceived. What the lame man really needed was healing. Peter saw his real need and ministered to it.

In explaining that God meets deeper and real needs, we are not sidestepping the fact that God can also meet "felt" needs. We can truthfully pray for, teach, and counsel people knowing that God will meet every kind of need.

There are two practical applications of this final lesson. The first has to do with how God meets our needs. Have you noticed that God is better at answering prayer than we are at praying? Jesus helps people with both felt needs and real needs, but he does so in a way often superior to our understanding. The order in which He addresses our needs may vary, but He is always willing and able to meet the real need. Eventually, He helps us address and alleviate the problems related to our felt needs too. Often the felt need is met in the more comprehensive solution that God gives us when addressing our deeper needs.

Often the felt need is met in the more comprehensive solution that God gives us when addressing our deeper needs.

The second application is that Christians, as God's representatives on earth, should recognize the real needs of people and try to address them. For example, as mentioned at the beginning of this chapter, some people continually ask us for a prayer blessing. However, it is better to teach them how to live and pray, so they can pray and then receive their own blessings directly from God. We are each equally God's very own children — we each can pray in Jesus' name. The Bible teaches us that all believers are priests unto God. We need no mediator other than the one whom God has already provided in Jesus. Teaching people to pray is far superior to repeatedly praying a prayer of blessing over them. Remember, it is better to teach a person to fish than to give him a fish.

Someone may feel he needs money, but what he really needs is Jesus' salvation, the wisdom to accept personal responsibility, and to become economically self-reliant. Another may feel his need for a healthy lifestyle, but what he really needs is to know the Savior who can clean up his unwise, immoral, or physically destructive habits causing his sickness. When the self-destructive habits end, his health can return. Jesus is the Health Giver who will help us clean up our lives. Someone who is often fired from his job may feel that he needs a better employment situation and fairer treatment. Perhaps what he really needs is an attitude change so that he better handles responsibility, works faithfully, and develops improved interpersonal skills. When Jesus helps him with his greater need, he could receive promotions instead of losing jobs. Many people have felt needs that remain needlessly unfulfilled. Those needs are met automatically when their more fundamental needs are graciously met by a wise and understanding Savior.

Jesus is better at answering prayer than we are at praying. He knows what we really need. In order to help people "walk" instead of being "crippled" by our own poor choices, Jesus deals with the real problems. The best help we can give people is to point them to the Savior, then follow Jesus' own example to address the more fundamental, basic, or real needs. This is the best kind of help — the kind of help God gives. As another example, teaching Christian leaders how to study the Bible and learn practical lessons from it for life and sermons is a longer-lasting and better gift than to present an inspiring lesson.

Teaching people to pray is far superior to repeatedly praying a prayer of blessing over them. Remember, it is better to teach a person to fish than to give him a fish.

As you read the drama of Peter and John's trip to the temple and remember the seven hidden lessons:

- Ask God to give you the wisdom and courage you need to go "up" to prayer.
- Pray systematically and at length.
- Know that God needs you and has plans for you.
- Understand crippled humanity
- Distinguish between a handicap and a beggar complex.
- Look straight at people.
- Give people what they really need, not merely what they ask for — especially by teaching them how to pray.

As in Peter and John's day, if we will take time to be with God, we, too, will have something to give that is better than silver or gold. Being a person of prayer positions us to give the finest gift to the "crippled" we meet.

In our next chapter, we will focus on perseverance in prayer. Sometimes we must persevere to get our answer, but God has a good reason for requiring that.

CHAPTER SEVEN
How to Persevere in Prayer

"… they should always pray and not give up."

Luke 18:1

For years, every time I read two particular stories in the Bible, they disturbed me. The first one, a parable Jesus told, was easy to understand, but it angered me. The second puzzled me because it was hard for me to understand. Jesus created the parable to teach an important point. The second story—a real event—vividly illustrates the parable.

I had not felt any peace about these stories for years. Then one day it seems, God opened my heart to realize the message in both stories was the same. Now, I delight in telling the rich truth that lies beneath the surface and experience great joy in sharing it.

God opened my heart to realize the message in both stories was the same.

A few years ago in Eldoret, Kenya, I retold both Bible stories giving the audience their choice of which one I told first. Accordingly, I began with the parable that was easy to understand which follows:

"Then Jesus told his disciples a parable to show them that they should always pray and not give up. He said: 'In a certain town there was a judge who neither feared God nor cared about men. And there was a widow in that town who kept coming to him with the plea, 'Grant me justice against my adversary.' For some time, he refused. But finally he said to himself, 'Even though I don't fear God or care about men, yet because this widow keeps bothering me, I will see that she gets justice, so that she won't eventually wear me out with her coming!' And the Lord said, 'Listen to what the unjust judge says. And will not God bring about justice for his chosen ones, who cry out to him day and night? Will he keep putting them off? I tell you, he will see that they get justice, and quickly. However, when the Son of Man comes, will he find faith on the earth?'" (Luke 18:1-8)

Here is the other story, a narrative, that was difficult for me to understand. It is the true story of the rough treatment Jesus gave to a woman in need. When you read how badly the woman was treated, you also might think it is offensive. However, in the end, you, too, will be relieved when reading the happy conclusion:

"Leaving that place, Jesus withdrew to the region of Tyre and Sidon. A Canaanite woman from that vicinity came to him, crying out, 'Lord, Son of David, have mercy on me! My daughter is demon-possessed and suffering terribly.' Jesus did not answer a word. So his disciples came to him and urged him, 'Send her away, for she keeps crying out after us.' He answered, 'I was sent only to the lost sheep of Israel.' The woman came and knelt before him. 'Lord, help me!' she said. He replied, 'It is not right to take the children's bread and toss it to their dogs.' 'Yes, it is, Lord,' she said, 'Even the dogs eat the crumbs that fall from their master's table.' Then Jesus said to her, 'Woman, you have great faith! Your request is granted. And her daughter was healed from that very hour" (Matthew 15:21-28 TNIV).

In essence, the Bible interprets the Bible — the parts of the Bible that are easier to understand than others help us with those parts that are more difficult. What Jesus said in His very clear parable of Luke 18 about "perseverance in prayer" helps us to understand the reason He treated the Canaanite woman the way He did in Matthew 15. The combination of these two stories is a powerful lesson about the process God uses to develop our perseverance in prayer. They show us what Jesus *taught* about perseverance in prayer and what He *did* to develop it in the Canaanite woman. We can notice and identify with the nine steps through which the woman passed.

Step 1: She Did Not Receive an Answer

"Jesus did not answer a word" (Matthew 15:23). In other words, there was only silence from heaven. Have you ever prayed and received no answer? Since this is such a common occurrence, we must realize that Jesus has a training process that we must learn. After learning this process, we will know what to do when we pray and He does not answer.

Jesus wants to develop persistence and tenacity in His followers. Unfortunately, receiving no answer deters some from continuing to seek or even follow Him. Jesus is willing to take that risk. He is more interested in having persistent followers than having a large crowd of weak ones. He loves everyone, but observation and experience teach us that He does not greatly use those who are impulsive or lacking backbone or character. It is with perseverance that the privilege of discipleship and the benefits of answered prayer come our way.

> Let us seek to understand His development program for us and learn to persevere.

If Jesus is that concerned about persistence, let us seek to understand His development program for us and learn to persevere.

Step 2: She Endured Rebuke by the Disciples

As if Jesus' silence were not enough, the story also tells us "his disciples came to him and urged him, 'Send her away …'" (Matthew 15:24). This represents another all-too-common experience — rejection from people.

We are not told why the disciples urged Jesus to send her away. Perhaps they were prejudiced against women, non-Jews in general, or Canaanites in particular. Alternatively, maybe they needed a break from the crowds since they all had withdrawn to that area to rest. Whatever their reasons, they seem annoyed by her persistence. Yet, in other places in the Bible, the disciples brought people to Jesus. For example, Andrew brought his brother Peter. On another occasion, the Greeks, who were foreigners, came saying, "We want to see Jesus." Disciples are followers of Jesus. They are supposed to follow Him and encourage others to *follow*, not tell potential followers to leave.

When teaching this lesson, I often ask a member of the audience to join me in a short drama. The audience member tries to get to Jesus while I portray the disciple who attempts to keep him away. I coach the other actor in the drama to keep trying until he eventually is able to approach Jesus. The drama helps me demonstrate the inappropriateness of hindering others. More to my point, it also emphasizes the need to persevere even when others oppose us.

These disciples did the opposite of what disciples are expected to do. Have you ever felt rejection from other believers? Have you ever felt like they were thinking, if not saying, "Send her away?" If so, you are not alone. Others have endured such treatment and learned to persevere.

There was another time when some mothers brought their children to Jesus for Him to bless and the disciples said they should not bother the Master. That time, Jesus intervened on behalf of the mothers and children saying, "Let the little children come to me" (Matthew 19:14). However, this time, when the woman pled for help, Jesus said nothing (Matthew 15:23). By His silence, He made room for the disciples to discourage the Canaanite woman. So they said, "Send her away ..." (Matthew 15:23).

The key lesson for us in this narrative centers on the woman's response. She did not allow the disciples to interrupt her search for the Savior's mercy and the healing of her daughter. When and where there are obstacles to our faith, we tend to make the obstacles the issue. God is interested in *our reaction;* and that should be our focus, too. The combination of others seeming to want to keep us away and God's silence seems like a double difficulty in our hour of need. Yet, God is intentionally training us to persevere.

It can be difficult to separate our *reaction* to adversity from the adversity itself. We cannot do anything about the hardships that God allows in our lives; however, we can do something about our attitude toward the hardships. Instead of allowing discouragement, bitterness, or wrong thoughts about God to creep into our hearts, we can handle adversity correctly by showing persistence; then God's purpose for allowing the adversity is complete. God removes the adversity and His mission is accomplished.

Step 3: She Suffered Further Resistance from Jesus

To our disbelief, Jesus appears to be ignoring her pleas. He said, "I was sent only to the lost sheep of Israel" (Matthew 15:24). This represents another obstacle we often experience as we grow closer to the Lord — feeling like God is rejecting us.

We are only told what Jesus said. We are not told of the tone of his voice. The fact that He even was willing to engage in conversation with a foreign woman may have given her some encouragement; or perhaps she had heard of His kindness before. When Jesus finally spoke, His answer was not that of encouragement, rather it seems it could have discouraged her. "I was sent only to the lost sheep of Israel." This appears as if Jesus was saying, "I was not sent to foreigners. I do not care about you. You are not important to me. You are not one of the elite. You are not one of the ones I came to help."

Have you ever felt like God was not answering your prayers? Did you think your concern did not matter to Him? Have you heard of others receiving answers to their prayers while your prayers remain unanswered? When that happens, it is important to remember God's training program. Your concern *does* matter to God; He is just testing and developing your perseverance, faith, and character.

> Your concern *does* matter to God; He is just testing and developing your perseverance, faith, and character.

There seems to be a curious development in this narrative. Jesus had evidently gone to the Tyre and Sidon area to rest, but His rest was interrupted. Why did He allow Himself to be discovered here? When He wanted to get away from the crowd at Nazareth (Luke 4:28-30) He was able to do so. By allowing Himself to be discovered here, was He intentionally demonstrating to all the Gentiles who would eventually read this story that He was available to more than just the lost sheep of Israel? Was He testing this woman? Was the situation pre-planned in order to illustrate the power of perseverance? The story's happy ending implies Jesus was willing for all this to happen.

Jesus is very clever. We must learn to recognize His hints of encouragement in the midst of obvious "rejection." In His training process, Jesus develops tenacity in His followers by blending the right amount of subtle encouragement in with the right amount of rejection. Even in the face of the rejection, we must remember to look for those subtle, encouraging signs.

In Matthew 15:21-28, we do not know of the encouraging sign that made this woman persevere. Perhaps it was simply Jesus' reputation. Nevertheless, the woman saw some indication of Jesus' concern, and held on to it by faith. It is as though Jesus, the Master Teacher, in teaching us to persevere is stiff-arming us with one hand and saying, "No, you cannot have this answer," while simultaneously encouraging us to come with the other hand by saying, "Yes, you can have it. Come and get it. Press in there. Persist. Keep praying. You can do it." When our prayer seems rejected, we must look for and seek to discern the encouraging signs.

On football fields across America, you will sometimes see heavy metal equipment made up of four or six vertical pads and several horizontal skids on the bottom. The purpose of this heavy device is to provide resistance to football players as they train. They need to have strong legs that work together in unison with other linemen to push back the opposition when they are in a football game. Players have to learn how to lower their center of gravity, hit those pads hard, and push. We can just imagine the coach shouting, "Come on! Push! You can do it. Get tough. Drive 'em back. Go get 'em! Shove!"

If mere progress across the field were the objective, the heavy framework would be left on the sidelines. The coach wants to see *progress in spite of the resistance!* To learn this, the players need to train with heavy equipment *and* hear shouts of encouragement from their coach. God's program for developing prayer warriors is like that. He allows resistance and obstacles, yet simultaneously, He is there shouting encouragement. He wants us to pray with vigor.

Step 4: She Showed Reverence Even While Seeking Her Answer

So far in our story, the woman has pressed on in the face of resistance; but now we begin to see a softer side to her. "The woman came and knelt before him" (Matthew 15:25). Her humility and reverence demonstrates an attitude to maintain — a model to follow. *She bowed before Him whether He answered or not.*

She bowed before Him whether He answered or not.

With her request rejected once and before she made it again, this woman knelt in humility before the Lord. It is easier to submit to the Lord when we receive answers to prayer. It is more difficult to submit to God when He does not answer our prayers.

Can we throw ourselves at His feet saying, "Lord, I want the answer to my prayer very much indeed, but I submit the matter and myself to You in humility. I love You unconditionally. It is You I seek. Though You slay me, yet I will trust You."

If we show reverence and worship only when we receive, is it possible that we are more interested in what we receive from God than loving God himself? Delays in receiving the answer are opportunities for us to test ourselves and ask, "Do we love God and His will or do we love just His answers?"

Step 5: She Surrendered to Jesus' Lordship

Throughout this narrative, the Canaanite woman kept calling Him "Lord" as when she said, "Lord, Son of David" (Matthew 15:22). "Lord, help me" (Matthew 15:25). "Yes, Lord," (Matthew 15:27). These expressions of reverence to our Lord represent submission.

The woman called Jesus "Lord" three times while showing reverence to Him even in the face of rejection and again before receiving the answer to her request. If she had only called Him

Lord once, it might be difficult to build the case that this woman was submitting herself to the authority and Lordship of Jesus. However, her consistency and reverence indicate that she truly considered Jesus to be her Lord. She used the title sincerely.

When Jesus teaches us perseverance in prayer, our belief in the Lordship of Jesus may be the only thing that keeps us praying instead of resenting the fact that He is not answering our prayer requests. Those who acknowledge Him as Lord will continue to persevere in prayer. Prayer is not overcoming God's reluctance; it is an exercise in claiming His will.

> We persist because we know He wants us to persist.

The insight that Luke 18 adds to our understanding of Matthew 15 helps us realize that Jesus is training disciples. Notice how He reacts to the woman's requests. He taught her and thereby teaches us to "always pray and not give up" (Luke 18:1). When we recognize that it is the Father's will that we persevere in prayer, we persist *because we know He wants us to persist*. We do not persist out of rebellion, selfish or self-willed praying, or resentment; but out of faithfulness. He encourages us to persist even while He seems to be resisting our requests. We pray persistently *because* He is Lord, not *in spite of* the fact He is Lord.

Step 6: She Prayed with Passion

Her prayer was not just cognitive — she put some emotion into it. Her first approach, Matthew says, was "crying out" (Matthew 15:22). Then the disciple accuses her to Jesus by saying, "For she keeps crying out after us" (Matthew 15:23). Later she pleads passionately, "Lord, help me!" (Matthew 15:25). She was praying fervently, earnestly, and from her heart.

Even though Jesus rejected the woman's first request for help, this brief, one-sentence prayer has less conceptual content and as much passion as her "crying out" in the other parts of the conversation. She consistently shows emotional urgency.

Our prayers are sometimes dull without raw, emotional feeling. Strong dedication is not the only thing needed in prayer; we must also pray for the right things. However, prayer can become formal, intellectual, and casual without passion as if the goal were *the act of praying* rather than *obtaining an answer to prayer*.

Can we control the emotional element level of our prayer? Yes! It depends on how much we want the answer. It is okay to be emotional and passionate about prayer. Prayer is much more than just emotion and passion. Yet, without passion, prayer may seem insipid or even preoccupied with just the action of doing it, without much concern about actually receiving the answer. Remember, the answer is what we seek. Prayer, in any other paradigm, is incomplete.

It is a paradox that God either resists our prayer or allows resistance from another source in the spirit world. He develops our persistence and our passion, and encourages us to pray and realize the answer He too wants us to receive. Both of these elements — resistance and encouragement — are taught in the Bible and validated by human experience. Giving us an answer as soon as possible is obviously not God's goal, or else every delay in an answer to prayer would be an indication of God's failure.

So, what *is* God's goal? God's eternity-oriented goal for you and me is to develop dependable, unshakable, persevering, totally committed, and confident statesmen to manage His coming Kingdom. That takes some doing. He is willing and He has the time. You will get your answer — that is what you want. God will achieve your character growth — that is what He wants.

Step Seven: She Reasoned With Jesus

The Canaanite woman was able to think clearly and quickly, when she reasoned with Jesus by saying, "Yes it is, Lord, but even the dogs eat the crumbs that fall from their master's table" (Matthew 15:27 TNIV). God seems to like it when we use our heads too. By saying, "Yes it is," she is not being defiant; she is reasoning. Proverbs 15:1 says, "A gentle answer turns away wrath." Of course, Jesus was not wrathful here, but the principle of maintaining a controlled reasoning attitude is upheld by this woman's clever and sound contention This woman's gentle and consistent reasoning in the face of the insult displays her perseverance from an additional angle — she used her head as well as her heart.

She refused to be insulted or deterred even when verbally "attacked" by the disciples and Jesus. After Jesus claimed that He was sent only to the lost house of Israel, He further said, "It is not right to take the children's bread and toss it to their dogs" (Matthew 15:26 TNIV). To this rebuttal, the Canaanite woman cleverly responded, "Yes it is, Lord. Even the dogs eat the crumbs that fall from their master's table" (Matthew 15:27 TNIV). When virtually called a foreign dog, she humbly and effectively used the same figure of speech in her response. She did not ignore what Jesus said; she used those same words in her argument.

God delights when we use our reasoning powers. He wants us to engage Him intellectually. Through Isaiah, He invites us: "Come now, let us reason together" (Isaiah 1:18). Our arguments or rhetorical questions do not intimidate Him. That is part of being honest with God. The Bible says we should love Him with all our minds. God's desire for us is honest, mental engagement in our prayers to Him, rather than merely saying all the right phrases.

> God delights when we use our reasoning powers. He wants us to engage Him intellectually.

Jesus is the tenderhearted, sympathetic, compassionate Savior and comforter. However, He can also be a tough trainer just like the coach of the football team we illustrated in Step 3. The lesson in this story is not so much comfort for beginners as it is a challenge for stronger sons and daughters. This passage portrays that He wants to develop tenacity, discipline, and character in us. The way He trains His disciples is different from the gentle nature He shows to the lost, the burdened, and the sorrowful and broken sinner whose grief He came to bear.

When appropriate, Jesus is a wonderful comforter. At other times, He administers appropriate challenges to strengthen our faith. The target audiences, the needs, and the results are all different, and Jesus knows what lessons He needs to teach and the principles He needs to use to teach them. All muscle builders know that resistance training is the key to making muscles stronger in the building process. God is developing spiritual muscle in His intercessors and knows that resistance is part of the process.

Jesus is the Master of reverse psychology. Jesus knew the spiritual training that the Canaanite woman needed. For us, He provides the correct amount of resistance that develops tenacity, perseverance, consistency, patience, passion, and faithfulness. His resistance neither crushes nor lets us coast on in comfort at existing maturity levels.

In training His children to persevere in prayer, Jesus is more concerned about permanent results than in relieving His trainee's temporary difficulty. He knows how the process works and is developing statesmen for His coming Kingdom.

Step 8: She Received the Lord's Promise Because of Her Faith

The woman's passionate persistence and reasoning power resulted in Jesus finally saying the words she wanted to hear, "Woman, you have great faith. Your request is granted" (Matthew 15:28). The indication the answer would come preceded the actual answer.

The word for faith and faithfulness is the same in Greek. If we have faith, we will be faithful. This woman had great faith and Jesus told her so. It was not until late in the conversation that Jesus' words indicated that the woman's faith had helped her pass His test of perseverance.

Jesus told her that because she had great faith, He would grant her request. Her faith is manifested in her persistence, passion, and quite-spirited reasoning powers. She had faith before she even met Jesus. However, her faith was further nurtured by meeting Jesus. After displaying her faith, she was rewarded with the promise from Jesus that her request would be answered.

The development of faith is a process. It was only after the test was complete that Jesus finally encouraged this woman. Through His encounter with this woman, He teaches us that if we endure the process and remain faithful in prayer, God will reward us with commendations and answers to our prayers. Determined perseverance both develops and demonstrates great faith.

Step 9: Jesus Did Exactly What He Said He Would Do

Not only did the woman hear the words that she wanted, but she also received the action that Jesus promised her. "Her daughter was healed from that very hour" (Matthew 15:28). She received the answer Jesus promised. That is the way God works; He is true to His Word.

God's Word and His actions are consistent. Jesus healed the daughter when He said, "Your request is granted" (Matthew 15:28). This shows that we can trust the words of Jesus.

Consider Jesus' promises to us. God's Word says that He forgives those who repent, heals our bodies, and that He will never leave us nor forsake us. Jesus said, "I will build my church," (Matthew 16:18) and He is doing all those things. Right now, Jesus is preparing a place for us in heaven. He will return to earth to take us to be with God forever. He keeps all His wonderful promises.

No parent likes to have his or her children in pain or discomfort. When our children cry for help, our parental instincts rush through our body and we want to respond quickly. It takes wisdom and strength on God's part to resist our requests and force us to grow in character, faith, and the ability to persevere in prayer. God cares enough about our development that He is willing to put us through His training process. He is our Father, but not only that; He is also our Trainer — a Master Trainer with lofty goals for each of us. Envision God as being even more eager than we are for the answer to come our way. He restrains Himself for a more noble purpose — our development.

We must not think that our Father does not want to answer our prayers. He most certainly does when the answer is consistent with His will. God's intention in the delay of the answer may be to help us determine whether what we seek is really His plan. On the other hand, it may be that He is developing a sense of determination within us. We have two choices: we can thank Him for giving us a chance to discover His will at a deeper level, or thank Him that He is developing greater perseverance within us. In either case, the result is good and at the right time, His good answer will come to wiser, stronger sons and daughters.

CHAPTER EIGHT

Intimacy with Our Heavenly Father

"Come near to God and He will come near to you."

James 4:8

I'm about to share something God has revealed to me over time with some ideas dating back a few years. He has taken me on my own journey of discovering intimacy with Him.

I want to share with you the ways that I relate to our Father in heaven. Possibly, these methods will be different from what you use now or be something that you have never heard of before. Nevertheless, if there are some "nuggets of wisdom" that you feel will help you to be more comfortable being closer to Him, I trust that you will let God apply them to your own relationship with Him.

At the end of the six-month sabbatical/missions trip to South Africa and India, I experienced the greatest surprise of the experiment. *It was a new closeness to God, feeling personally familiar with Him.* My new and deeper level of intimacy with our Heavenly Father, upon reflection, is a direct result of my increase in daily prayer time.

Intimacy with God does not require a sacrifice of genuine respect, amazement, and awe at His glory, grandeur, and excellent greatness. Yet, our view of God is incomplete if we only respect His greatness and awesome power without also fully appreciating His gentle, soft, parental, and tender side.

Balance requires both aspects; you cannot have imbalance and be whole. To develop an accurate concept of God in our spirits, we must balance our perceptions of God's strong and dynamic side by our grasp of His tender and approachable side.

Two Aspects to God's Greatness

During the four months in India, I enjoyed introducing my audiences to two glorious thoughts: *God is big!* and *God is near!*

- If He were only big and powerful but not near and caring, He *could* help us but *would* not.

- If He were only near and caring but not big and powerful, He might be able to *sympathize* with us but *could not help* us with our problems.

> We must balance our perceptions of God's strong and dynamic side by our grasp of His tender and approachable side.

The combination of His great power and His nearness makes Him so wonderfully unique.

This is extremely different from the Hindu concept of many violent and distant gods whose requirements force their helpless followers who struggle to satisfy the gods in a never-ending effort to avoid their anger. In addition, it is a subtly different thought process for many Western Christians. Their idea is to revere God more for His greatness but not so much for His approachability. The *true* God is both big and able to help and near and willing to help.

The people in the audience were happy to hear these profound and wonderful theological truths. I shared these grand ideas in terms they could easily grasp, and never used words that were hard to understand.

The Bible says, "Come near to God and he will come near to you" (James 4:8). From the use of the word "near," we can assume that God wants a close, relationship with us. He prefers that our relationship with Him be close, not distant; soft, not hard; warm, not cold; friendly and intimate, not adversarial, resentful, or characterized only by awe, respect, fear, and reverence. Those responses are natural when we have a relationship with a holy God. However, it is important not to miss the friendliness and intimacy that God provides.

Seeing things from God's perspective is what we want. We cannot fully understand our intimate relationship just by considering His creative power, majesty, wisdom, and perfect knowledge. God's greatness also includes His tender side. He is also near, warm, friendly, tender, accepting, and approachable. When appreciating God's tender side, our perception changes. If we are willing to see things with God-given perception, we will be able to appreciate the ideas in the following paragraphs.

A Unique Opportunity for a Paradigm Shift

After returning from India with experiences abroad fresh in my mind, I took three days to be alone with God. I asked God to give me His own debriefing — I needed to process what I had learned from Him through prayer. I also wanted to understand what I had learned about the process of learning through prayer.

By imagining myself in God's throne room, it made my praise more meaningful than merely saying the familiar words of praise that I had used for many years.

The increased power in preaching and teaching together with new insights into old truths during the six months abroad were so profound that I did not want to slip back into my previous pattern. I wanted God to show me His priorities and value system. Also, I wanted to know what was of value and of no value to Him so I could set my course on the correct path and pursue what God wanted. I was determined to adjust my own value system to conform more perfectly to His. I was seriously asking for a paradigm shift. My prayer was answered, and within a few days, it transformed the way I thought of my heavenly Father in relationship to me.

During the six months in India and Africa in which I increased my daily prayer, I continued to feel closer and closer to God. It became easier to spend the increased amount of time in prayer each day while learning to enjoy a more relaxed pace, moving from praise to prayer, lingering as long as I wanted on each point. I knew I was experiencing a spiritual change.

To ensure that I did not miss the opportunity to draw close to God, I started my morning prayer times during the latter weeks of my sabbatical by imagining myself at the base of a raised platform on which God sat on His glorious throne. I would say something like:

"Father, here I am in the midst of Your glorious splendor that streams from Your mighty throne. In all the light, brightness, color, shimmer, fragrance, and glory of this place, and in the midst of the sound of multiple voices singing, exclaiming Your greatness in praise so that the ground trembles with thunderous volume, I, too, lift my voice in awe at Your greatness and majesty. I lay myself before You and, with my face on the ground out of profound reverence and humility, I acknowledge Your superiority and exceeding greatness."

By imagining myself in God's throne room and expressing myself this way, it made my praise more meaningful than merely saying the familiar words of praise that I had used for many years.

After praising God in this way, I usually proceeded to another step. I would say:

> "And now with caution and awe, I lift my head from the ground to look upon Your beauty and lovely face. I see You smile and nod to me and receive it as Your invitation to ascend the steps, which I now cautiously do. I approach Your throne and note You are still smiling and encouraging me to approach even closer. I climb up on Your lap and lay my head against Your shoulder. While placing one arm over Your shoulder and the other around Your neck, I whisper with deep feelings in your ear, "Daddy, I love you. I love you, Daddy."

After several moments of intimately speaking with God, I descended from His lap and platform and proceeded with my normal, daily routine of prayer and intercession.

Then, on the morning of January 2, 2003, more than a week after my three days of debriefing alone with God, I proceeded to pray as described above. However, there was one major change: I had a deep longing to linger on God's lap; so I told Him and He invited me to stay. To my delight, I spent the remainder of my prayer time that morning staying on His lap and accordingly changing my vocabulary to that of a child speaking to his daddy.

I spent the remainder of my prayer time that morning staying on His lap and accordingly changing my vocabulary to that of a child speaking to his daddy.

The Adjustments of Taking Time to Linger on Daddy's Lap

It is easier to pray practiced prayers (clichés) when God is in heaven and we are on earth, or when we are in a crowd or distant from the throne. However, praying in clichés is nearly impossible when we are on His lap talking with our Daddy. Clichés help us continue to say words and help make our prayer sound acceptable when we are praying aloud; but they do not contribute to the depth of private, personal prayer. Talking with Daddy forces us to be real and focused and to think about saying something meaningful.

Wandering minds and clichés are even more inappropriate when climbing up on Daddy's lap and talking directly into His ear. Just imagine leaning against His shoulder and talking intimately. It would be extremely out of place to speak common phrases *there* with your mind somewhere else. I am embarrassed when that happens to me. It is an awesome and holy privilege to be on that lap. When we speak in Daddy's ear, every word uttered and thought expressed takes on new depth and richness. We view the universe and the challenges we face on earth differently from Daddy's lap. Problems appear very small, non-threatening, and easy to solve from there.

The Power of Words

Words are powerful. When we use words like *holy, exalted, lifted up, high, mighty, glorious,* and *awesome,* we honor God in His splendor. Without thinking, the use of those words may cause us to perceive God to be distant.

Abba is another powerful word. It is used very few times in the New Testament since the New Testament was written in the Greek language. *Abba* is the common familiar Aramaic word for "Father" that the Jewish people would have used in their everyday family relationships and conversations. Some Bible scholars take its unique and very limited usage in the Greek text to mean the more familiar and less formal expression that we would translate as "Daddy" or "Papa" in contemporary usage.

Many times when Jesus prayed to His Father, the Gospel writers used the Greek word *Pater* for "Father." So the one very unique setting in which Mark by the Holy Spirit used the Aramaic *Abba* as Jesus prayed, may have been intended to emphasize Jesus' intimacy and close dependence on His Father. Jesus was in deep agony in the Garden of Gethsemane as He faced the horrible crucifixion the next day. In such depth of emotion, Jesus needed to sense the presence of His Father in the most intimate way. I believe Mark used *Abba* here to show the depth of intimacy Jesus had with His Father at this darkest hour in His life.

The Apostle Paul emphasizes our being God's sons twice in his writings. In Romans he says, "… you received the Spirit of sonship. And by him we cry, 'Abba, Father.' The Spirit himself testifies with our spirit that we are God's children" (Romans 8:15-16). According to Galatians, we are sons privileged to use that name. "Because you are sons, God sent the Spirit of his Son into our hearts, the Spirit who calls out, 'Abba, Father'" (Galatians 4:6).

Since Paul wrote his letters to the churches using Greek, it seems strange that he would use *"Abba, Pater"* in those two letters, placing the Hebrew word for "Father" before the Greek word. What significance did he and the Holy Spirit have in mind? One can only guess. But, many Bible teachers believe, as I do, that the use of *Abba* is intended to connote the more intimate and childlike expression "Daddy."

It is a ministry of the Holy Spirit, who is the Spirit of adoption, to assure us that we are sons and daughters of God. If I am correct, the use of *Abba* in Romans and Galatians indicates our acceptance by God as His little children. Compared to Him in spiritual matters, we are as infants and small children. He is available to be near and dear just like loving human daddies like to be to their little children. It is obvious from these Scriptures that He wants us to think of Him and ourselves in this way.

When I was a missionary candidate preparing for our first term in the Orient, the Lord increased my courage by inviting me to call Him "Dad." As I was growing up and into my adult years, I had usually referred to God as "Father." But when I was preparing for overseas mission work, being invited to call Him "Dad" gave me courage to face the unknown. That was a great step forward in my journey toward intimacy with the heavenly Father. Since then, to my comfort and God's delight, I have found great joy in occasionally calling Him "Dad."

"Dad" is what I called my earthly father from age 10 and older. I loved my dad and hugged him often, but the years of cuddling with him on his lap were over by then since I had become a bigger boy. Our hugs had become manly and full of bravado with frequent back pounding.

Therefore, when I began to call God "Daddy" years later, it was another step in becoming childlike before Him to recognize my weaknesses, foolishness, and ignorance as compared to Him. Not only did I learn from this great experience, but also I drew closer to Someone I loved, trusted, and with whom I felt comfortable being affectionate in a childlike way. I became deeply aware of a new aspect to an already wonderful relationship.

While the meaning of *Abba* may be subject to some debate as to whether it means Daddy or Father, no such ambiguity exists with our being God's "children." Jesus said, "… unless you change and become like little children, you will never enter the kingdom of heaven. Therefore, whoever humbles himself like this child is the greatest in the kingdom of heaven" (Matthew 18:3-4). To call God "Daddy" requires a childlike attitude toward Him. Again Jesus said on the way to Jerusalem, "… how often I have longed to gather your children together, as a hen gathers her chicks under her wings, but you were not willing" (Matthew 23:37).

Each of these verses contributes to our understanding of a close relationship where a little one readily runs to be close to and safe with a parent. If we take the "little child" from one verse and the running to safety under the mother hen's wing from the other, it is easy to picture a little boy or girl running to the lap of Daddy God for comfort and protection. Even Jesus, when revealing his humanity before enduring the cross, struggled to do the will of the Father. It was then that the Holy Spirit through Mark chose to show Jesus referring to God as *Abba,* or "Daddy."

> Daddy wants us on His lap, but we are the ones who hesitate.

As we pray, we have no question about the ability of the powerful Creator to work whatever miracles are necessary to answer our prayer. The question is seldom, "*Can* God do this?" It is usually, "*Will* God do this?" The contrast between talking to the Creator and talking with Daddy is that the Creator *could,* and Daddy *would.* Daddy has always been approachable, available, and willing. It was not the Mother Hen who wanted to maintain distance, but rather the little chicks Jesus was talking about when He said, "but *you* were not willing" (Matthew 23:37 emphasis mine). Jesus wanted intimacy. In other words, Daddy wants us on His lap, but we are the ones who hesitate. God is very good at answering the cry of our hearts even when we don't know what to pray or when we express ourselves poorly; Daddy answers prayer better than His little children can pray. He knows that part of what we need is just to be on His lap. So He invites us there.

Knowing that, as we submit our prayers to Him asking for His kingdom to come and His will to be done, Daddy will act favorably in our behalf. This helps us see how praying to Daddy, in addition to addressing Him as the mighty and powerful God, adds the element of tenderness, love, and favor.

These descriptions are not easily understood by the exclusive use of fancy words often used in prayer. The distance between sinners and a holy God is created by the sin of the sinner. However, even after becoming members of God's family, any distance between God and ourselves is created by us, not God.

Our sin, or *our* hesitancy to be intimate with Him, is the reason for any distance between us. God will never hold us at a distance when we approach Him even though He is the awesome and great Creator. He takes particular delight in being our Daddy.

When I first lingered on Daddy's lap during my prayer time, calling and thinking of Him as Daddy, I discovered some life-changing truths. By getting down from His lap or, worse yet, never getting on His lap, I had unconsciously created distance between Him and myself. In the early stages of discovering these truths, I returned to my role as a professor and intercessor too soon and did not remain a little boy dependent upon his Daddy. Nevertheless, more lessons were yet to be revealed by becoming Daddy's little boy.

The Others on Daddy's Lap

Later, as I prayed for Char, my wife, I found I perceived her as a little girl also on Daddy's lap. I found my prayers for her were much more tender, delicate, and caring. I wanted Daddy to hug, strengthen, and answer her prayers too. It was not difficult for me to imagine many of Daddy's little boys and girls romping, playing, or seeking comfort there, all of them with hurts and problems that Daddy could fix.

Another Picture of Intimacy

The idea of touching God may seem too intimate at first thought. This is even truer when we think of a lingering, familiar, or prolonged intimate touch. For further insight, consider one of God's names. One of the Hebrew names of God in the Old Testament is *El Shaddai* that is generally translated "God Almighty." The name could refer to "God of the mountain" or, originally, probably "breast." Some scholars think it means "Many-Breasted One," graphically illustrating God's abundant ability to nourish all His little boys and girls.

Char and I conducted a three-day pastors' conference in Salur, a town in northern Andra Pradesh on the east coast of India. One afternoon while Char was teaching, I went for a walk through the market area that included a vegetable section where there was an open space for discarded vegetable pieces. A young family of pigs was eating and rooting noisily through the useless particles. This location must have seemed to them like pig heaven. The sow's belly was covered with well-supplied breasts, and the squealing scampering piglets always seemed to want more nourishment. Fascinated, I watched for a while.

The sow lay down on her side and positioned herself in such a way that a whole row of hungry piglets could wiggle, squirm, and cuddle up to fountains of overflowing nourishment.

As I think about that scene and of *El Shaddai* as the "Many-Breasted One" and relate them to the verses in Matthew that I wrote about earlier, I think of a loving Daddy. This Daddy calls His little chicks under His wings to find security and comfort as we saw in the word-picture of the mother hen. He also calls all His little boys and girls for unlimited nourishment.

How could the little ones enjoy, experience, or find that kind of comfort unless they were willing to cuddle, snuggle, and press close to flesh? Of course, God is Spirit and you cannot physically cuddle with Spirit. However, the scriptural symbolism allows for this mental image.

I have shared above many scriptural metaphors describing our childlike dependence on and relationship with God. Jesus also gave us another cluster of metaphors when He said, "Do not be afraid, little flock, for your Father has been pleased to give you the kingdom" (Luke 12:32). In one sentence, we are described like sheep, children, and citizens. Many of God's aspects are best understood by using such descriptive words or picturesque images. Yet He is much greater and bigger than only one metaphor can convey. The solution is to use multiple figures as Jesus did. God is so beautiful and complex that this is required of human languages.

Another image that we can see in our mind to describe God is "The name of the Lord is a strong tower; the righteous run to it and are safe" (Proverbs 18:10). Therefore to portray just this one part of the multi-faceted relationship we have with God, we can combine images of the safety under the mother hen's wings, soldiers running from battle to the security of a fortress-tower, and the abundant protection and nourishment provided there for all of Daddy's (*Abba's* and *El Shaddai's*) children. Can you imagine many of Daddy's little boys and girls — His soldiers — being roughed up in battle? If so, imagine them needing to run to the security of His strong and encircling arms to find sustenance as they press against, cuddle, and snuggle at His soft, warm, and nourishing supply. That is intimacy, and Daddy loves it. It is His delight to draw us to Himself in all these ways.

Asking Daddy Our Requests

Another aspect of lingering on Daddy's lap is the new and intimate perspective I gained about asking Daddy for favors. Any child who is confident in the arms of his loving Daddy is not afraid to ask his Daddy for what he wants. As I remained on Daddy's lap, I kept thinking about all the things that I had asked God to bring me over the last several months. However, as I was using the intimate language of a child, the distant way that I made past requests seemed cold and artificial. Therefore, to be consistent with the intimacy of my "new" location and the relationship I had with Him, just as a child asks for a cookie, I made each request as if I were the child asking for a cookie. As I prayed about each of my usual requests, I remembered, in my mind, to remain on Daddy's lap and speak of my desires to Him in a childlike manner. I felt more confident that Daddy was listening and that He would take care of each request.

> I felt more confident that Daddy was listening and that He would take care of each request.

Daddy's Correction

Eventually, I arrived at the personal prayer request that God would prune me so I could become more fruitful. Jesus taught that His Father was the Gardener and that "every branch that does bear fruit he prunes so that it will be even more fruitful" (John 15:2). So I said, "Daddy, you are the Gardener and I am the branch, please prune me."

One of the ways God shows us that He is genuinely our Father and that we are His sons and daughters is by His willingness to correct us. Char and I taught our sons to say and mean, "Okay Daddy" or "Okay Mommy" when we were either instructing or even punishing them. It was not enough for our children to physically experience the punishment we administered as parents. We wanted our children to willingly embrace the correction at a spiritual level — we wanted them to truly receive the instruction. As God's son, I wanted to readily receive God's correction rather than resent it internally while merely enduring it physically.

These thoughts led me to ask Daddy, as a willing child might surrender to the instruction and correction of his father, "Daddy, realizing who You are to me and knowing I am safe in Your arms, as needed, correct me. I want to be pruned so I can become more fruitful." This was not because I am sadistic or masochistic but because pruning is the biblical process through which we become more fruitful. Through submission, I wanted to be more fruitful. In that moment of the closest intimacy I had ever experienced, I prayed, "Daddy, correct me," and I gained a new understanding of Hebrews 12:5-11. Later, I consulted it to make certain my experience was scripturally true. It was.

"... you have not forgotten that word of encouragement that addresses you as sons:

'My son, do not make light of the Lord's discipline, and do not lose heart when he rebukes you, because the Lord disciplines those he loves, and he punishes everyone he accepts as a son.'"

Endure hardship as discipline; God is treating you as sons. For what son is not disciplined by his father? If you are not disciplined (and everyone undergoes discipline), then you are illegitimate children and not true sons. Moreover, we have all had human fathers who disciplined us and we respected them for it. How much more should we submit to the Father of our spirits and live! Our fathers disciplined us for a little while as they thought best; but God disciplines us for our good, that we may share in his holiness. No discipline seems pleasant at the time; it is painful. Later on, however, it produces a harvest of righteousness and peace for those who have been trained by it."

This is precisely what we need from Daddy.

Children who love and trust the fairness of their fathers willingly accept loving correction.

The Bible says, "There is no fear in love. But perfect love drives out fear ..." (I John. 4:18). We do not have to be afraid of unfair treatment from our heavenly Daddy. No child likes correction, but children who love and trust the fairness of their fathers willingly accept loving correction. Those who have the benefits of correction are more likely to be correct just like those who are pruned are more likely to be fruitful. Course alteration (correction) is vital for us to arrive at our destinations. Whether we are in a spaceship, steering down a highway, dribbling down the basketball court, or attempting to be our best possible self — to be all we can be — let's accept and welcome our Daddy's correction.

This is an amazing benefit of intimacy with God. If we are intimate with our heavenly Father, we become more trusting and open to the process of being pruned, corrected, and producing fruit. If we embrace the process, we will hit the target — we will be all we could be by becoming our best possible selves. Our positive and intimate relationship with God gives us a positive attitude toward His correction. Perhaps we do not accept correction from just anyone, but certainly, we accept it from our Daddy who is very wise. Some believe that older people cannot learn new things. However, older people who are intimate with their Daddy can.

Ultimately, it is a compliment when God corrects His little child. As mature adults, unlike little children, we accept His "correction training" as a compliment. It is our privilege to accept this kind of corrective attention from our perfectly fair and loving Father.

Ultimately, it is a compliment when God corrects His little child.

Obtaining and Maintaining Balance

To think of God as only powerful and distant lacks balance. To think of Him as a doting father who will always treat us like spoiled children with no requirements or controls is also inaccurate. The ideas in this chapter help us balance our view of a powerful God by adding the tender, gentle, and personable side of His character. Most of us know we need to show respect to our holy Creator. However, God is not only your Creator but also your heavenly Daddy.

In this chapter, I described my lifelong journey of discovering that God is my heavenly Daddy. It is a journey Daddy has led me through over many years — even decades. What I have described to you is *my* story.

Your story — your pilgrimage of getting to know God as your Father or Daddy — will be different from mine. Yet I believe God is eager for you to make your own discoveries of Him as your eternal, heavenly Daddy. If you have never sat on His lap, would you consider this encouraging aspect of your relationship? Knowing who your Dad really is and, more perfectly, what He is like can give new confidence to you.

This kind of thinking is different from our normal understanding of a human's relationship with a holy and grand God. Understanding these intimate aspects of our relationship with God requires a significant conceptual adjustment. When Elijah had a public "power encounter," he called fire down from heaven, defeated, and killed the prophets of Baal and Ashterah on Mount Carmel, but he first "repaired the altar of the Lord which was there" (I Kings 18:30). "Repairing the altar" is an expression full of meaning. Elijah did not need to, nor did he, build a new altar, but neither did he use the altar in its dilapidated condition. This seems to be a good model for us when we want to perfect or further develop our ideas. When we learn new ideas, we do not need to throw out all we knew or held dear. New truth should enhance and add new dimensions, depth, and understanding to old truth.

We, too, can add a newfound appreciation for God as our Daddy to our knowledge base without undervaluing His might and majesty. Combine the new and old truths of God's closeness with ideas of His great power, and the combination will serve you well.

The universe looks different from God's lap. Earthly problems look different from this vantage point — they look very small, non-threatening, and easy to solve. The Holy Spirit, the Spirit of truth, teaches us to do readily what Paul says: "Do not conform any longer to the pattern of this world, but be transformed by the renewing of your mind" (Romans 12:2).

What I thought was going to be a six-month educational learning experience became a spiritual experiment with multiple levels of discovery. Life with God is full of surprise and discovery. Spending more time in prayer surprised me with its new sense of closeness with God. I invite you to step forward on your own path of discovery to see what new insights our Father — Daddy — has for you. Perhaps you will join me on His lap.

CHAPTER NINE

The Making of an Intercessor

"He rewards those who earnestly seek him."

Hebrews 11:6

The experiment began in Africa with the question, "What would happen if a *teacher* prayed?" Wanting to become a *praying teacher* increased my interest and participation in prayer, but I still saw myself essentially as a teacher. A *praying teacher* may focus much more on prayer but the primary motivation is still to pray for the success of teaching.

An *intercessor* committed to intercession is freer to focus on *God's* issues and less worried about *his own* prayer topics because they are now God-driven in a new way. Intercessors find fulfillment by keeping God's agenda the focus of their prayers. Their other gifts or roles become less the focus than the new leading role of being an intercessor.

What would happen if becoming an intercessor became your focus and whatever else you did became secondary?

A Major Shift in Self-Perception

After about a year of focusing more on prayer, I realized I was beginning to redefine myself. This process continues to this day. But what is the difference?

Self-perception — how one sees himself, his purpose, and his lifestyle — influences behavior. All perceptions have tremendous emotional power. As humans, we naturally tend and seek to live in a manner that is consistent with our perceptions. They influence our beliefs, values, thoughts, and finally our actions.

The self-perception as a *teacher* who prays is not the same as that of an *intercessor* who teaches and watches God open doors and work in human affairs. It was an improvement to begin to view myself as a *praying teacher* versus seeing myself just as a *teacher*. This is because anybody, including a teacher who considers praying a significant part of who he is, is positioned to become much more effective in the use of his or her gifts. Yet, growing to see myself as an *intercessor* who *also teaches* was another advancement in my thought process. I began to see myself principally as an intercessor. I began to experience personal fulfillment in praying, no longer because praying was necessary to help me teach better, but because praying helped bring God's will — whatever it was — to Earth. My new perception makes my increased prayer time seem natural and right. Simply stated, it is what I do because it is who I am — I pray more because that is what intercessors do.

> Simply stated, it is what I do because it is who I am — I pray more because that is what intercessors do.

Perceiving myself as a teacher who prays transpired as I began to pray more each day. Increasing my prayer time required major schedule changes. I had been busy, and then I became busier. Now, however, these hours in prayer seem more natural. The new way I see myself as an intercessor makes the hours of intercession fit better with who I am. Scheduling my new priority of praying more is consistent with my perception of doing what intercessors do.

Praying At Night

I have used various prayer schedules in order to complete my four hours a day prayer time. For example, for a year or two I got up in the middle of the night to pray for an hour and went back to bed. Then, at 6:00 A.M., I would pray an hour before breakfast, and would pray two more hours before going to work. My current routine, however, is to pray two and one-half hours before breakfast, and the pray the remaining time after breakfast before beginning my other activities for the day.

It occurred to me that several years ago a professor friend told me he thought the day would come when God would awaken me in the middle of the night for extended periods of prayer. That thought was so unnatural to me at that time that his words had little effect on me. It was not until long after I had begun getting up in the middle of the night to pray for my first hour that I recalled what my friend had said.

Beginning to think of myself as an *intercessor* rather than as a *teacher* made praying at night seem like the appropriate thing to do. It was not that I liked sleep any less; but it was because I valued more what God could do and was doing. Since my aim is to see God fulfill more of His agenda through me, I pray more and work harder to arrange my schedule to make this possible.

Praying more is the strategic plan I am experimenting with to try to increase the fruitfulness that God has planned for me. Praying at night or praying in the early morning is a tactic — how I implement it in my life. *Strategy* deals with the broader deliberate plan while *tactics* get those plans fulfilled. Effective people are intentional; they have strategies and tactics. When something is important to us, we are willing to develop tactics to implement our strategy. This is why self-perception is so important to an intercessor; like anyone else, he does what he needs to do to fulfill who he is.

Psychologists tell us that we often interpret events in terms of our expectations. Beliefs condition perceptions and we look for what we think we will see. It was not until after I had begun to pray in the middle of the night that I began to notice how many times Scripture refers to praying at night. That was an amazing eye-opening discovery after reading the Bible all the way through each year for 40 years! The verses were there all along, but I had not noticed them — maybe because I had not wanted to notice them.

Here are some examples of how the Bible refers to praying at night:

- Abraham must have been talking to God at night when God told him to look at the stars (Genesis 15:5).
- Jacob wrestled and prayed his well-known prayer at night (Genesis 32:22-26).
- Psalms refers to praying while lying in bed (Psalm 63:6).

- Jesus often prayed at night. At least once, He prayed all night and then chose His disciples the following morning (Luke 6:12-13).

- Jesus had just been praying at night when He walked on the water to His disciples (Mark 6:46-48).

- The church in Acts was praying at night when Peter was awakened by an angel and miraculously released from prison (Acts 12:6, 12).

Since my schedule and workload are as full as they are, praying at night has practical advantages. For example, if I wake up in the middle of the night, I use that time to pray as I go back to sleep. In addition, praying at night also makes much better use of the time if I have difficulty sleeping. Who would have thought of prayer as a great solution for insomnia?

At night, we are not interrupted. Just as important, we are not distracted by the thought that we might be interrupted. In other words, at night we can pray freely without any need to hurry. Praying in the daytime is often subject to interruptions by a family member or phone call. Nighttime or early morning is a unique time. At night, you are not likely to be required to do anything else. The events and conversations of yesterday are through and the appointments or deadlines of the next day are not yet upon you. You are free of daytime constraints.

Praying at night also allows for the expression of urgency. The widow in Luke 18 symbolizes persistence, diligence, and insistent prayer. Jesus' interpretation of that parable we looked at in Chapter Seven includes the rhetorical question: "Will not God bring about justice for his chosen ones who cry out to him day and night?" (Luke 18:7)

Nehemiah was urgent in prayer and used the fact that he was praying day and night as part of his pleading with God. "Let your ear be attentive and your eyes open to hear the prayer your servant is praying before you day and night for your servants the people of Israel" (Nehemiah 1:6).

David used similar language, "O Lord, the God who saves me, day and night I cry out before you" (Psalm 88:1). "By day the Lord directs his love, at night his song is with me — a prayer to the God of my life (Psalm 42:8).

Isaiah invites intercessors or "watchmen" to "never be silent day or night. You who call on the Lord, give yourselves no rest, and give him no rest till he establishes …" (Isaiah 62:6-7).

Paul refers to "sleepless nights" (2 Corinthians 6:5), and it would be hard to imagine that he did not use some, if not all, this time to pray. In Paul's list of sufferings about which he "boasts," he mentions that he has "often gone without sleep" (2 Corinthians 11:27).

So whether you use praying at night as a practical scheduling convenience or as a means to express urgency in prayer, remember to consider its potential in making effective prayer doable. If love for comfort is an enemy of your prayerfulness, if you have time-constraints in the daytime, or if you want to make more time for yourself to press harder into greater effectiveness and fruitfulness as a Christian, praying at night may help you. It is biblical, practical, and may be a powerful weapon in your battle for spiritual fruitfulness. Consider it.

Choosing a New Self-Perception

How important is our self-perception especially when it comes to prayer? Why is it important to think of ourselves as intercessors? What would happen if we saw ourselves primarily as intercessors — partners with God — and everything God did through us was produced out of our time spent with *Him*?

When our minds are on our careers or other earthly matters, we process the contents of our prayer and use spiritual forces through prayer from our own career-oriented perspectives. We pray so our careers go well. However, since much of what we do is an expression of who we perceive ourselves to be, career-oriented prayer may still be man-centered or even a gimmick to obtain self-centered aims.

What would happen if we identified ourselves principally as intercessors before God rather than defining ourselves in terms of our own career or family status? Would it mean that our lives become more *about Him* and less about ourselves? Can we learn to delight in being a less-opinionated, more-neutral human tool used by a wise God?

The first part of my transition — from seeing myself as a teacher who prayed and then to being a teacher who prayed more in order to have more fruitful ministry — took place in a day or two as I changed my prayer pattern. I made an intentional and abrupt transition on my part in South Africa. However, the next change to currently being first an intercessor and a teacher second took place over time and seemed to occur gradually as I found myself enjoying my increased prayer time more and more.

Sometimes in the privacy and darkness of the early morning, after my time of worship and praise, I am then ready to begin making petitions. I stop walking, click my heels together, and give a military salute to the Commander-in-Chief. In my best macho voice I say, "Private Ron Meyers, intercessor first-class reporting for duty, Sir. What is the agenda today?" This, too, is consistent with my new self-perception.

No two of God's children are alike. I cannot tell you what God has in mind for you. But I can tell you that if you sense a desire in your heart to witness greater fruitfulness in your life and service to God, you will see some amazing transitions taking place in your life when you try increased prayer as a strategy. Gradually, desiring and seeking God's agenda will become more important to you. The greater fruitfulness you desire will motivate your increased prayer. More lives will be changed for God's glory. And one day, you may begin to see yourself more as an intercessor than having any other major pursuit in life.

God, your heavenly Father, will use His own means to lead you to what He wants you to be. However, right now, you can begin making this transition to committing yourself to spend more time with God in prayer. It does not have to be any certain length of time. If you currently pray for 30 minutes daily, perhaps you could double that to an hour. If you spend an hour in prayer daily, perhaps you could add **Think about how you can increase your prayer time in a way that fits your prayer style.** 30 minutes or even another hour. If you are the type of person who prays as you go about your daily work, think about how you can increase your prayer time in a way that fits your prayer style. Experiment with ways to increase your prayer time to see what works best for you.

Only God knows what your new self-perception will be one of these days. Moreover, He will take great delight as your desire to know Him increases and you begin to seek Him more intensely. If knowing God is truly your desire, prayer is the way to express it.

Tips for Intercessors: Helpful Hints for Effective Praying

Over the years, I have learned that there can be a number of physical obstacles to effective praying. People distract us. Telephone calls interrupt us. Some of our distractions relate to our locations. Others obstacles are due to our not knowing how to pray. Still others problems relate to keeping our minds focused on God. We each have to solve our own set of challenges in this regard. Nevertheless, this section shows a few practical lessons about tactics that may help make our prayer more effective.

Find a Place to Pray

In order not to disturb my wife Char or feel inhibitions in praying, I often pray in the garage at our home. There is enough room for me to walk easily around our parked cars. The five-watt light hanging from the ceiling allows me to see the prayer Scriptures that now hang on and dominate the walls of our garage. Plus, the light does not glare in the night or early morning hours.

> I recommend finding a place to pray in which you feel free in your spirit to pray with liberty.

Please do not think of me as a super-spiritual or unusually dedicated person. It is just that since I really want to pray, I take the necessary measures to do it. I also find that early in the morning the streets are empty enough that I can walk and pray with freedom when the weather permits. Interestingly, even though I travel a lot and find myself in many different nations and cities, God is concerned enough about prayer that He always helps me find a place to pray. Whatever your taste or situation, I recommend finding a place to pray in which you feel free in your spirit to pray with liberty.

Use Scripture to Present your Case

As I walk and pray in the garage, I often use the Scriptures to "reason" with God. I present my arguments to Him for an answer. I have never found He was intimidated or irritated by this. Instead, He seems to enjoy my persistence that He do what He said in His Word He would do. These paragraphs could be entitled "How to wrestle with God" or "How to use God's Word in prayer." Here are some examples of how this might sound, though, of course, each day the prayer comes out differently. Each paragraph has a lesson of its own. If you were to join me in my garage, this is what you might see and hear.

I often begin with the verses that are placed on a shelf on the east wall, "Jesus told ... a parable to show them that they should always pray and not give up" (Luke 18:1). I may pray, "Lord, the reason I am out of bed and here again insisting on an answer to my prayer is that You, yourself, taught us to not give up. I am respectfully holding You to your Word. You want me to do this. I insist on your answer and Your complete involvement in every detail of this situation. I do so with the full confidence that this is what You want me to do."

The next Scripture in line reads, "If you remain in me and my words remain in you, ask whatever you wish, and it will be given you" (John 15:7). I may pray, "Lord, to the best of my ability, I am remaining in You and allowing Your Word to shape my attitude and prayer goals. What I am asking for is consistent with what Your Word says I should pray for. Since I remain in You and Your Word remains in me, I am asking that this thing I am praying for be given to me in Your time. You said You would give this to me, and I receive it with thanks."

On the next shelf down are two more verses. I read, "You may ask me for anything in my name, and I will do it" (John 14:14), and pray, "Lord, You said I could have anything; and what I am asking You for is in no way displeasing or dishonoring to You. It is something You want me to have and have promised me You would do it."

The next Scripture in line is this one: "I tell you the truth, my Father will give you whatever you ask in my name" (John 16: 23). I may pray, "Father, Jesus Christ Your Son and my Savior told me You would give me what I ask for in His name. Not for me alone, though I know You love me, but also for the sake of the promise He gave, give me my request. There is no way I can picture You not doing this."

The three promises mentioned above come directly from John Chapters 14, 15, and 16. Additionally, in these three verses, Jesus was discussing *ministry concerns*. He was not discussing material possessions. It is important to keep in mind that *when our prayers are ministry related*, Jesus says we will have the answers. These powerful promises to answer our prayer are not to be misused for just any type of careless praying. Some people misunderstand these promises to mean that they can go "shopping" at will for anything they want.

Then I turn to the south wall where I read this Scripture placed above several gadgets hanging on the wall: "This is the confidence we have in approaching God: that if we ask anything according to his will, he hears us. And if we know that he hears us — whatever we ask — we know that we have what we asked of him" (I John 5:14-15). I may pray, "Lord, thank You for this awesome assurance that You are going to do this thing I am requesting. I rest in You and know that You are listening and working in behalf of my request."

Further to the right along that same wall and above my workbench is this verse: "The prayer of a righteous man is powerful and effective" (James 5:16), and I pray, "Lord, I would not claim to be a righteous person except that Your own Word says I am made righteous through Jesus' blood. I lift my voice to You, not because I know how prayer works, but I know that when I pray, You work; and when I don't, You don't. Hear this prayer and answer. I do not know why You say this exercise is powerful and effective, but I believe You, and my experience has shown that it is true."

On the garage door are several verses. One reads: "If any of you lacks wisdom, he should ask God, who gives generously to all without finding fault, and it will be given to him" (James 1:5). I may pray something like, "Lord there are so many times when I do not know how to pray or even what to pray. Please give me wisdom as I seek to intercede for the things that are important to You. What is Your agenda today? What concern is on Your heart today? How may I serve Your purpose in prayer today? Thank You that You do not fault me for praying this way. Thank you that You are generous. I need You to be generous. Display Your generosity and goodness in a gracious answer to prayer today. Don't let my lack of wisdom hinder or limit Your mighty involvement among humans. Instead, give me the wisdom to pray the right way. Give me the words that are fitting to be expressed to such a mighty and wise God — prayers that are worthy of Your attention and answer."

Another verse on the garage door is " — the God who gives life to the dead and calls things that are not as though they were" (Romans 4:17). "Lord, everything that we see was once only someone's dream. I "see" my prayer being answered and the thing I am asking for becoming a reality. I agree with You that this thing that does not exist now will exist as You make it a reality. You are the unchanging and unchangeable mighty Creator. Just as You created in the past, You continue to create. Create clean hearts and open minds. Create opportunities to serve and open doors. For those in danger, create mechanisms of escape. Breathe life into discouraged hearts. Bring fresh energy into dead hopes. We trust You, the God Who gives life to the dead."

On the other wall of the garage hangs a ladder. Six verses of Scriptures are displayed on it. The first one I read is: "… to him who is able to do immeasurably more than all we ask or imagine" (Ephesians 3:20). I might pray, "Again and again, You have already demonstrated this truth to me. Already You have answered prayers far better than I have prayed. I trust You to continue to do what you do so well. I do not want to restrict You. Keep on surprising me. My part is to do Your will. Your part is to do what You want to do more wisely than I know how to verbalize — do what You want to do on earth."

I read, "What is impossible with men is possible with God" (Luke 18:27) and I pray, "Father, I know I can do little about this situation myself, but that is not an issue. You can do something — anything — and I trust You to do what You can do. I know You can answer my prayer. I am glad I am not limited by what is impossible to me as long as I trust in You."

Next, I see this verse: "Those who hope in the Lord will renew their strength. They will soar on wings like eagles; they will run and not grow weary, they will walk and not be faint" (Isaiah 40:31). I continue praying, "I take great courage from this promise today, Lord, because I get tired. However, I trust You to renew my strength, both physically and spiritually, and I will continue to pray, hope, trust, and intercede on behalf of Your will here on earth. I will not stop. And I thank You that You will help me."

Next, I may say, "Lord, in the spirit of Jabez I pray for increase, '… bless me, and enlarge my territory! Let Your hand be with me'" (I Chronicles 4:10). During the years I saw myself as a teacher, I would say, "I am a teacher, I ask You for more influence along with better, deeper, and longer-lasting impressions on more people. I want a larger territory, a bigger classroom, and more students because more influence means more people are going to get to know You. Lord, with Your hand with me, I know I can succeed. Your hand makes all the difference. Lord, keep Your hand on me." Now that I see myself more as an intercessor, I pray more for more than just my teaching. Nevertheless, increased influence in the visible and invisible realms remains on my agenda because it remains on His.

"Father, in the spirit of the tenacious Jacob, who wrestled with You in prayer long into the night, I too insist, 'I will not let You go unless You bless me' (Genesis 32:27). Hosea tells us, '… as a man, he struggled with God … he wept and begged for His favor' (Hosea 12:3-4). As a man, I, too, struggle with You. I weep and beg for Your favor. Lord, You are going to hear more from me. I will not stop praying. I will not stop believing. I will not stop bringing these petitions before You. I will not let You go unless You bless me. I do all this with the confidence that, strange as it may seem, I am persisting in an exercise that You want me to continue. I will not let You go unless You bless me!"

These Scriptures are full of tremendous and powerful ideas. As the months go by, I find more verses that I add to the garage décor. It helps me to turn these thoughts over in my mind as I pray. As I notice the Scriptures there each day, it adds to the changes taking place in my perceptions of myself as an intercessor. My soul feeds on these powerful promises from God. I had thought of placing prayer Scriptures on the walls of my garage while still on sabbatical in India, but I did not realize then how powerful their influence would be on me. I did not know that they would become effective, conceptual prayer tools.

Naturally, there are many other things to pray about besides our exercises in holding God to His Word. Nevertheless, these illustrations will help you see the influence of God's Word on prayer when we use it with increased determination. The book of Hebrews says God "… rewards those who earnestly seek him" (Hebrews 11:6). I believe that, and I act on it. You can too. We need to learn to hold God to His Word in prayer.

Avoid Holy Tones, Platitudes, and Clichés

A friend of mine recently told me this story. One day when he was in college, he went into the student cafeteria to eat lunch. He collected his food, and sat down at a table with two of his friends. Before eating, he bowed his head to give thanks to God for his food silently, as he had done countless numbers of times. A few seconds later, he abruptly realized that instead of praying he was mindlessly counting! He had already reached number seven before he became aware of what he was doing. As he told his friends what had just happened, they all had a big laugh.

Have you ever been praying for a while when you suddenly became aware that for the past several minutes, your mind had been somewhere else even while you kept mouthing words of prayer?

The holy tone of my voice mocks me for sounding so sincere and being so empty while my heart is not in it and my mind is not on it.

I find at times that my mind wanders from the task at hand, and I am merely speaking empty words — even spiritual-sounding clichés — into the air. The holy tone of my voice mocks me for sounding so sincere and being so empty while my heart is not in it and my mind is not on it. I am embarrassed each time this happens, so I repent and begin over again.

This is an all-too-common problem. It may be because we either slip into a rut because we get used to saying certain words in prayer, or we forget we are talking to a real Person.

The Old Testament says that God knew Moses face-to-face. When Moses prayed, he was keenly aware that he was talking with God face-to-face. It would have been completely out of place for that great man to speak in empty clichés masked with artificial holy tones. That is not praying.

Envision God Listening Intently

When we pray, God our heavenly Father turns his face toward us and we have His full attention. He watches us and is eager to receive our requests and act on them. When He is hovering over us with tender compassion, staying interested with our concerns, and listening carefully, it would be an insult for us to think about something else and merely mouth words. We are to love God with all our minds as well as with all our heart, soul, and strength (Luke 10:27). How do we get real with Him?

I find that using my imagination to picture myself in God's presence really helps. This is not the same as using New Age or eastern religions' visualization techniques to try to receive a supernatural vision or visitation from God. That form of meditation is occultist, and the visions people receive may be of demonic origin. God warns us not to have anything to do with anything of the occult. Throughout Scripture, true heavenly visions are always initiated by God and never induced by a person's self-seeking effort. Therefore, I seek to remember that God is right there with me.

I simply think about the biblical idea that God is interested and listens to me. The ability to imagine is a God-given quality. We can use our imagination to help us plan and create beautiful works of art and surroundings. We can also use it to invent new tools to help us work and play more efficiently. What better use of our imagination could anyone make than to help us stay focused on communicating directly with God when we pray!

When I am praying, I visualize several models or images in my mind. As we discussed in the previous chapter, when I think about how small and weak I am and compare that to how big and strong my Father (Daddy) is, I imagine myself talking to Him while I sit on His lap. When I think about my friendship with God, I imagine myself in a man-to-man embrace much as when my grown sons and I hug each other. When I worship Him, and sometimes when I seek His favor, in my mind (and sometimes with my body), I am flat on my face before His mighty throne expressing praise and petition. While in that position, I seek His full involvement in all my earthly decisions because of His goodness, power, and wisdom.

When I catch myself mouthing empty words with my mind wandering, I visualize the following image that helps me to refocus my attention: God, my Father, is sitting at His desk administrating the affairs of the universe or at the head of the table in the boardroom. I, an adult, am sitting on a chair at the side of the desk and we are talking intelligently together. He is listening with attention and expects me to listen in the same manner too. At the same time, He is directing the activities of hundreds of messengers, administrative assistants, angelic beings, and others who hurry in and out of the room in a constant flurry of kingdom business. Nevertheless, His ability to direct those affairs is in no way an interruption to our intelligent conversation. He is good at multi-tasking.

In this image, I am a mature adult and He deserves that I focus on the kingdom business I am there to discuss. Much more than our minds are at work when we are in prayer, but to be mindless about the serious business of prayer is also wrong. That is why this image works for me; it helps me keep my mind (as well as my words) on target. When we keep our minds on our direct interaction with God; we are using our time well; and when we are not, we may be wasting time.

Intercessors are God's power tools.

Ezekiel 22:30 tells us that God, because of His holy character, *must* punish sin and is looking for intercessors. He is seeking those who are willing to stand in the gap and intercede for the land. "I looked for someone among them who would build up the wall and stand before me in the gap on behalf of the land so I would not have to destroy it, but I found no one." God is looking for intercessors. Hanani the seer said to Asa, "The eyes of the Lord range throughout the earth to strengthen those whose hearts are fully committed to Him" (2 Chronicles 16:9). Intercessors are God's power tools.

CHAPTER TEN

The Motivation of an Intercessor

"But when you pray, go into your room, close the door, and pray to your Father, who is unseen. Then your Father, who sees what is done in secret, will reward you."

Matthew 6:6

The really big changes over the course of my life have taken place through prayer. I learned the power of personal prayer at age six through a unique answer to a private prayer. When I was 19 years old during the summer of 1963, I learned the power of systematic prayer when I began to pray one hour a day. Soon, my outlook changed dramatically. I began to read the Bible an hour a day, increased my prayer time to two hours, began caring more for others, and became much more passionate in my pursuit of God.

Years later, in the spring of 1979, I fasted and prayed for 40 days in order to see the Korean church where I worked freed from administrative and spiritual bondage. As a result of that time of prayer, I experienced more change in myself than in the church or the administrative situation. I became less likely to argue, judge, and state my opinions. Currently, I pray four hours a day to see if it will make any difference in my career. As you can see, this process of change continues today through prayer.

God can work alone but usually does not. He invites and wants our participation in His work which is done through prayer.

God does not want to control everything and everyone like a puppeteer controls a puppet. Some of what He does, He does in partnership with praying sons and daughters. God wants us actively involved. We wait *for* God too many times instead of waiting *on* God. We do not initiate enough. We give up too easily. We stop praying too soon.

My life experiences and the reading of God's Word have led me to a thoughtful yet unexplainable belief: *God answers prayer.* It is an awesome thought that God acts when we pray. In an attempt to grasp the magnitude of this commonly stated but little understood idea, consider this: When we do not pray about a situation, it often remains the same or becomes worse, but when we pray about it, the situation improves. Consequentially, I have come to believe that:

- When we pray, God acts.

- When we don't pray, God does not act as much.

- In some instances, God acts *because* we pray.

The purpose of this book is to make the point that prayer makes a difference; if you pray, you can make a difference. Of the many motives for prayer, the most important is that prayer changes things.

Does my Emphasis on Time Spent in Prayer Mean I Am Works-Oriented?

This question has been asked by my students and has come to my own mind many times. It is at the heart of the prayer experiment. Let me clarify what it usually means to be "works-oriented."

We all know that we are saved by grace through faith and not by good works. However, many believers continue to try to gain further acceptance from God by doing good works. As a means of gaining salvation, good works will not work. God already loves and accepts us fully without any further works on our part. Praying, giving, or serving more cannot make Him accept us more than He already does. We are already fully accepted as His beloved; He has "seated us with him in the heavenly realms" (Ephesians 2:6). To think we earn acceptance from God by increased "works" is to be "works-oriented." Grace is not like that.

Yet, doing good works as a response to God's love still has a biblical basis. In Matthew 5:16, Jesus said, "Let your light shine before men, that they may see your good deeds and praise your Father in heaven." James 2 instructs us to make works an evidence of our faith. In other words, when we have faith in God, we receive the salvation that He gives us. We demonstrate our faith by loving Him and others and obeying His Word. This is the proper way to think of "works." We *want* to do the things God desires such as pray. Therefore, prayer and even increased time spent in prayer are valid forms of performing "good works" for God.

I cannot fully explain the relationship between Scripture's instruction to pray and God working in response. Yet, He does. It is even harder to explain how God appears to give more in response to our disciplined and increased time spent in prayer — our "works." However, it is abundantly evident that He does.

Since when do you have to be able to explain *how* a thing works in order to believe that it *will* work? We all use computers, but only a small percentage of us understand how they work. We use them because they work. The same is true of prayer. Without understanding how or why God does more when we increase our prayer time, we can still believe it and adjust our practice accordingly.

Without understanding how or why God does more when we increase our prayer time, we can still believe it and adjust our practice accordingly.

It is not an attempt to be cute to raise this question and then say there is no explanation. We lack the understanding to explain how or why God works to answer prayer — it is something we must learn to live with. After having prayed for two hours a day through 37 years of ministry, I began to pray twice that much. With that change, I also began experiencing at least twice the number of God's miracles in my life. The reality is this: When I pray, God works; when I do not pray, God works less. However, when I pray more, He works more. In spite of the unanswerable issues, I would rather He answered prayer and worked more than not answering prayer and working less. I will just live with the mystery of how prayer and answers relate.

If you are curious about this idea, conduct your own experiment in prayer. If your experiment is realistic based on where you are in your career growth and in the Lord, then the purpose for which I have been sharing my experiment will have been fulfilled. I am trying to "bait" you. I want to invite you — even entice you — to conduct your own test. I think I can predict what God will do. However, I cannot predict what you will do. The bigger question is whether you will try something new.

Two Awkward Puzzles

Just like you, I, too, want everything that I do to be noble and pure. I would like to be so in love with God and so committed to seeing His Kingdom come and His will done that I naturally give myself to praying constantly without thinking. However, it does not work that way for me. And apparently, this is true for others too. I have had to learn to become comfortable with two practical puzzles that I cannot resolve.

The first one is that I do not want the desire for good works and their reward to be my only motivation. I do want a reward, but I know that should not be my only motive. At the same time, I am not willing for the desire to avoid the wrong motive of *only* wanting to be rewarded to deter me from praying more. I will boldly pray more.

> Watching the clock helps me pray more. Therefore, I will watch the clock.

Bearing more fruit brings more glory to God than bearing a little fruit or none at all. Praying more produces more fruit and God does indeed relate to humans in a *quid pro quo* relationship. He says, "If you do something, I will do something. If you pray, I will answer. " I accept His terms. I pray and He works; I pray more and He works more. Sure, sometimes this makes me feel awkward, but I will not stop because of that. In other words, my valid fear of just seeking a reward for praying is not strong enough to avoid being disciplined to pray for a set length of time.

Throughout the experiment, *timing my praying is precisely the action that is helping me pray more and receive significantly more answers*. Deng Xiaoping said, "The cat that catches the mouse is a good cat." Translation: whatever works is better than whatever does not. My human weakness simply makes watching the clock necessary. Lofty wishes that this were not the case does not help me pray more. Watching the clock helps me pray more. Therefore, I will watch the clock. Jesus evidently valued measuring the time spent in prayer. He asked His disciples in Matthew 26:40, "Couldn't you men keep watch with me for one hour?"

Incidentally, God sends His answers to prayer in such a clever way that they often seem like events occurring quite independent of anything we do. His works often seem like they happen by accident. I would easily conclude they were coincidences except for the fact that they occurred more frequently when I prayed more, and they occurred less frequently when I prayed less. Based on that evidence, I choose to pray more. I like the "coincidences."

I have come to terms with the second puzzle in not only scheduling and measuring my prayer time, but also in encouraging others to do it as well. To do that, I must talk or write about it. I confess, I have never heard of or read about anyone else who talks or writes as openly about quantifying his personal time in prayer as I now do. However, I feel compelled to share my testimony so it will stimulate interest in prayer while giving God glory for what He is doing.

I am in the process of learning to be an intercessor who prays and watches God work. I trust the Lord to give me the wisdom necessary to balance the principle of Matthew 6:5-6 that instructs us to pray in secret with the other principle of being open enough with my students and readers that it motivates them to do good works. I seek more and more to simply pray, obey, and get out of the way.

Why Prayer Is Not Entirely a Matter of Quid Pro Quo

I have run 30 marathon races, and each of them have different finish times. Why does one person who puts his best effort into each race run different speeds in different races? It is simply because each race has multiple factors, and each race time depends on the combination of those factors for that race. Those factors include, but are not limited to, the amount of training, sleep, diet, shoe weight and fit, personal body weight, race layout, weather, and crowd encouragement. Naturally, runners do what is necessary to have each factor work toward their advantage, and experience increases performance. It is the same with prayer.

Praying for extended periods of time also involves multiple variables. If the conditions taught in Scripture are fulfilled, it is reflected in God's actions. The number of answers increase and the quality of those answers improve. If the conditions of Scripture are not met, increased prayer time will have little or no effect. The conditions of Scripture — the moral variables — need consideration.

In a *quid pro quo* exchange, you receive something for something — each part is measured, controlled, and exchanged. If prayer were strictly *quid pro quo*, you would receive more automatically and unconditionally, or the quality of the answers would increase because of your additional prayers. *Prayer would become a mere currency by which you exchange a certain amount of human energy for an amount of God's miracles.* This would easily reduce praying to a works-oriented purchase of God's blessings where we earn the miracles God does on our behalf when we pray.

This is not the way prayer works. My prayer experiment deals mostly with quantity of prayer; and my focus in this book has been on the quality and intensity as well as the volume of prayer. Nevertheless, some other life-related conditions exist that we dare not omit. What are the scriptural qualifications for becoming the kind of person whose prayer God answers? We cannot randomly decide we will pray more and expect that God will work more. There are spiritual requirements. God is blessing all He can — all that we allow. As in preparing for and running a marathon, remember the following multiple prayer factors found in the Bible:

- Strive for earnestness, intensity, sincerity, perseverance, and tenacity.

- Consult God's wisdom for He has a plan and will for your life.

- Treat your spouse well. The Bible makes it clear that there is a direct relationship between treating your spouse correctly and receiving answers to prayer. Peter gave advice to spouses, "So that nothing will hinder your prayers" (I Peter 3:7).

- Create a good attitude towards others. If we have sin, hatred, unforgiveness, or bitterness toward others, our prayers will be hindered.

- Obey God's laws. This verse seems clear: "If anyone turns a deaf ear to the law, even his prayers are detestable" (Proverbs 28:9).

- Hear the plea of the poor. God does not hear those who do not hear the poor. "If a man shuts his ears to the cry of the poor, he too will cry out and not be answered" (Proverbs 21:13).

- Keep your spirit and thoughts on the prayers that you pray. Mindless mouthing of many words does not make prayer effective. "And when you pray, do not keep on babbling like pagans, for they think they will be heard because of their many words" (Mathew 6:7).

- Be selfless, not selfish. James makes it clear that asking incorrectly or using the answer for our own selfish benefit produces no answer. "When you ask, you do not receive because you ask with wrong motives, that you may spend what you get on your pleasures" (James 4:3).

- Maintain a moral and ethical quality of life. A holy and godly life does not earn answers, but a moral quality of life lived outside of the prayer closet does influence the answers to prayer.

It is a tragedy when these (and possibly other conditions not mentioned) are met and you lack answers due to prayerlessness. If you fulfill these character qualifications, you have an opportunity — a unique privilege — to take another step and be a big winner. God "rewards those who earnestly seek him" (Hebrews 11:6). Also, if we "come near to God," he will "come near" to us (James 4:7). Clearly, we can initiate prayer, and God will respond. Take the character and behavioral factors mentioned here into consideration. Nevertheless, answers to prayer are never earned or deserved. They are gracious gifts from a merciful God.

Evidences for a Difference

To complete my experiment in increased prayer time, I decided it needed to continue after I returned from my missions work abroad and resumed my regular routine. I had reaped the benefits that increased prayer time brought to my life while working abroad, and I wanted to see if I could duplicate it while in the United States. What changes took place? What did God do under the new prayer schedule that had not occurred under the earlier one?

Answers to prayer are never earned or deserved. They are gracious gifts from a merciful God.

Increased prayer produces increased involvement in our lives by a God who "is able to do immeasurably more than we can ask or imagine" (Ephesians 3:20). Our tendency to see the works of God as unexpected coincidences is a natural reaction if we are not sensitive to the ingenious way He works. However, I was watching for them, and so can you. Here are 11 "coincidences" that apparently occurred as a direct result of increased prayer within only a year *after* our return from abroad. They provide evidence that God was increasing opportunities for service and fruitfulness; He was enabling me to do more for Him.

- The dean of my school at Oral Roberts University asked me to teach in an intensive course program in a sister university in Sweden. This led to influence with ministers and missionaries in Europe and the former Soviet Union.

- I thought of an appropriate title and found a publisher for my book, *Habits of Highly Effective Christians* along with its mate, *Habits of Highly Effective Christians Bible Study Guide.*

- I created a website called www.ChristianHabits.com. It now offers many Christian materials to the world such as seminars, lectures, African Pastors Training Project page, and a Christian conversational game called "Treasure Hunt."

- Some of the materials on the website have been translated into other languages.

- A medical missions group consulted me regarding training interns who hope to use their professional skills in ministries abroad.

- I addressed 120 ORU students during their summer missions at their special spiritual retreat before their departures.

- I became the associate minister for a Chinese congregation in Tulsa, Oklahoma, that put me in regular contact with the Chinese community in a ministry setting for the first time in several years.

- I had written a 40-chapter collection of essays in Chinese while I was in China. It is now on its own website called www.mailangsuibi.com with a connecting link to my www.ChristianHabits.com website.

- I was given the opportunity to have *Habits of Highly Effective Christians* translated into Malagasy and distributed throughout the island nation of Madagascar.

- I was invited by four different Malagasy ministers, including the president of the Evangelical Ministerial Association, to present six three-day conferences for pastors and church leaders in the capital and other major cities of Madagascar.

- I was introduced to a ministry that would help publish an African edition of *Habits of Highly Effective Christians*.

When measuring your new levels of fruitfulness, please use this caution. Increased prayer does not mean you will be more fruitful than another person will be; it means you will be more fruitful than *you* were before. Measure and compare the "before" and "after" of the same person — *yourself*. Do not compare your ministry results with another person's ministry results. Each person's desire is to become as fruitful as he or she can be.

I challenge you to conduct your own experiment with increased prayer. My hope is that it leads you to increased fruitfulness — the complete fulfillment of your potential.

Not a Harsh Taskmaster

For the most part, in this book I have emphasized the work, the battle, and the persistence sides of prayer. As soldiers and ministers called by God, prayer is a big part of our work. And He is worthy of our diligent, earnest, and zealous efforts. However, there is another side to prayer — our Father's devotional, soft, and gentler side. Because of this, I have determined that on my weekly day of rest I will pray two hours instead of the usual four. Even an intercessor needs a day of rest. Here are several observations regarding God's gentle character.

As we learned in Chapter Eight about God being our Daddy, it is a greater privilege to be a son or daughter of God than to be a servant of God. To celebrate being His son or daughter is to celebrate God's redemption, adoption, and Fatherhood. The glory in being His servant makes place for my self-expression, contribution, work, and, in some instances, pride in my work. To celebrate our sonship more than servanthood — our position more than our accomplishments — shows that we worship Him as our Father more readily than we relate to or fear Him as our boss. He *is* our boss (Lord), but more importantly, He is our Father.

> To celebrate our sonship more than servanthood — our position more than our accomplishments — shows that we worship Him as our Father more readily than we relate to or fear Him as our boss. He *is* our boss (Lord), but more importantly, He is our Father.

When we worship, we express *our love for Him*. Yet, according to Scripture, it is an even greater thing to think about *His love for us*. "Greater love has no one than this, that he lay down his life for his friends" (John 15:13). Jesus did that for us; we did not do that for Him. "We love because he first loved us" (I John 4:19). In trying to be faithful in worship, it is easy to concentrate on our love for Him. We must never forget the reason we love Him is that He first loved us with such a superior love.

In my eagerness to obey Jesus' instruction to love God with all my heart (emotions), soul, mind (the intellectual aspects), and strength (Mark 12:30), I sometimes lose sight of the wonderful truth that God loves me. I work hard to keep my schedule of regular, daily prayer hours. Even when I am tired, I keep at it. Occasionally, I sit or lie down, continue praying, and then fall asleep. I have learned that when I wake up to remember that I am doing my best. I then begin praying where I left off without feeling as though I need to punish myself or that I will be punished by the Lord.

God reveals His tender and gentle care for me when I try too hard, push myself too much, or overwork and cause myself harm. Jesus said, "Come to me, all you who are weary and burdened, and I will give you rest. Take my yoke upon you and learn from me, for I am gentle and humble in heart, and you will find rest for your souls. For my yoke is easy and my burden is light" (Matthew 11:28-30). When our burden seems too heavy, it is probably because in our eagerness to please God, we have taken on a burden God did not intend for us to carry. God's yoke is easy. Yes, there is work to do, and we will not hold back from work — even hard work. However, God also intends for us to rest appropriately.

A good example of this is when I had an 18-mile training run scheduled one hot Saturday. As usual, I began my early morning prayer routine. I was about three minutes into expressing my love for God, when His Spirit reminded me that it was going to be a hot day. I had known this, but had still wanted to pray first. It was as though He said He would still be there to hear my prayer later in the day when it was too hot to run. I love Him for being so practical. This was not a new practice to pray *after* I ran in the early part of a warm day — but it was a new thing for God to coach me to do so when I had already begun to pray. I appreciate Him even more when He shows me that He has practical expectations. In my zeal to put Him first, I had begun to pray; in His tender love for me, He coached me to run while it was still cool. He is wonderful.

Another time, I woke up in the early hours of a Saturday morning, and was unusually tired from an extremely exhausting week. I had kept up with all my regular work and prayer schedule throughout the week. Contrary to my normal routine, this particular morning I felt I was *not* to pray, but to go back to bed. Psalm 127:2 says, "For he grants sleep to those he loves." I went back to bed and slept soundly. I woke again prepared to pray, but felt the Lord saying to stay in bed and rest. I drifted in and out of sleep fully aware that time was passing but that God wanted me to rest.

During one of the times, I was awake and expressing my love to Him. I sensed that "Daddy" was holding his little child in His arms admiring *His* handiwork. As I lay there in bed in His arms, I felt His acceptance, approval, pride, and happiness that I was earnestly seeking Him. I knew that if I got out of bed and went to the garage to pray, I would be relying on my ability to pray and not obeying His request for me to rest. I would have failed God had I ignored Him when He was holding me in His arms speaking to me about His love for me.

How many times have we seen young parents holding their children in their arms just admiring the beauty of their — really God's — handiwork? Would we want to deny our heavenly Father the same joy? I basked in God's attention and love. I felt I better understood Zephaniah's word to Israel on God's behalf: "He will take great delight in you, he will quiet you with his love, he will rejoice over you with singing" (Zephaniah 3:17).

The enemy acts to produce a slavish attitude in us. He drives those who follow him with a firm hand. If we let him, he would drive us to do the same when striving to please even our heavenly Father, in spite of the fact that the very word "Father" suggests we are not slaves, but sons and daughters. You and I will strive to be hard-working and faithful servants, but we will also remain confident, content, and joyful sons and daughters. For all our efforts to be faithful and passionate in prayer, we do not believe works-oriented intercession means as much to Daddy as our love and friendship.

Proud of God

One morning during the first semester back in the U.S. as I was walking and worshipping in the garage, I heard myself say something that amazed me. I said, "I am so proud of you, Dad." The sentence crossed my lips before I had time to think about what I was saying.

Throughout the semester, I had been feeling closer and closer to God. Sometimes, I was almost afraid others would not understand what I was trying to say when I tried to talk about the new depth I felt in my friendship with God. After making the statement, "I am proud of you, Dad," I came to think that just as any son delights in being proud of his dad, it is entirely appropriate for us to feel proud of God and say so. Had I thought about it before saying it, maybe I would not have said it aloud. I was glad I had let the feeling gush.

We can say He is the "glory and the lifter of my head," because that is written in Scripture and has a familiar ring to it. Nevertheless, to say something unconventional like, "I am proud of you, Dad," forces us to think. Spending increased time with God has brought many good changes. I hope some of these changes made my classroom ministry at the university more effective; I know these changes are making my life better.

More to the point in writing this book, I hope my experiment in prayer encourages you to conduct your own experiment. I can think of no more effective way to convince you than to share the great changes that have occurred for me and hope you will seek the same for yourself.

The changes are so deep in the unexplainable levels of my psyche and spirit that I cannot tell you how it works, but I do feel more like an intercessor and less like a teacher. I still teach, but it comes out of my intercession.

What are possible good motives for prayer? Here are several possibilities:

- Love for God

- Love for people

- Concern for people

- Desire to help people avoid eternity in hell

- Desire to fulfill one's own personal potential

- Pursuit of God's reward for those who pray

- Desire to see God's kingdom come and His will done

These are all good prayer motives and each can glorify God. Each of us can make our own personal list. However, the one different motive from all those motives is this one: *prayer makes a difference*. We need to make a difference and prayer allows us to do that.

Look around you. Can you see anything that you feel would bring more glory to God if it were different than it is now? Well then, you too have a motive for prayer. The day will come when we rule and reign with Jesus Christ, but we do not have to wait until then to start. Can we not already here and now begin to change things and administrate Kingdom concerns through prayer?

CHAPTER ELEVEN

Where Are the Elijahs of the Lord God?

"Elijah was a man just like us."

James 5:17

Elijah and his soon-to-be successor had crossed the Jordan River. Within minutes, a sudden visitation from heaven arrived — a chariot and horses of fire. Without hesitation, the prophet Elijah went up in the chariot and dropped his cloak to Elisha, indicating he was passing his ministry on to his beloved disciple. At that point, Elisha "picked up the cloak that had fallen from Elijah and went back and stood on the bank of the Jordan. Then he took the cloak that had fallen from him and struck the water with it. 'Where is the Lord, the God of Elijah?' he asked. When he struck the water, it divided to the right and to the left, and he crossed over" (II Kings 2:13-14).

Elisha asked a question: "Where is the Lord, the God of Elijah?" Of course, the answer to Elisha's question is that He is on His throne just as He has always been. However, today, when God is looking for prayer warriors, the more important question is *"Where are the Elijahs of the Lord God?"*

Similarities exist between the spiritual condition of Israel in Elijah's time and the spiritual condition of our nations today. All nations, as Israel was then, are under attack by a hateful enemy who wants to destroy them. Israel needed an Elijah; today's nations need men and women like Elijah.

Who was Elijah? What was he like? What do we need to know and become if we want to be *an Elijah* in our generation?

Elijah Was a Man Just Like Us

Elijah was one of the most powerful and important men in the Old Testament. His prayer life, miracles, courage, and the powerful showdown in the contest with Baal and Asherah in opposition to Yahweh on Mount Carmel are recorded in some of the most picturesque narratives in the Bible. He was a great man who did great things for God.

Yet the New Testament says, "Elijah was a man just like us" (James 5:17). If Elijah were different from us, we would have an excuse from doing or even trying to do what he did. The excuse for not being as powerful an influence in our day as Elijah was in his time is effectively removed by this short sentence that is rich with meaning: "Elijah was a man just like us." This New Testament comment helps us interpret the Old Testament story. It also challenges us to be more like Elijah.

> If Elijah were different from us, we would be excused from doing or even trying to do what he did.

As we challenge ourselves to be more like Elijah, realize that Elijah faced difficulties just like the ones we face. For example, imagine that one day, Elijah's son came running to him, saying, "Daddy, daddy, my puppy is lost. Where is my puppy? How can I find my puppy?" Another day, Elijah's wife came running up to him, "El, the water in the creek is so muddy I can't get the laundry clean. I wash and wash and the clothes get muddier and muddier. What can I do?" Another time, Elijah's neighbor came running up to him, "Elijah, fine fellow you are! Your sheep are eating my grass. If you don't get your sheep out of my field, I am going to have one of them for dinner." Elijah faced the same kinds of situations we face. Although he had domestic challenges like ours and he was a man like us, he lived a godly life of prayer and spiritual accomplishment. We can, too.

Where are the Elijahs of the Lord God? Even though you are a normal human being and have daily responsibilities, will you take time to be spiritual? *Will you be an Elijah of the Lord God today?*

Elijah Was Not Charmed or Preoccupied with Earthly Finery

In any generation, some people seek material affluence. However, Elijah did not seek wealth; he was content with the simple things of life. This trait of Elijah's character is revealed in a conversation between the king and his messengers as they discussed Elijah. "The king asked them, 'What kind of man was it who came to meet you and told you this?' They replied, 'He was a man with a garment of hair and with a leather belt around his waist'" (II Kings 1:7-8).

Do we really need to know what kind of clothes Elijah wore? No, but it is important that we understand Elijah's character. The description of his unadorned clothing helps to tell that story. What he wore reflected his value system.

The Old Testament has several references about fine clothes. It tells us that not only did fine garments exist, but also explains how some people valued them and would risk their lives to keep them. For example, Achan hid a beautiful Babylonian robe in the floor of his tent along with silver coins and a wedge of gold that were all stolen from Jericho. He paid for that mistake with his life. Not that it was wrong to have nice clothes or value them, but Achan had stolen the items after the battle of Jericho even though Joshua had specifically told him not to do it. The high value that Achan placed on those clothes increased his temptation to steal and then hide them.

Gehazi, Elisha's servant, had the same problem. He ran after Naaman's chariot and lied in order to again receive beautiful Babylonian garments. His wrong value system led him into temptation.

Jacob favored his son Joseph and gave him a beautiful coat of many colors. Doing that, though, was unwise because Joseph's brothers were jealous of the coat. Joseph would not have been wrong to wear the gift; however, but to brag about his dreams indicates that Joseph was too impressed with himself. That story shows that the clothes that we wear can indicate personal character.

The Bible does not expressly say that Jezebel wore lavish garments, however, it would be difficult to imagine Jezebel fixing her hair and painting her face only to wear shabby clothes. We can assume that she, too, had fine clothes.

Joseph, Mordecai, and Daniel were all given royal robes to wear by someone who valued the clothing. However, none of those three cases reflected the value system of the person wearing the clothes since they had received them as gifts.

Wearing nice clothes is not wrong. We all should want to look good for God's glory. After all, the Bible does say that man looks on the outward appearance — the first impressions we give about ourselves are usually what people see. Our clothes are important statements about our tastes. We do not want to discredit our Christian message by shabby appearance. However, material things, including clothes, are not to be our *focus*. Elijah, too, could have worn long, flowing, beautiful robes had he chosen to do that; however, he was content with a garment of hair and a leather belt. He was not preoccupied with finery.

The Bible tells us that God blesses us by providing daily, adequate provisions. Working hard, being honest, and having clean-living habits combined with avoiding expensive bad habits give economic advantages to God's people. David reminds us that God delights in our "well being" (Psalm 35:27). Furthermore, John wished blessings for his readers when he wrote, "I pray that you may enjoy good health and that all may go well with you, even as your soul is getting along well" (III John 2).

The Bible's concept of prosperity is portrayed in the fruitful trees planted by streams of water (Psalm 1:3) and that the path is made straight (Proverbs 3:6). These models include much more than just financial blessings. The Bible teaches that God will provide and take care of us, not that we will always have many material possessions and expensive clothes. Furthermore, the blessings God gives to those who tithe and give liberally to God's work are well known to Christians today. However, those blessings are not limited to material or financial matters. Some Christians have many material blessings; but that does not make those people more blessed.

Jesus taught that the pursuit of material prosperity and money could interfere with spiritual pursuits. "No one can serve two masters. Either he will hate the one and love the other, or he will be devoted to the one and despise the other. You cannot serve both God and money" (Matthew 6:24).

Jesus also taught the value of living simply and said, "Do not store up for yourselves treasures on earth, where moth and rust destroy, and where thieves break in and steal" (Matthew 6:19). A few verses later He said, "But seek first his kingdom and his righteousness, and all these things will be given to you as well" (Matthew 6:33).

Paul, following Jesus, wrote to Timothy about the "false doctrines" believed by those who do "not agree with sound instruction of our Lord Jesus Christ and godly teaching" (I Timothy 6:3). Among the errors that Timothy was advised to avoid was thinking that "godliness is a means to financial gain" (I Timothy 6:5). Paul continues, "But godliness with contentment is great gain ... For the love of money is a root of all kinds of evil ... not to be arrogant nor to put their hope in wealth, which is so uncertain, but to put their hope in God, who richly provides us with everything for our enjoyment" (I Timothy 6:6 and 6:17). Elijah's behavior, Jesus' teaching, and Paul's emphases are all consistent with each other.

The 1950's poverty theology I grew up with and the prosperity theology I experienced upon return from China in the 1990s are both out of balance. We are to use money to serve God; not use God to gain money. Rejoice in what God gives you and do not be embarrassed, preoccupied, or possessed by it. What types of things do you talk about to other people? If you talk frequently about material possessions, that could be an indication that you value them too much. Do not let any pursuit of material or financial gain interfere with your more important pursuits of God's kingdom and His righteousness.

> We are to use money to serve God; not use God to gain money.

Where are the Elijahs of the Lord God? Where are those who will not be caught up in the pursuit of financial prosperity, but rather will seek first the kingdom of God? *Will you be an Elijah of the Lord God today?*

Elijah Addressed Important National Issues

After enduring three and one half years of famine, Elijah finally went to meet Ahab. Ahab began the conversation with a question accusing Elijah of causing trouble for Israel. "'I have not made trouble for Israel,' Elijah replied. 'But you and your father's family have. You have abandoned the Lord's commands and have followed the Baals'" (I Kings 18:18).

Another time Ahaziah, Ahab's son, sought advice from the god of Ekron concerning his pending death. "But the angel of the

Lord said to Elijah the Tishbite, 'Go up and meet the messengers of the king of Samaria and ask them, "Is it because there is no God in Israel that you are going off to consult Baal-Zebub, the god of Ekron?" Therefore, this is what the Lord says: "You will not leave the bed you are lying on. You will certainly die!"' So Elijah went" (II Kings 1:3-4).

Elijah spoke as God directed him to speak; he was not just expressing his own political opinions. Nevertheless, it appears that Elijah was aware of and had opinions about events of national importance to Israel.

Elijahs today should prayerfully prepare sermons with the Bible in one hand and the newspaper in the other. We need to know the Bible and what it says about current events. We must skillfully use the Bible so our sermons have the authority of "This is what the Lord says." We too must wait on God for a fresh, vital word to speak into the situation; speaking out of our own opinion without a current word from God could be presumptuous.

Unless we are also reading the newspaper, or listening to the national news, we will not know the important issues of the day. That knowledge gives the Holy Spirit an opportunity to lay the burden of His concerns about national events on our hearts. Know the issues. Have an informed opinion. Know what God says about contemporary issues, both from the Bible and prayer. Then, have the courage to speak out the word of the Lord on meaningful subjects.

What is God's opinion of the tort laws in your state? What does He think about the tollways? What is God's attitude toward the rights of homosexuals and lesbians? What is His position on sex education in public schools? How is "under God" justified in the Pledge of Allegiance to the flag in a nation that believes in separation of church and state?

Those issues should concern American pastors. If you live outside the United States, what laws does your nation need to pass to turn the ore and stones in your hills and mountains into streets, bridges, and good public schools? Have you thought this through? Do you pray about these things? Have you ever expressed your views to your congressional or parliamentary representative?

Where are the Elijahs of the Lord God? Will you become aware of local, national, and contemporary issues while finding God's will in the matter, and speak out for Him with authority? *Will you be an Elijah of the Lord God today?*

Elijah Spent Much Time Alone With God

Earlier in the story of Elijah, God initiated the events leading up to the Carmel Mountain drama by telling Elijah to go away from the normal activities of life for a special time alone with God. Here is how it happened. "Now Elijah the Tishbite, from Tishbe in Gilead, said to Ahab, 'As the Lord, the God of Israel lives, whom I serve, there will be neither dew nor rain in the next few years except at my word.' Then the word of the Lord came to Elijah: 'Leave here, turn eastward, and hide in the Kerith Ravine, east of the Jordan. You will drink from the brook, and I have ordered the ravens to feed you there.' So he did what the Lord had told him" (I Kings 17:1-5).

Even though Elijah handled domestic responsibilities at home, the time came when he needed extended time alone with God away from normal daily activities. We do not know how much time passed between Elijah delivering his message to the king and his departure for the Kerith Ravine, or how long he stayed there. Of the three and a half years between Elijah's announcement and the contest on Mount Carmel, we might guess that Elijah spent a number of months alone with God.

Not only is this true of Elijah, but of every other significant, spiritual figure of biblical record — they spent a considerable amount of time in seclusion with God. Each person derived his understanding, authority, and confidence from that place. The miracles that occurred in the lives of those prayer warriors are directly connected to the lengthy and meaningful time they spent with God.

Where are the Elijahs of the Lord God? Have you discovered the value and productivity of spending lengths of time alone with God in prayer? *Will you be an Elijah of the Lord God today?*

Elijah Discerned God's Plan and Prayed Accordingly

The New Testament often gives us additional insight into the narratives of the Old Testament. In this case, it is James, not the Old Testament historical record, who informs us that Elijah actually prayed for no rain to come. The historical record says that Elijah claimed, "There will be neither dew nor rain in the next few years except at my word," but according to James, Elijah also *prayed to that effect.* "He prayed earnestly that it would not rain,

> When it does not rain, we usually pray that it *will* rain. What kind of prophet would pray that it would *not* rain?

and it did not rain on the land for three and a half years." Then later on Mount Carmel: "Again he prayed, and the heavens gave rain, and the earth produced its crops" (both quotations come from James 5:17b and 5:18).

Upon careful examination, the reason Elijah was "powerful and effective" (James 5:16) or successful in his prayer life was that he was actually cooperating with God in prayer and praying according to God's plan. Neither the New Testament nor Old Testament history tells us how Elijah knew that he should pray that way. Nevertheless, according to God's agenda, Elijah recognized God's plan and prayed that it would not rain. That seems like a strange prayer. When it does not rain, we usually pray that it will rain.

What kind of prophet would pray that it would not rain? A prophet who knows God's plan, that's who!

God wanted to defame Baal, the Canaanite rain god. God's plan worked perfectly. The prophets of Baal could produce neither rain in the valleys nor fire on the mountain. When God's purpose was complete and Elijah and God had everyone's attention, he prayed for rain — the next phase of God's plan. This required Elijah to completely reverse his direction in prayer to fulfill the second phase.

What kind of a prophet would pray one way one day and turn around and begin to pray exactly the opposite the next day? A prophet who knows how to move with God through the phases and stages of God's plan would do that; a prophet who partners with God and prays according to God's plan would do that. In each instance, Elijah was merely following God's agenda for that specific time.

The wisdom of God is, after all, far superior to the plans of men. This is why we should submit our wills to Him and seek His plan. Some of us do the will of God — what God has shown us to do — for too long. We have no right to assume that we will always be where we are or that we will always do what we are doing. We should be sensitive to God's Spirit and be ready, as Elijah was, to move to the next phase, pray a new way, and do new things.

What is God's plan for your community, church, family, or your career? What would happen if you began to pray according to God's plan? What would your church or community be like 10 years from now if you knew and prayed according to God's agenda for the next 10 years? Elijah at Mount Carmel shows us how God releases His power in the affairs of men who pray according to His direction. The prayers they pray are not limited to only those that they can imagine. God is "able to do immeasurably more than we can ask or imagine" (Ephesians 3:20).

Where are the Elijahs of the Lord God? Will you find out what God wants to do through you now, today, and then pray and move with God accordingly? Will you be listening when God moves to the next phase and again pray accordingly? *Will you be an Elijah of the Lord God today?*

Elijah Publicly Challenged the Political and Religious Systems

The time had finally come to confront publicly the false religions of Baal and Asherah head on. Can you imagine just how bold and confident Elijah felt to meet the king in a designated prominent place — and all because of his hours alone with God? Here is what Elijah told the king. "'Now summon the people from all over Israel to meet me on Mount Carmel. And bring the four hundred and fifty prophets of Baal and the four hundred prophets of Asherah, who eat at Jezebel's table'" (I Kings 18:19).

While in Madagascar during the summer of 2004, I heard about a group of Christians who publicly confronted the Shamans in their community. Up until then, the Shamans had been able to cause people to levitate whenever they wanted. However, the Christians told those who trusted in evil spirits that the true God would get in the way, and this time, they would not be able to cause a man to rise. When the Shamans were unable to make the person levitate, all of the observers were able to see that God's power was greater than that of the evil spirits. The Bible records many successful power encounters such as Moses and the plagues (Exodus 7–11), Elijah on Mount Carmel (1 Kings 18:16-46), and Paul at Ephesus (Acts 19:11-20). Powerful encounters are still occurring today in Jesus' name.

> Elijah had the courage after spending months alone with God in prayer to publicly confront the established religious system of his day.

Elijah had the courage after spending months alone with God in prayer to publicly confront the established religious system of his day. He had the courage to criticize the prophets of Baal while they prayed. He also had the courage to pour water on the sacrifice he was about to offer to God — three times! He had the courage to have the 450 prophets of Baal and the 400 prophets of Asherah killed in the Kishon valley below. After all this, he again ascended Mount Carmel and began to pray for rain.

At the end of the day, everyone knew Jehovah was the one and only true God. They also knew He was a God of might and power. All this was possible because God found a partner who was willing to let God be in charge and, as a result, Elijah was useful to a mighty God.

Christians are not to put God to the test foolishly, presumptuously, or in unwise, humanly imagined contests. However, Elijah was moving in the will of God. God also led Moses in the public demonstration of God's superiority. When God leads and gives us the courage, we, too, can bring glory to Him by moving obediently and boldly.

Where are the Elijahs of the Lord God? Will you take the time to find out what God wants to do in your community and then publicly, obediently, and boldly represent Him? *Will you be an Elijah of the Lord God today?*

Elijah Received Encouragement from God in a Moment of Weakness

The excitement surrounding Mount Carmel must have been tremendous. It would have made a strong impression on any participant or observer: the fire coming down from heaven to consume the sacrifice, the slaying of 850 false prophets, and the miraculous and timely rain. It had to have been very exciting for Elijah, but how did he handle the emotion of the following days?

Thankfully, most of us do not face the additional challenge Elijah faced after his victory — Jezebel threatened his life! However, God strengthened him with a specially prepared meal. It allowed Elijah to travel the distance to Mount Horeb, as far to the south as Mount Carmel had been to the north. There, in a cave at Horeb, Elijah experienced something each of us needs to learn: how to deal with the human emotions that follow a mighty move of the Spirit of God.

"There, he went into a cave and spent the night. And the word of the Lord came to him: 'What are you doing here, Elijah?' ... He replied ... 'I am the only one left, and now they are trying to kill me too.' There was a powerful wind ... but the Lord was not in the wind ... there was an earthquake, but the Lord was not in the earthquake. After the earthquake came a fire, but the Lord was not in the fire. And after the fire came a gentle whisper.'" (I Kings 19:9, 10c, 11c, and 12).

With the congregation gathering, the musical instruments playing, the dancers dancing, and the crowd worshipping with joy, it is easy to be caught up in the glory of the Lord's presence.

Even though we prepare our sermons as well as we can, preachers know that there are many times God enables us to preach far better than if we only used our own knowledge and rhetorical skills. Preachers have always rejoiced in the glorious presence of God and His ability to deliver His Word persuasively and with liberty to their congregation.

The next day when the excitement from the message wanes in our memory, our emotions can take a dive. All the energy of yesterday seems long ago and far away. The "day-after emotional valley" is a preacher's career hazard. For example, it is not wise for people in ministry to make an important career decision the day after an emotionally charged ministry activity. The human creature is not designed to fly high with emotional excitement day after day. We must be able to hear the encouraging voice of the Holy Spirit the day after a day of ministry if we want to minister to God's people week after week. We must be able to work our way through the valleys if we want to celebrate the joy of the Lord with God's people again.

Elijah was able to discern which sound he heard at the cave that contained the voice of the Lord. It was not in the wind, earthquake, or fire — it was in the whisper. When Elijah heard it, he went to the mouth of the cave and God spoke to him. In addition to calling down God's fire, we must also remember to listen for God's whisper.

What is the routine, emotionally dangerous day in your career?

What is the routine, emotionally dangerous day in your career? Is it the day after the board meeting? Is it at the end of each semester? Is it on Saturday after working hard Monday through Friday? Whichever day or period it is, identify it and plan to allow the Holy Spirit to carry you through it. He will, if you listen and let Him.

Where are the Elijahs of the Lord God? Will you hear the voice of the Lord in the emotional valley that follows the ministry mountain-top experience? Will you hold steady through the emotional ups and downs of your work? *Will you be an Elijah of the Lord God today?*

Elijah Was Involved in International Developments

After settling the problems of Elijah's emotions, God revealed to Elijah three major appointments. God was still at work in the nations, had a plan, and revealed it to Elijah. Here is what God said to Elijah. "'... anoint Hazael king over Aram. Also, anoint Jehu son of Nimshi king over Israel, and anoint Elisha son of Shaphat from Abel Mehoiah to succeed you as prophet. Jehu will put to death any who escape the sword of Hazael, and Elisha will put to death any who escape the sword of Jehu. Yet I reserve seven thousand in Israel — all whose knees have not bowed down to Baal and all whose mouths have not kissed him'" (I Kings 19:15-18).

You may think that it is impossible for everyone to be involved in an international ministry. Not so. I told you about praying in my garage in Chapter Nine. Your regular place of private prayer can become your "World Center for International Intercession." I have a "World Center for Prayer" at my house. We also park our cars in it. Most people would call it a garage, but there is something much more important that happens there than just parking cars. According to the verses on the walls and door of my "prayer center," I try to pray things that influence nations and governments. Some of them are in the following paragraphs. You may read them as illustrations of how to use God's Word in prayer and hold God to His Word in a way He likes and encourages.

"The prayer of a righteous man is powerful and effective" (James 5:16). I read this verse and pray something like, "Lord, I realize that when I pray for the nations and their governments, peoples, families, pastors, churches, Christians, and missionaries, I know that it is a very big prayer for a little person like me to pray. You said prayer is powerful and effective. I do not pray because *I* am big. I pray big prayers because *You* are big. I trust You to hear my prayer and move in the world."

"Rise up, O Lord! May your enemies be scattered; may your foes flee before you" (Numbers 10:35). After reading this verse, I may pray, "Lord there are enemies of the gospel and enemies of Your church strongly working in many places in the world against Your kingdom. Please rise up and scatter those who oppose You, Your church, and Your people. You said that no weapon that is formed against us will prosper. We need You in this generation to break the weapons of the enemy."

On the inside of our garage door is this verse. "They will never be silent day or night. You who call on the Lord, give yourselves no rest, and give him no rest until he establishes ..." (Isaiah 62:6-7). I see it and may pray, "Lord, I confess I am just a human being with human frailties. I get tired when I pray. I am tired now. I know that You give rest to Your children and we are not to overdo. I also know that I am to love You with all my strength. That means I will push myself sometimes. Pushing myself — using all my strength — means I will get tired. I want Your answers. I want You to move, to act, to respond, to bring Your kingdom to earth and to be fully involved in human affairs. Please, Lord, receive my feeble effort to involve You mightily in this situation for which I am praying. I will not let You go unless you bless us. Your own Word tells me I should not let You rest until You answer."

Another verse reads, "See, today I appoint you over nations and kingdoms to uproot and tear down, to destroy and overthrow, to build and to plant" (Jeremiah 1:10). I read a part of that verse, originally spoken to Jeremiah and now attached to the inside of our garage door, and pray, "Lord, the forces of unrighteousness are working through people to harm Your Church. Good people are being threatened, injured, and persecuted. In mercy to Your people, uproot those enemy forces. In compassion for Your own children, tear down those powers of ungodliness. In power, destroy the enemy. In victory, overthrow the adversary. Build Your church. Plant Your kingdom. Show all the kingdoms of the world that You alone, oh Lord, are God."

On the wall is this verse: "Ask of me and I will make the nations your inheritance, the ends of the earth your possession" (Psalm 2:8). Read Psalm 2:7 and you will notice that the context indicates that verses 8 and 9 are addressed to the "Son," not to us. "Father, You told your Son He could have the nations for His inheritance and the ends of the earth for His possession. Praying *in His name*, I ask You for the nations and the ends of the earth *for His sake*. May Your Spirit watch over the face of the earth today just as the Spirit watched over the face of the earth at the time of creation. Call out people to love and worship You. Give Your Son the nations. Give Your Son His inheritance."

We need to remember Elijah, Daniel, Isaiah, and Jeremiah. They all had messages not only for Israel, but for other nations as well. Why should we pray *just* for our own nation? Get a globe or a world map, or at least look at one and make a list of the nations. I have my own weekly routine. I begin with Iceland and pray my way through each nation of North America, Central America, the Caribbean, South America, and Africa on Mondays. On Tuesdays, I pray for each nation in Europe, Middle East, Asia, and the Pacific regions. I pray for each nation and their government, pastors, churches, Christians, peoples, missionaries, and families.

All of this happens as I walk a path around and between our cars in our garage in Tulsa, Oklahoma. If I can have a World Center for International Intercession in my garage, you, too, can have an international ministry in your place of prayer if you want one. A job, health, age, or other factors and responsibilities may hold you back from physically going abroad, but prayer knows no boundaries. With prayer, you can travel the world from nation to nation and influence the spiritual atmosphere at any time.

Through entreaty, you can bind spirits, release God's blessings, cast down evil imaginations, bring every thought under control, and break down barriers to the work of the gospel. As an intercessor, you can uproot, tear down, destroy, and overthrow. In your place of prayer, you can build and plant. I suggest you become the founder of a new "Center for Prayer and World Evangelism." When we get to heaven, come on over to my place for a while, and we will talk about what you did.

> I suggest you become the founder of a new "Center for Prayer and World Evangelism." When we get to heaven, come on over to my place for a while, and we will talk about what you did.

We lived in Korea for 13 years. During this time, we noticed that political struggles for power affected many Christians as well as non-Christians. Political division seems to have reigned on the Korean peninsula for centuries. There used to be three simultaneous kingdoms in Korea. Now, after many years of political arguments, there are still two Koreas. Additionally, pastors and elders compete *inside* the church. Deacons and ordained deacons struggle for authority. Denominations divide over these struggles. There were more than 80 Presbyterian denominations in Korea during our years there! Furthermore, I felt that I, too, was influenced by the desire for authority.

In my private times of fasting and prayer in a wooded area in south Seoul between 1983 and 1986, I can remember walking back and forth on a path praying that the power of Authority would be broken in the land. "Authority" was, I felt, the name of the evil spirit that was causing power struggles and so much competition. I prayed the Lord would reduce Authority's grip, his power would be broken, his influence canceled, and he would no longer be able to divide good people. I prayed that way for several years until our family moved back to the United States.

I shared this prayer pattern with several Koreans since our return to the United States. They confirmed that such a prayer was necessary. What would happen if we could see the spiritual battle in the nations and use the mighty power of prayer to combat the adversary? Only God can equip us for this kind of battle. Seeking Him to show us how to pray and how to fight effectively will help reduce the hours of wasted prayer and increase our hours of efficient prayer. The difference between *effective* and *efficient* is that *effective* gets the job done, while *efficient* gets the job done with the least amount of wasted effort. I want to learn how to be efficient in prayer. Praying against the unseen forces of unrighteousness in the nations is an efficient method.

Where are the Elijahs of the Lord God? Will you look at the nations of the world and become a part of God's army of intercessors? *Will you be an Elijah of the Lord God today?*

Elijah Trained Future Ministers and Mentored a Successor

Not only was Elijah a spiritually discerning and prayerful man, he evidently had some administrative and teaching abilities, too. He was active in training a successor as this Scripture says, "So Elijah went from there and found Elisha, son of Shaphat ... Then he (Elisha) set out to follow Elijah and he became his attendant" (I Kings 19:19-21).

Elijah traveled regularly to specific places and trained younger, prospective prophets. "The company of the prophets at Bethel ... The company of the prophets at Jericho ..." (II Kings 2:3 and 2:5). Even though Elijah was a busy prophet, he took the time to train a successor while spending time with groups of prophets at Bethel and Jericho. Training others and preparing successors in ministry both take time. However, if we want to follow Elijah's example and influence our generation plus those of the future, we must make this investment.

God's work is vast. We will not finish the job in our generation. We must devote some time to allow the next generation of ministers to stand on our shoulders and do a better job in their generation than we did in ours. By being transparent with them, we can help them avoid making some of the mistakes we made.

When we make fewer mistakes, the Holy Spirit does His work better. As we mature in ministry, we learn that we will not always be *the sage on the stage* — the one with all the wisdom and answers. The time will come for a senior minister to be *the guide on the side* — the mentor off the stage passing the responsibility on to the next generation. Elijah trained not only groups of prophets but also a successor.

Where are the Elijahs of the Lord God? Will you take time to mentor younger servants of the Lord so they can carry on the next generation's work? *Will you be an Elijah of the Lord God today?*

Elijah Was Worth Chariots and Horsemen

The mentor and his protégé continued on their journey on the far side of the Jordan River. "As they were walking along and talking together, suddenly a chariot of fire and horses of fire appeared and separated the two of them, and Elijah went up to heaven in a whirlwind. Elisha saw this and cried out, 'My father! My father! The chariots and horsemen of Israel!' And Elisha saw him no more. Then he took hold of his own clothes and tore them apart" (II Kings 2:11-12).

> We will not always be *the sage on the stage*. The time will come to be *the guide on the side.*

What is the symbolism of being called chariots and horsemen? Earlier, I shared that Elijah was a man just like us. Yet Elisha calls him "the chariots and horsemen of Israel."

Chariots were powerful weapons of warfare in Elijah's day. Not only could archers shoot arrows and spearmen throw spears from chariots, but also the chariots themselves were weapons. The wheels of some chariots were equipped with blades capable of cutting down many foot soldiers. Additionally, the warhorses in front of the chariot, striking with powerful hooves, added to the power of this instrument of war. A chariot in those days was like today's intercontinental ballistic missile capable of going a great distance. It was like the contemporary "smart bomb" with the explosive power of a huge bomb directed at its stationery land target with the precision of a laser beam. It was also comparable to something even more sophisticated in military technology — a Patriot missile that is capable of hitting and exploding a fast-moving rocket before the incoming projectile can hit its target. Israel was under spiritual attack and God needed an Elijah to be a strong instrument of spiritual warfare. Elisha recognized Elijah's vital role and called him, "the chariots and horsemen of Israel."

Nations today, as then, are under attack by invisible forces of unrighteousness. Evil spirits seek to destroy God's people and Church. Invisible spiritual forces continually blind and bind non-Christians. Today, God needs men and women who, like Elijah, will be powerful, spiritual weapons rushing to the effective defense of all that is precious to God.

The militant church of God must fight against the spirits of jealousy that breed discontent. We must fight the spirits of lust that urge people into various forms of perverse sexual sins. We must rise up against the religious spirits that lead people into demon and devil worship, and other deceptive spirits that lure people into witchcraft, materialism, atheism, and false religions.

> Today, God needs men and women who, like Elijah, will be powerful, spiritual weapons rushing to the effective defense of all that is precious to God.

Will you do today for your nation what Elijah in his day did for his nation? Will you become a strong spiritual weapon that God can use to tear down the forces of unrighteousness that attack your nation? If you are willing to do the difficult spiritual work in the invisible kingdom, you will be doing the work of an Elijah. You too will be as chariots and horsemen.

Where are the Elijahs of the Lord God? Will you enter into an invisible spiritual war and bring destruction to those forces that are trying to destroy your nation? *Will you be an Elijah of the Lord God today?*

CHAPTER TWELVE

The Centerpiece of Ministry

"The prayer of a righteous man is powerful and effective."

James 5:16

Prayer is the centerpiece of spiritual ministry. Real battles are fought alone with God. We wrestle with God in prayer even though He is not actually our opponent. He is training us. He is our Father! He wants us to wrestle and win.

The forces of unrighteousness are the enemy. Our fight against the enemy is our urgent, persuasive, and critical appeal to God. Prayer against spiritual forces of unrighteousness — spiritual wrestling — is our urging God to fight for us against them, the unseen spiritual adversaries listed in Ephesians 6:12. There Paul says, "For our struggle is not against flesh and blood, but against the rulers, against the authorities, against the powers of this dark world, and against the spiritual forces of evil in the heavenly realms."

As we wrestle with our heavenly Father in prayer, it is serious work and quite different from wrestling in play with an earthly father. The only similarity with wrestling in prayer with our heavenly Father and playing on the floor with our earthly father is that our heavenly Father, just like an earthly father, is teaching and toughening His children to face the challenge, exert energy, and win the contest.

Our prayer battles, whether we win or lose, determine successes and failures in our everyday lives. The devil does not like it when people of prayer invade enemy territory. He fights back. In this chapter, we will read of events that illustrate these ideas while we note that God's plans and answers are better than our own.

Including Prayer in a Mission Statement

In *Habits of Highly Effective Christians,* I explained how writing a mission statement helps us by not only defining who we are but also by keeping us on course to reach our goals. Decisions about our life, our use of time, and our use of other resources are easier to make if we have carefully defined who we are in a mission statement. We then make daily decisions according to our perception of who we are.

Applying this principle to my new attitude toward the importance of prayer has significantly changed the way I structure my use of time each day. Since my original personal mission statement did not reflect my newly developing prayer emphasis, I changed the statement to fit my new sense of values by writing the following addendum.

Addendum to My Personal Mission Statement

Prayer is my most important activity to help make God's kingdom come to earth. I match this belief with the daily practice of giving prayer more priority in importance, time, and sequence than anything else I do. Of my own choosing and with a sense of privilege, I gladly arise in the night or early morning to ensure that I complete my predetermined number of daily prayer hours. I continue to pray after breakfast as necessary. Imperfect human that I am, I watch the clock so that prayer is increased. Logging so many hours in prayer is not the goal; increasing my prayer is. I exercise holy discipline and self-control in this intentional personal commitment, fully confident I am heard based on the truthful Word of God.

> **Prayer is my most important activity to help make God's kingdom come to earth.**

My appointment with God is first and takes me longer than anything else I do in the day.

I know prayer is addressed to Him who is able to do immeasurably more than I can ask or imagine. Jesus said He would do whatever I asked in His name if I remain in Him and His words remain in me. Jesus instructed His disciples to always pray and not give up. The prayer of a righteous man is powerful and effective. Those who hope in the Lord will renew their strength; soar on wings like eagles; run and not grow weary; and walk and not be faint. I know that with men, many things are impossible, but with God, nothing is impossible.

Since my practice of prayer illustrates its importance, I risk possible misunderstanding when I speak openly about my commitment to prayer. I desire by word and example to challenge Christians to pray. Talking about my prayer life is not the goal; it only serves the higher objective of stimulating others to pray.

As a partner with God, I do not make requests that are inconsistent with His plan. I seek always to know His agenda and pray accordingly. Passion in prayer is important, but accuracy is more important. When the right direction for prayer is known, I persist, insist, labor, plead, reason, and persevere in the spirit of Jabez who prayed, "Oh that you would bless me and enlarge my territory! Let your hand be with me ..." (I Chronicles 4:10) and with the tenacity of Jacob who said, "I will not let you go unless you bless me" (Genesis 32:26).

In prayer, I do not overcome God's reluctance, but rather grasp His willingness. Spiritual forces oppose me, but they can be overcome. To be fruitful in God's kingdom brings more glory to God than to be unfruitful, and, as Jesus said, to bear much fruit is even better (John 15:2, 8). Therefore, with neither shame nor selfish ambition, I pray with confidence to be more fruitful for Him.

As with any personal mission statement, the process of creating it gives the writer a better idea of who he or she really is. Personal mission statements are not so much goals as they are self-descriptions. No sane person will behave in ways that are inconsistent with his or her self-perception. Therefore, by writing my mission statement and now this addendum, I am able to focus more easily on being who I am — the self my personal mission statement defines. Seeking to be unwavering in passionate pursuit of God, the mission statement has been a help to me.

The Valleys of Death

On Saturday, May 29, 2004, I ran the Andy Payne Marathon in Oklahoma City, Oklahoma. Several hours later, I boarded a plane for Atlanta. I was bound for a two-month trip to Madagascar, Zimbabwe, and Papua New Guinea (PNG) that included 10 seminars for pastors and Christian leaders. I slept okay at a motel near the Atlanta airport, called Char the next morning to chat, and boarded the plane for a 17-hour plane ride to South Africa.

I slept for only four hours before meeting Eddie Robinson of the World Missions Centre at the airport. I spent the day with him discussing missions work, strategy, trends, and the seminars scheduled for Madagascar. I went for a prayer walk in his quiet neighborhood that evening and then went to bed early. The next thing I knew, I was up at midnight and noticed that my irregular heartbeat seemed even more irregular! First, let me give you some background.

I first noticed an irregular heartbeat about three months prior to this episode. A physician friend of mine volunteered to listen to my heart, and then recommended that I see my own doctor. My doctor tested the beating patterns of my heart with an electrocardiogram. This test revealed fluttering atria and an irregular beating of the ventricle. The upper chambers of my heart were quivering instead of pumping regularly and the lower chambers were pumping, but not in regular rhythm. This heart disease is called atrial fibrillation. I met with a cardiologist, a heart specialist, and received a three-dimensional heart exam using an echo-measuring sonic camera. The echocardiogram revealed that I had a faulty mitral valve. Each beat of my heart allows some blood to pass back into the atria in the upper heart instead of pumping all of the blood out into my body.

To my surprise, the cardiologist recommended that I continue my exercise program, including running marathons! Even if the heartbeat was irregular, he reasoned, it was still better for the heart to be strong than weak. Following doctor's orders, I continued my exercise program — including the three marathons that I had already scheduled for that spring. The big question was whether I should proceed on my proposed trip to Africa and PNG since my schedule included being in some remote areas far away from hospitals and cardiologists. The trip, planned for months, also included meeting people in three nations who were expecting me. My cardiologist advised me that it was safe for me to proceed as planned.

My decision to go, however, required some thought. Since I train missionaries, I am more aware of not only how I *think* about Christians taking risks, but also how I personally *handle* risks. Would I die for the gospel? Yes, of course, but not all deaths of gospel workers are necessary. We are not to tempt God. We are to temper our zeal with knowledge.

I did not want to go on an eight-week trip to remote areas if it meant that I would be tempting God. My cardiologist assured me that, while atrial fibrillation was serious but treatable, the treatment could wait until I returned to the United States. I took medication to sedate my heart slightly so that it would not be over exerted. Then after I returned home from my trip, I had planned to take a blood thinner so blood clots would not form in the atria that were not pumping normally. Now, let us get back to the midnight adventure in South Africa.

In Eddie's home in Pretoria, I lay on my bed and listened to the irregular pumping of my heart. I noticed that my heartbeat was even more irregular than it had been before I went to the doctor. Was it the marathon I had just run? Was it the 17-hour flight from Atlanta? Was it the missed night's sleep? Was it the sleeping pill I had taken on the plane? Had the sleeping pill reacted with the other medicine I was taking? Was it a combination of all of these?

As I reflected on these possibilities, I noticed that the irregularity had suddenly stopped. In fact, everything had stopped! I heard no heartbeat at all! Because I wear earplugs at night to help me sleep, I am able to hear my heartbeats quite distinctly. However, now, I heard nothing. I began to feel something abnormal in my legs; then, my arms. I held very still and prayed, "Lord, are you taking me home?" As the deadening (no pun intended) silence prevailed, I cried out, "Lord, help me!" My heart then began to pound very strongly. My whole chest shook with sudden and abnormally vigorous activity.

I began to rethink whether I should proceed with my trip. My schedule included being on the road for eight weeks living in remote areas. Was it wise to proceed? I walked slowly into

Eddie's living room and lay on the floor to gather my thoughts. After several minutes, I decided to discuss the whole thing with Eddie. I called out to him and he came into the living room. I had him put his ear on my chest. After some discussion, we decided to go to a hospital that specialized in heart conditions which was about 10 minutes away. For three hours, I experienced an electrocardiogram, blood tests, consultations, phone calls, and lengthy waits. During this time, I watched the irregular patterns on the heart monitor with inward agony. Early in the morning, the doctors eventually agreed with my cardiologist back home: proceed on the trip and take an aspirin a day to help mildly thin my blood.

As I look back now on that event, I believe the enemy attacked me. The 10 conferences eventually held on that trip in Madagascar, Zimbabwe, and PNG were well received; in fact, many people expressed how much more effective they thought their ministries would be as a result of hearing the teachings. Furthermore, I was invited to teach more seminars in all three of those nations. However, the enemy does not want God's servants to succeed. Attacks will occur, and when they do, maintaining prayer is essential for survival. Nevertheless, the attacks on me continued, and so does my story.

After successfully completing seven conferences in Madagascar and two in Zimbabwe, I prepared to leave for PNG. I was to fly through South Africa and then another third of the way around the world through Australia to Goroka in the Eastern Highlands of Papua New Guinea. The trip before me involved thousands of miles with two days of travels and layovers and an eight-hour time change.

During the last two days in Zimbabwe, however, I had developed chest pains. When I twisted my body in certain ways, coughed, sneezed, or lifted a suitcase, my chest would hurt. I asked the pastors in my final session in Zimbabwe to pray for me. And pray, they did. One man came from the audience, placed his hands on my chest, and prayed fervently. When I asked him why he had done that, he said that the Lord had told him to pray for my heart. I was encouraged.

After boarding the plane from South Africa to Australia, I took another sleeping pill. By the time we landed in Brisbane, I was exhausted. I made sleeping arrangements and ate dinner. As I got ready for bed, I again heard my heart beating very irregularly. Because of my chest pains, the fuzziness in my head, and my extreme exhaustion, I thought that I was dying.

Out of a sense of responsibility, I wrote two notes: one for the hotel personnel and one to my wife should I die. Below are the notes.

To whom it may concern:

In case of an emergency, please contact Char Meyers (pronounced Shar) at either of these two numbers [here I wrote out our home phone number and Char's work number] in the United States. She is my wife in Tulsa, Oklahoma (USA), and I have been having atrial fibrillation for three months. The doctor said I could make this trip safely, but I have been having chest pains.

July 8, 2004
Ron Meyers

Dear Char,

I do not know if this is serious or not, but I have a chest pain if I cough or lean over the right way (wrong way), or put pressure on my chest.

I am not afraid to come home to my dear Savior, but I would extremely regret leaving you to be a widow to go through temporary pain until we are reunited in glory land. You have been the delight of my life, and I regret to let you down.

I have no other regrets. God has been good to me to give me 54 more years since I recovered from rheumatic fever at age six.

July 8, 2004, 10:22 p.m.
Ron Meyers

When I woke up in the morning, I realized that I was still alive! I wrote the following addition to the above letters, shoved them all into my briefcase, and did not tell anyone about my near-death experience.

July 9, 2004, 8:45 a.m.

I feel weak and fuzzy in my head. I only slept two hours and 45 minutes during the night. I have prayed desperately for both wisdom and courage: wisdom to not foolishly plunge forward on this trip if my health is at risk, and courage to finish this project even though I seem to be under a spiritual attack. The chest pains are not as bad as the psychological strain of trying to be both wise and courageous.

Ron Meyers

Later that morning, I was still dizzy as I stood in line at the Brisbane International Airport. It was quite a sobering experience to be a physically strong man having trouble standing or carrying a briefcase and a light bag. I prayed desperately that the Lord would stop me from going to a remote area if it were unwise to proceed with the trip.

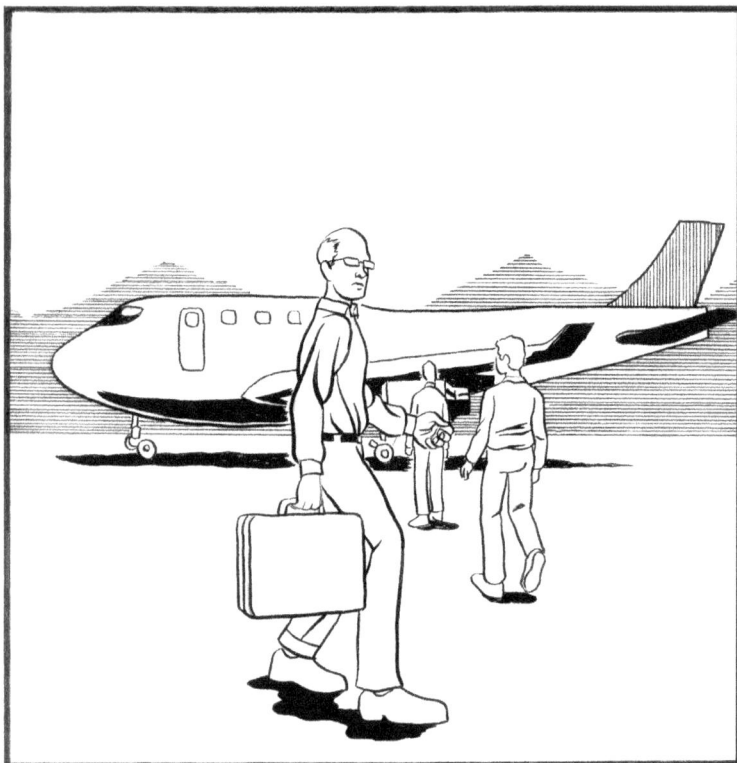

Hours later, in Port Moresby, PNG, as I walked to my next departure gate, I felt even more weak and dizzy. I pled with God for an answer. Was I being foolish in my zeal to continue the trip? Should I turn back? The plane bound for Goroka was late. Was God giving me more time to decide not to go? I kept praying and still the pain in my chest continued every time I coughed. Finally, it was time to board the plane. I gathered my belongings, and with a lump in my throat and tears in my eyes, I walked to the plane. As I boarded the plane, I quoted Scripture from the King James' version I had memorized as a small child. "Yea, though I walk through the valley of the shadow of death, I will fear no evil: for Thou art with me; Thy rod and Thy staff, they comfort me" (Psalm 23:4).

I was embarrassed to begin my relationship with my PNG host, Reid Crow, by telling him about my difficulties. Since I thought it would be a terrible first impression, for the first hour of our drive through the mountains, I let him tell about the tribal wars and dangers of travel in the highlands. For example, Reid showed me the house where a pastor's hand had been cut off recently as an act of tribal revenge. Halfway to Kainantu from Goroka, I began to tell Reid of the problems I had endured in the last four days. I also knew I needed to tell Char so she could be praying for me. I also wanted her to hear from me one more time before I went to heaven. After we reached Reid's home, I sent Char an e-mail. Then Reid and I prayed, and we each went to bed.

That night, I slept like a rock. In the morning, I felt no chest pain, tightness, or dizziness. In fact, I took part in my normal prayer routine and read some e-mail. By that time, Char had written to inform me that our medical friends at home in Tulsa reported that any chest pain I was having had to be something else other than my heart. An irregular rhythm is a rhythm problem, not a muscle problem. In other words, they believed that I had not been near death during my trip. Rather, I must have just been travel weary and had gone too long without sleep.

The enemy had tried to "hitchhike" on a normal problem, lying to me, and trying to trick me into aborting what turned out to be a glorious two weeks of ministry to very fine, mature men and women of God. Now I understood why God had not told me to remain in the U.S., South Africa, Zimbabwe, or Brisbane. I **The centerpiece of ministry is not our feelings, and neither is it feeling timid when Satan lies to us. The centerpiece of ministry is prayer.** *thought* I might be having a problem, but God knew better. The centerpiece of ministry is not our feelings, and neither is it feeling timid when Satan lies to us. The centerpiece of ministry is prayer. Through prayer, God's servants can know His will and act on it.

Proving that there is a direct link between increased prayer and any one of the miracles of God protecting, blessing, or anointing me described in this book is difficult. However, the remarkable increase in miracles happening in my life seems to correspond to the increased time I spend in prayer. If I wanted to be scientific about it, I could temporarily decrease my prayer time to the pre-July 9, 2002-level just to see if the number of miracles would decrease. However, I would run the risk of being less fruitful for a season. What opportunities with eternal consequences might be lost during that time? Even though I cannot explain the answer, I do not want to take the chance. I would rather continue with my prayer regimen.

The valleys I have described were difficult experiences. Nevertheless, those experiences require careful evaluation since the spiritual ministry that followed was so wonderful, exhilarating, and fruitful. During the whole trip, all 10 conferences ended with great joy and celebration. Training pastors in other parts of the world, even with the valleys factored into the equation, provides me with more satisfaction than I can express. I cannot place a price tag on the spiritual freedom to connect with fine men and women of God. I know my effort to walk through my valleys has increased their ministry effectiveness. I will continue to pray my way through them.

A Bonus Conference in Zimbabwe

After I arrived in Harare, the capital of Zimbabwe, I was told that the conference was cancelled. However, I would be conducting a conference in the church of my host pastor in the small community of Norton. My visionary host pastor wants to build a church organization that will serve Zimbabwe and Southern Africa. Even though his church was not in the capital city, I was happy to contribute to the development of his staff and ministry team at that early stage in their organization. The Lord blessed the conference in Norton; the people were receptive, and I was content with what the Lord was doing.

Several days into the Norton conference, I found myself praying about the missed conference in Harare. Now, I generally do not complain about lost opportunities to serve even when I am inwardly disappointed. Therefore, for me to be still thinking about the conference in Harare that did not happen was out of character. Nevertheless, I continued to pray about the pastors in Harare and felt almost embarrassed to be dwelling on that missed opportunity. At the Holy Spirit's prompting, I prayed that if it were possible, I would still like to schedule something for the pastors there. What did the Lord have in mind? I decided to mention the idea to my host.

Notice how interestingly God answered the prayer He had placed in my heart. Before I even mentioned the subject to my host, he asked me to attend a conference in Harare with him the next week! My host was scheduled to speak at two sessions, and he wanted me to speak at one of them. Sensing this was the work of God, I quickly agreed. Learning about the pastors' conference that someone else had planned in Harare also helped me understand the reason why my own conference planned for Harare was cancelled.

The organizer of the conference was a recent ORU graduate and knew my wife through a graduate program there. He said he knew me too, though I had only heard of him from Char. After giving instructions to the presenters, he politely asked me to greet the group. By the end of my 10-minute greeting, two more presenters asked that I be given one of their speaking slots. This meant that within a 72-hour period, I would present three times at a pastors' conference where I had not been scheduled!

In each of those three sessions, I was happy to speak to God's servants. The appreciation they expressed in return was enormous. In fact, I received an invitation to return for another conference the following year. My unplanned participation in the Harare pastors' conference reinforces my conviction that ministry comes out of prayer.

My unplanned participation in the Harare pastors' conference reinforces my conviction that ministry comes out of prayer.

Prayer is the centerpiece, and from that center flows anointing, insights, and various types of help and opportunities that the Lord gives to us. When we seek through prayer to serve Him and His people, He makes a way. Having access to God through prayer is better than any other "inside" organizational contact. The strings that Jesus pulls are better than any we can manipulate. Having access to the Father in Jesus' name increases one's influence in pursuing a Kingdom-related career and is better than any other connection here on Earth.

Promotion comes from God. Regardless of what kind of career you have, seeking God and His Kingdom is superior to seeking career advancement. God rewards those who earnestly seek Him. The public does not need to know about our secret struggles in prayer in order for us to be near God and to be all we can be for Him. Jesus said it all when He said, "Then your Father who sees what is done in secret will reward you" (Matthew 6:6).

A Fiery Dart Narrowly Missed

Months after I left Zimbabwe, I accepted an invitation to teach for a week in a Christian university in Sweden. During fall break at ORU, I flew to Sweden. As I walked into my hotel room in Uppsala, Sweden, I was surprised to see that the television was already on and displayed a message welcoming Dr. Ron Meyers to Uppsala. I was impressed. Additionally, I enjoyed seeing a basket of fruit. I felt ready for a week of teaching pastors and missionaries one of the most helpful courses for those who communicate the gospel message in multicultural settings — Missionary Anthropology.

For the first time, I had added another component to the course: an emphasis on incarnational missions. This element emphasizes the need to live with and experience the same everyday life difficulties as the people to whom you are ministering. Jesus, at incarnation, did not come just to visit; he came to *live* with us. His model is still great for missionaries today. I want my students to know that their actions speak louder than their words. Their life actions have the potential to make a great impact on their students. I was looking forward to the week.

I picked up the television remote and scanned the channels to see what was available. I recognized some programs to be movies, children's programs, documentaries, and news. But then I ran across a pornography channel. Never in my life had I seen anything like this. Shocked, I turned the television off — and it stayed off the entire week! Unfortunately, I had acted too late to stop the images which I had seen from entering my mind and being forever impressed upon my memory.

I have taken great care over the years not to look at pornography because of its addictive nature. Even though it may be available at every turn in the U.S., we have the freedom not to view it. In Sweden, I was not presented with alternatives: I saw it. This was bad enough, but here is the worst of it — *while I was watching, I had liked it!*

As an eager Christian, I try to protect my mind from evil so I do not look at that sort of thing. I have told pastors on four different continents how pornography can hinder spiritual growth if allowed to enter our minds. Furthermore, at that time I was a 60-year-old seasoned and experienced preacher. I had been in the ministry for 39 years. How could it be that I liked seeing such filth?

Char and I have a healthy intimate life. I do not know, and do not want to know, the secrets of other married couples. It is difficult for me to imagine any married couple being happier, freer, or more content than we are. The thing that bothered me about what I saw in that hotel room was that the sexual expression I had watched was not like my own involvement in my own marriage. The images that were burned in my memory forced me into someone else's intimate experience. I began to think about things that I should not think about. I did not like what was happening to me. I did not like where my thoughts were taking my mind. I did not want to think about those things. I was forced to see and then think about things I had not chosen to see. I decided I needed to clear my head.

Needing to get some fresh air, I ran 10 kilometers in a picturesque setting surrounded by beautiful yellow maple leaves with just enough cedar trees to complement the already-breathtaking view. The beautiful scenery reminded me of Canada where we lived for five years.

Even though I was diligently trying to clear my mind of those toxic thoughts, they continued to poison my mind. I passed women along the path, and I thought about them in a completely different way — most of it was unacceptable. I could not see them as dear daughters of a loving God for whom I needed to pray. Disturbingly, I imagined them as sex objects and potential partners. Those thoughts were very uncharacteristic for me. I came back to the room exhausted and ready for sleep. I decided that I would have to face those evil giants tomorrow.

When I arrived at the host university the next day, I met wonderful students and delightful people and managed to pray and teach my way through the day. While praying during my walk that evening, I was having unclean thoughts once again. I was even attracted to the mannequins modeling women's clothing in the store windows. I felt trapped by the images in my mind that had distorted my thinking. Being a man who was tempted at such disturbing thoughts was not the man I wanted to be. Again, I went to bed with the realization that I would have to fight the demons tomorrow.

The next morning during discussion, a Swedish lady happened to mention the sinister problem of pornography in Sweden. I immediately told them about my own difficulties. The students offered to pray with me, and I gladly accepted. Can you imagine young, international students from various nations in Europe gathered in Sweden praying for me to be set free from the demon called pornography? During the prayer time, one of them said, "You need to renounce it yourself," and I gladly and immediately did. I said, "I renounce those images in my mind. I renounce the experience and the attack from Satan. I resist him and run to you, Father." If a veteran prayer warrior and missionary like me was pulled that quickly into the pornography trap, imagine how easy it is for a non-Christian or someone new in the faith to become trapped.

I usually am able to pray my way through difficulties even if it takes some hours of prayer alone with God. However, the same Bible that says we should get alone to pray also says we are to confess our sins openly. The release I needed did not come this time through solitary prayer — it came through confession and group prayer. Like anyone, I dislike embarrassment, but I dislike bondage even more. It is better to turn to loving Christians for prayer than to be bound by spiritual forces that can be stronger than we are. Confession is a small price for us to pay for freedom, especially since Jesus has already paid a much greater price.

> The release I needed did not come this time through solitary prayer — it came through confession and group prayer.

I had been asked to preach at the Wednesday evening service that week. During lunch, I asked the dean of the sponsoring university if it would be appropriate for me to preach on the subject of keeping our minds pure and use my personal experience as an example. He said he felt it would be quite helpful.

The Lord enabled me to use this experience with pornography to show others how I fought the battle that they must fight daily. My personal experience enabled me to speak on a topic crucial to their spiritual improvement. Before that experience, I would not have been qualified to minister to them in an area so essential to their character development. However, personally experiencing (important in incarnational missions) what the Swedes themselves told me they went through gave me the insight I needed to say something of value to them. Furthermore, I would have never escaped an evil mind trap had it not been for the power of confession and the prayers of those loving students who were willing to minister to a brother at a time of personal need.

I did not realize when I prayed about teaching on incarnational missions in Sweden that I would endure 46 hours of that kind of mental torment. However, it sensitized me to their needs, challenges, and unique difficulties. If I did not love God or pursue Him so earnestly, my struggle might not have mattered so much. My experience in dealing with pornography helped me to be sympathetic — not judgmental — toward anyone else experiencing a similar problem. The devil would just love to destroy an intercessor — or any of God's servants — with this type of fiery dart.

Choosing Another Marathon

I had not been allowed to play high school basketball and football, so running marathons satisfied my desire to compete. I enjoyed several things about racing: training for the competitions, the diversion from day-to-day responsibilities, traveling with Char to each event, the joy of facing challenges, and collecting trophies and marathon T-shirts. These experiences are all still great memories.

Since my first marathon in 1999, many additional ministry opportunities had opened. My trips abroad during the June and July months became longer, and they required more planning, corresponding, and preparing. I also increased my daily prayer time, which meant less sleep and fewer daytime hours to work. Then I became a consultant to a team of future medical missionaries, the Associate Pastor for English Ministry at the Tulsa Chinese Christian Church. In addition, I was already a full-time professor at ORU. Adding new responsibilities without cutting back on any current commitments meant that I was stretched too thin. The final straw that broke the camel's back was the discovery of my irregular heartbeat that I discussed earlier. I knew I had to cut back on something.

The problem was that I liked all the things I was doing. I did not want to stop any of them. Consequently, one day in Africa, while running, I decided how I would determine what activity I would stop doing. I would use the "eternal value" criterion. The final two choices came down to either cutting back on my prayer time or not running marathons. I realized I could stop running marathons and leave earth with no remorse. However, if I cut back on my prayer time, I could well regret it when I left earth. I hated to stop running, but I decided not to race any more. Incidentally, for physical exercise, I still run six miles four times a week.

It may seem like no big deal to decide to stop running marathons, but there is a reason for telling you this story. I enjoyed people asking me about marathons. For the first time in my life, I had a sport in which I excelled. Marathons provided me with a talking point — a contact with people. I will even admit that I enjoyed the respect people seemed to give me for my accomplishments. I not only ran marathons, I won a fair number of prizes for my age group. I usually finished in the top 25 percent overall, which means I ran the marathons faster than many who were much younger.

However, given the choice between that fun and the sense of eternal accomplishment with my extended time of prayer, I chose prayer. I had to make a decision, difficult as it was, that was consistent with my belief system. I believe prayer is the most important thing I do, and I did not want to cut back on it. I now run another type of race. Some day, I hope I will hear the cheers and receive the prize for which marathon prizes on Earth are mere shadows. I am not minimizing earthly marathons, but when forced to choose, I chose the heavenly.

> Some day, I hope I will hear the cheers and receive the prize for which marathon prizes on Earth are mere shadows.

You, too, have things that you must evaluate as you schedule your priorities. What is the eternal value of the items on your list that compete for your time? Would it not be reasonable to weigh these decisions in terms of their eternal consequences?

Increased Territory

One of the verses in our garage states, "Ask of me and I will make the nations your inheritance, the ends of the earth your possession" (Psalm 2:8). Another verse on a shelf states, "Oh that you would bless me and enlarge my territory. Let your hand be with me …" (I Chronicles 4:10). Since returning from South Africa and India in 2002, these decorations in my garage are part of the scriptural basis for my continued efforts to accomplish all that God has planned for me on Earth. Those verses are deep in my spirit.

I have heard it said that we do God's will too long. We keep doing what He has told us to do and may not be open to the new things that He may have in store for us. Also, I remember a quotation from a fine senior minister who said to me, "I never figured I had the right to assume that I would always do whatever I was doing." This elderly, seasoned man of God had been a pastor, served as a missionary, served as a dean of a Bible College, performed district supervisor duties in two different districts, and acted as a temporary general supervisor for an entire denomination when needed. He was an amazing man whose talents were used in a number of different capacities. So, his words had a deep effect on me: *"I never figured I had the right to assume that I would always do whatever I was doing."*

With those words in my heart and the above verses repeatedly urging me to pray for the nations and for increased ministry, I should not have been surprised when the Holy Spirit answered the main question of my experiment in prayer: "What would happen if a teacher prayed seriously?" He said, "You have prayed for the nations as your inheritance and the ends of the Earth for your possession. Do you care enough about receiving your inheritance that you would go there and take possession? Do you care enough about an enlarged territory that you would go there to receive it?"

God was beginning to open more doors than I had imagined. I was already speaking or being invited to minister in the Ukraine, Palestine, and Sweden, as well as nations in Africa, Asia, and the Pacific. It was easy for me to say, "Yes!" when He called us to Africa. Clearly, God was beginning to answer my question about what would happen if a teacher prayed seriously.

Aiming for "Immeasurably More"

Another verse in our garage states, "To him who is able to do immeasurably more than we can ask or imagine" (Ephesians 3:20). This verse confirms to me that the most important thing that I can do is pray. As I ponder the words "immeasurably more," the following profound observations become points of interest and value to me. "Lucky breaks" are neither "lucky" nor "breaks." Blessings have nothing to do with chance; they are deliberate favors from a sovereign God.

- **God is able.** Of course He is able to do "immeasurably more" than we can since He is wiser, stronger, and better than we are.

- **God is huge.** The difference between what *we* can ask for or imagine and what *God* can both imagine and do — the difference between His ways and thoughts and ours — is huge.

- **God is willing**. That He is willing to do immeasurably more is implied by telling us that He can. He would not tell us He could do it if He would not.

> That He is *willing* to do immeasurably more is implied by telling us that He can. He would not tell us He *could* do it if He *would* not.

- **God lets us choose.** As we may readily observe, some people press for, and therefore experience, God's blessing of "immeasurably more."

- **God lets us reject.** As we may equally and readily observe, some people neither press for, nor receive, God's blessing of "immeasurably more." Some live beneath their privileges.

- **God gives us equal opportunity.** His promises regarding prayer are equally available to all. You, too, can experience "immeasurably more."

- **God understands our limitations.** God being able to do "immeasurably more" implies God knows that, even at our best, we still ask for immeasurably less than He is able to give.

- **God is powerful.** Our imaginative powers are seriously limited in comparison to God's for He does "immeasurably more."

- **God's goodness**. God, in His goodness, does not want us to limit ourselves to receive only what we can imagine.

- **God's will**. Praying for God's will is better than praying for our will since our will is immeasurably less than His.

- **God understands.** Praying according to the Holy Spirit's prompting is highly useful since the Holy Spirit would never prompt us to pray for anything except God's will. We do not understand enough to use just our own humanly originated prayer.

- **God surprises us.** If we pray, God does immeasurably more than we imagine or ask. That means we should necessarily experience repeated surprises — we did not even imagine what God could think and do.

- **God is giving.** We should not be surprised *that* we are surprised; we should only be surprised by *what* any given surprise is. We could not have imagined the answer — that is why it is a surprise. If God does more than we can imagine, surprises should be normal.

- **God provides gifts.** We should learn to expect and pray for surprises. His "immeasurably more" is worth seeking, and we do not want to limit Him to the narrow confines of doing only what we are able to imagine.

In view of these statements, it is simple to see that we need to do whatever we can to release God's ability and willingness to do "immeasurably more" in our lives. In addition, we need to stop doing whatever is blocking or limiting Him from performing "immeasurably more" in our lives. What if prayer releases God's willingness to do "immeasurably more" and prayerlessness blocks it?

These thoughts gave me anticipation as I prepared for Sweden, Ukraine, Armenia, Ethiopia, and Palestine. They motivate me even more now that I have resigned at ORU, moved to another continent, and look into our future in Africa.

Working to Live or Living to Work?

Some people work to merely live. They only want to be happy — for a long time — so they work hard to live. Pity such a person who has no other purpose other than simply to live! He will burn up many efforts in mere self-preservation. Working just to live does not lead to becoming your best possible self. Such a self-centered life is not worth working so hard just to maintain. Because of the shallowness of his goals and purposelessness of his efforts, he could easily lack self-worth and may be prone to other negative tendencies. Pity the person who has found no greater purpose than to live for one's own enjoyment.

There is a far greater value in finding a grand task more important than you are, more important than life itself. If you can find such a task, you have the privileged opportunity to live to work; your purpose to live is to do the task that gives your life meaning. What you accomplish with your life defines and outlives you. It makes your life worth living.

Blessed is the man who finds something that demands his best production. His thoughts are not inward. Instead, they are upward toward God and outward toward others. His value in life contributes to his optimism. He has the advantage that, even if he is mistaken on minor points, he will keep working at it until he gets it right. He will correct his course, improve his skills, and eventually achieve success.

I have found a superior task for which I live. It is to be God's partner through prayer to bring His kingdom and will to earth. That work — prayer — is the centerpiece of service and is worth living to do.

I have found a superior task for which I live. It is to be God's partner through prayer to bring His Kingdom and will to Earth. That work — prayer — is the centerpiece of service and is worth living to do. God is the source, a limitless and wonderful resource, of all good. Prayer is the means humans have to tap that resource. Because of prayer, humans can experience many marvelous blessings. When we contemplate what God can do, why would anyone not want to pray?

CHAPTER THIRTEEN
Acknowledge God

*"Trust in the Lord with all you heart and
lean not on your own understanding;
in all your ways acknowledge him,
and he will make your paths straight."*

Proverbs 3:5-6

Recently, I camped out in the wilderness, slept in a small tent, and marveled at the night sky with its beautiful display of stars. I appreciated the fact that God is very big and wise, and that I am very small. This is similar to the phrase of the children's song, *Jesus Loves Me*, "… they are weak but He is strong."

Why is it so important to recognize God's adequacy and our inadequacy? What advantage belongs to the person who recognizes these two truths? What relationship exists between God's perfect adequacy and our human need for help, God's greatness and our dependency? Are they not counterparts in a wholesome union between the weak and the strong, frail humans and a great God, the ones who appreciate and the One who is appreciated?

 The human need for strength leads those who *need* strength to appreciate the One who *has* strength. In other words, the need to be strong will lead weak humans to *acknowledge a strong God*. If we merely understand that and *acknowledge God*, then God will happily use His strength in our behalf and make our paths straight. If having a straight path is the result, I surely want to learn how to acknowledge Him

By praying, we acknowledge God's ability to help us and express our need for His help. We acknowledge God by admitting that we are mere weak and foolish humans with potential for doing evil. We acknowledge God by realizing He is good and without imperfection or possibility of change. Prayer is the surest, most important way humans acknowledge Him. Acknowledging God and praying go hand-in-hand. This chapter is an explanation of how acknowledging God is the basis of a life of prayer. What a profound difference it can make! What a powerful influence it can be!

Most of this book has been practical and full of my personal stories. But practitioners should also be reflective. To *only* reflect on prayer is to only *think* about praying, a weakness we want to avoid. On the other hand, to only practice praying has another kind of deficiency since we may not be praying as effectively as we could or should. This chapter will help us think deeply about the reasons we should pray and why we should live a life rich with prayer. Proverbs 3:5-6 has solid reasons why we should give ourselves more fully to prayer.

Growing in Acknowledgment of God

Wise King Solomon in Proverbs says, "… in all your ways acknowledge Him." The more spiritually mature and aware of God we become, the more we acknowledge both God's greatness and our failures. Our acknowledgment of God should grow. It may begin with *reluctant admission*, and lead us through a series of other responses to eventually feel *fervent love for* or *delight in* God. Growth in acknowledgment of God — increased awareness of our inadequacy — is not a sign of weakness; it is a sign of strength. It demonstrates we have the courage to face truth. In this case, it is the truth of our need.

> The more spiritually mature and aware of God we become, the more we acknowledge both God's greatness and our failures.

From day to day, or even from incident to incident, we may temporarily advance or lose ground. If we are unwilling or slow to acknowledge God or if we forget to acknowledge God, we regress. However, if we are quick and eager to acknowledge Him in our situations, we will rapidly progress. Our desire must be to fit in with His plans. Our goal is to be His willing prayer partner who works toward the fulfillment of His plans. We work faithfully with Him until His plans are complete. Then we rejoice in their fulfillment. As we progress in acknowledgment, our awareness of Him is greater; and we are happiest to let God be God. This is as it should be.

Char and I lived for five years in Beijing where students were taught there is no God. Millions of people in the world do not admit or know of His existence. Knowing that He exists is an important first step to acknowledging God. The challenge of acknowledging God is to live in a manner consistent with that knowledge — to live as though we realize God is God and that we are not God. In other words, submitting to or acknowledging the God who is there is our great challenge. It is difficult for the human will to yield to another person. The human ego does not like to submit to anyone. It is not our nature to recognize authority. If God did not exist or was a mere creation machine — not a personal God — we could be our own god and do whatever we wanted. Some people prefer that way of life. But acknowledging God requires accepting His authority, and it is a paradox that as long as we submit to Him, we have more authority.

> Feeling hopeless can force us to seek solutions and improvement, while contentment may lead to laziness and lack of improvement.

Making Good Use of Hopelessness

We must rethink the idea of hopelessness. Hopelessness is not hopeless. Hopelessness is a prerequisite to fulfilled potential. We usually think it is sad and unfortunate for someone to feel desperate, but there is a positive side to feeling hopeless. Life's problems and difficulties that lead to despair are actually good since they help us see that we need God in our lives. Feeling hopeless can force us to seek solutions and improvement, while contentment may lead to laziness and lack of improvement. Most of us must become hopeless before we turn to God. We must sink to the bottom before we turn to the One who can lift us. We must use despair by combining it with a *double knowledge*— we must know ourselves as well as God.

Acknowledging God entails appreciating God's divine power *and* admitting our own personal weaknesses. Unless our appreciation for God goes hand-in-hand with acknowledging our faults, we will not pray for His guidance and help. Instead, we will rely on our strength. Seeing the stars in the night sky and remembering how great God is — and realizing how little man is — is a pleasant way to discover the two truths. Wouldn't it be better to quickly acknowledge both His power and our lack of it and move on to His glorious provisions? Wouldn't it be better to seek His help than try in vain to fix things ourselves?

To acknowledge God requires becoming honest and transparent, willing to recognize, admit, and confess our sins. The more perfect our acknowledgment of God is, the more transparent we become and the more easily we admit our need of Him in every situation. Such a realist values prayer and other forms of seeking God. Such a realist quickly admits human helplessness and turns immediately to God for help. Such a realist can easily trust God with all his or her heart rather than lean on his or her own understanding.

Acknowledging God's greatness, power, wisdom, and goodness fulfills the first requirements of Solomon's wise counsel: "Trust in the Lord with all your heart." Acknowledging human weakness and inability fulfills the second requirement: "lean not on your own understanding" (Proverbs 3:5). We become more eager to pray because we are more willing to trust someone stronger than we are. Trusting God and leaning not on our own understanding may not seem most reasonable, but it actually is.

I assure you that knowledge of His holiness and our sinfulness — His greatness and our dependence — has direct impact on our daily lives. When incidents like my experience with pornography in Sweden occur, they reveal a stark contrast between God's holiness and greatness versus our weakness and sinfulness. The rational response to recognizing this great difference is to pray for His help because He can and *wants* to help. Prayer, in our weakness to call on Him in His strength, is the most logical, reasonable, and sensible human response. By acknowledging God through prayer, weak persons become powerful.

Friendship with God

Another perspective to consider is our personal friendship with God. Those who acknowledge God do not try to hide from Him. When we get alone with God in prayer, we are the most free to be very honest with Him *and* with ourselves. Only those people who acknowledge God are able to be honest with themselves and admit who they are as a human in the presence of a Holy God. They alone are most fully themselves and this allows them to reach their most true and full potential. They enjoy mental and spiritual health and a perspective that others do not. Only God's humble friends can possibly be at their best; those who rely just on themselves will never be all they could have been.

Acknowledging Him places us on the path of great progress. This happens because acknowledging God requires repentance. Repentance is not a popular word, but it is good for us. Our initial repentance was the beginning of what we later realize has become a necessary continual process of growing in our ability to be honest with God. We demonstrate this by our willingness to constantly confess our need for Him.

As our acknowledgement of God grows, we increase our ability and desire to see Him become more involved in our everyday lives. Because of our intimate relationship with God, His involvement in our life becomes increasingly clear to us. God seems to play a game with us: He is with us but allows us to discover Him through the fingerprints that He leaves all around us.

Acknowledging Him and His wisdom — even in circumstances we don't yet understand — can become so habitual that, in times of darkness when we don't know God's reasons, we still know there *is* a reason. We trust Him. When there is no explanation, the prudent are content with the element of mystery; they know the secret will be revealed some day. We seek to know God's reason for events in our lives because we want to learn what God is teaching us through experiences that He allows. Even before knowing the reason, or even if we never know the reason, we find comfort knowing that there is a reason.

Letting God Be God

Human pride is at the heart of refusing to acknowledge God. Pride is the refusal to submit ourselves as creatures before God. Our foolish human pride leads us to make ourselves *god substitutes.* Paul described those who would not acknowledge God in Romans: "For although they knew God, they neither glorified him as God nor gave thanks to him, but their thinking became futile and their foolish hearts were darkened. Although they claimed to be wise, they became fools …" (Romans 1:21-22). Paul correctly associates the act of ignoring God with futility, foolishness, and thanklessness.

The last part of the verse at the head of this chapter states, "in all your ways acknowledge him, and he will make your paths straight" (Proverbs 3:6). That is the *New International Version* translation. However, an interesting change was made in the publication of *Today's New International Version*. In this translation, that same verse says, "in all your ways *submit to* him, and he will make your paths straight" (Proverbs 3:6, emphasis mine). Acknowledgement of God requires the conscious act of becoming submissive to Him. When we acknowledge Him, and recognize Him and His authority, we do the appropriate thing; we submit to Him. Keep this in mind as you read the rest of this chapter. Throughout this chapter, I use the word *acknowledge*, but the biblical concept is closely associated with *submission*.

We will have a much more fruitful life if we recognize God, admit our weaknesses, confess our sins, and live with the reality of the existing God, His authority in our lives, and His power to bless. More importantly, we must realize He is the only One who can give meaning to life. If we do not acknowledge God, we abandon the hope for a meaningful life. We attempt

> We either abandon control and gain purpose, or strive for control and sacrifice any real meaning in events going on around us.

to be content with or pretend to ignore the meaninglessness of life that does not acknowledge God. A meaningless life is not real life. The mere physical existence of biological life is not life. Ignore God and endure meaninglessness. Acknowledge God and find meaning.

By not believing in God or His reasons, we are refusing to acknowledge God's involvement in our lives. This can force us into the dangerous, dense forest of purposeless fate. Some, in their pride, prefer the dangerous, dense forest. In that world, they get to be god. Nevertheless, in supposedly gaining control over their lives, they suffer a greater loss — the loss of meaning that stems from purpose.

Instead of choosing a purposeless fate, it is far superior to choose humility. Humility is the best response for a weak human before an almighty God. It leads to the solid footing of knowing God is sovereign. We either abandon control and gain purpose or strive for control and sacrifice any real meaning in events going on around us. The wise will forsake their insistence on control. In releasing God to be God, they rest in His lofty, sovereign purposes and find life's meaning.

Acknowledging God and Experiencing Dominion

Our family owns an undeveloped and overgrown property in a very remote area. My wife and I recently camped there and worked hard clearing paths through the extremely thick and thorny brush. I never, under normal circumstances, would choose to do that difficult work for anybody at any price. The hot sun, bugs, bees, sore hands, prickly branches, sweat, sore muscles, and hard stony ground under our tent during the cold nights would be too much pain to deal with on a daily basis. However, the pride we felt in owning, sawing, and chopping to cut a value-adding path made us ready, even eager, to overcome those difficulties. The task became a challenging *extreme sport*. When we *own* a project and see its meaningfulness, we endure inconvenience much more successfully.

> Accomplishments we make by being a servant under God are far greater than what are possible when you are in control without Him.

The same principle applies to the dominion we sense in working with God as His servant under His authority. Even before we reach our eternal state, we are here on Earth already building His eternal kingdom. If we merely work to live biologically or live only for ourselves, we miss this dynamic. If we are living to do God's work, living to accomplish a kingdom-related noble purpose, we gladly endure the difficulties that may arise in choosing a purposeful life.

I concluded Chapter Twelve with remarks about those unfortunate people who worked merely to live. We were created to aspire for more significance than that. Acknowledging God leads us to realize our Creator gave us dominion on the earth. Discovering this essential aspect of our created nature — exercising some form of dominion and self-expression — gives us the dignity and self-worth of accomplishment. Understanding the dominion aspect of our human nature as we acknowledge God actually enables us to do much more than we otherwise would. The accomplishments we make by being a servant under God are far greater than what are possible when you are in control without Him. Vice-regency under *Him* is paramount if we want to be at our best. It is essential to be the *junior* partner if the partnership with God is to involve Him at His best.

Acknowledging God as a Courtesy to Him

The other day, a burning log fell off the grate and rolled onto the hearth but not onto the carpet. I might have thought it was just luck, but it was written in Proverbs 3:6 to acknowledge God and recognize His involvement to protect our home. Instead of thinking the incident was mere chance, I chose to acknowledge God as my Protector. My wife often expresses thanksgiving to God even when she finds a good parking place. She has learned to acknowledge God, appreciating His attention to the particulars in her life. She does not ignore, minimize, or fail to be conscious of His favor. Being thankful to God is being courteous to Him.

When someone walks into the room, we acknowledge him or her. We are courteous even if it is with just a nod. When we ignore someone, we insult him by acting as though he were not there. We may try to excuse ourselves for not acknowledging the person in the room because our attention was temporarily focused on other things. Treating people like that is, at best, impolite.

We must learn to ignore *other* things, not God.

If we are ignoring God, it is because we are focusing on the wrong things. To pretend as though God were not there or that He were not involved in our affairs is to ignore Him. Too many times, we are unthinkingly impolite to God. We must learn to ignore other things, not God.

We are each special to God. It is not embarrassing to say, "I'm special," because in the same breath we can add, "And you are special." I am special, but I am no more special than anyone else is since each of God's children is special. If we are each special to God, ignoring Him is even more discourteous; our acknowledgment of Him is even more satisfying to Him.

God Entices Us to Pursue Him

During my years at ORU, for one week each March I added 16 hours to my regular schedule by teaching our Doctor of Ministry students. One year, during that hectic week of shuttling between two buildings and juggling two separate teaching programs, our washing machine water hose burst and sprayed water everywhere! Our laundry room, breakfast nook, and kitchen were all under water that caused us to remove a recently installed floor. Two days later, the ignition switch in my car stopped working, stranding me in the grocery store parking lot. How did I interpret these things? I looked for a God-acknowledging way to respond to the difficulties I was experiencing. Could I find God's fingerprints? Hoses break. Ignition switches malfunction.

During that already unusually busy week compounded by minor setbacks, I chose to acknowledge God by trusting Him and allowing Him to hold me steady through the recovery and repair process. As I submitted to God and the circumstances that He allowed, He made my paths straight. He worked with us to bring our house and car back to normal. We survived! So far, the greatest consolation I have found is that my faith in God is tough enough so the problems I face in life do not threaten it. Another benefit of facing hardships is that we gain a chance to develop patience and perseverance through these very difficulties.

> God works secretly, not because He does not want our thanks or to be known, but because *He likes to let us be the discoverers*.

God plays hide and seek with us. He conceals Himself and we look for Him. Even though He is invisible, our faith tells us that He is there in spite of what our circumstance may seem to be saying. With our eye of faith, we grasp that He is doing something; we value His hidden activity in our affairs; we recognize His handiwork; we perceive His sovereignty; and we seek to understand His plans. Such a view allows us to detect His presence, find the hidden good, discover the hints of His involvement, and redefine what people call "coincidences."

This is all possible for the believer who is determined to acknowledge Him in all his ways. God likes to be the anonymous donor — the Secret Doer of good. God works secretly, not because He does not want our thanks or to be known but because He likes to let us be the discoverers. He knows it is more fun to discover something than to be told about it; the Master Teacher likes to keep His students active in a constant state of learning by discovery.

Christian character and its virtues flow from our acknowledgement of God. Strength, humility, brokenness, and love for Him are all possible in their purest form because we acknowledge who God is, what He is like, and what He wants us to be like. We cannot love the One we do not acknowledge. By acknowledging God, "we know that in all things, God works for the good of those who love him" (Romans 8:28). Acknowledging God directly affects our interpretation of everything that happens around us. We will look for the good in the bad, the silver lining in the dark cloud. I would not want to outlive my ability to acknowledge God since it is He who gives meaning to life. Life is meaningless unless we acknowledge Him.

Celebration of God

For therapeutic purposes, sometimes counselors recommend that a counselee prayerfully imagine a scene or situation from his or her past and ask God to reveal how He was quietly present in it. As God answers this prayer, the counselee is able to understand how Jesus was involved in past events. We, too, can review our past as God reveals it to us and realize that He works even when we are unaware of his presence. Acknowledging God, even long after the fact, means that we recognize that He was an active part of our past. By examining and learning from our past and then acknowledging God's past involvement in our lives, we can have confidence in whatever the future brings.

> Acknowledging God, even long after the fact, means that we recognize that He was an active part of our past.

Looking over my own life, I have had no trouble *picturing* God as my Daddy, holding me as His little boy, pulling me close in an all-encompassing hug. I was lost in His embrace. I could easily visualize my heavenly Dad with His arm around my shoulders as He led me through my teen and early adult years. His strong arm was guiding and protecting me, showing me how to develop the unique gifts and skills He gave me. Today, as an older adult, my Dad is still there with His arm around my shoulders guiding and protecting me as He did when I was younger. He encourages me and allows me to explore, express, and fulfill the creativity He gives me as I walk the path of providing a godly service.

Looking into the future, I can readily envision Him supporting me as I age by helping me to avoid the boulders and ruts in the path. During this time, whether I am strong, stooped and weak, or even when I stumble, He will be there; and I can lean on Him for strength and support to press on. One day, I may grow so weak that I will not be able to continue. At that time, He will be there, easing my body down to rest — not collapsing in failure but gently reclining me to rest when the task is finished. In that same moment, He will take my spirit to be with Him forever, and then the permanent, eternal state will begin for me.

We can both visualize and celebrate Father God's involvement throughout those stages of our lives. Acknowledging Him gives us peace about our past, present, and future, bringing a sense of design and purpose to our lives. Leaving Him out of the *photograph* we see in our mind robs us of seeing the complete picture that is only possible when we *see* the quietly invisible Participant. Who would want to miss seeing the true picture? He is very active in the scene and is, in fact, the most important character in it!

Celebrate God! God is actually everywhere, but sometimes we do not have a constant, conscious awareness of His presence. Having constant conversations with Him in our minds helps us practice His presence in our lives. By doing this, we honor God even when we are not specifically setting time aside to pray. Quietly speaking and listening to Him is one approach to acknowledging Him in all our ways. He *is* with us; and He likes it when we *acknowledge* that He is with us. Welcoming God into every moment of our life is a way to celebrate God and is one of the higher forms of acknowledging Him.

Some dimensions of life require unique skills or even special training in order for us to fully value and implement them. For example, those who study music appreciation have learned how to appreciate the full value of music. They hear the melodies, harmonies, rhythms, contrasts, and recurring themes that others may miss. In much the same way, the paragraphs of this chapter are a short course on God appreciation. If we reflect on these thoughts, we can train ourselves to appreciate God and His participation in our professional and personal lives. When we learn to appreciate the value of God's symphony played out in the score of our daily activities, the melody in our heart is music to God's ears!

Focusing on the Best

In our life, there are good things other than God — for example, things like food, shelter, clothing, work, and beauty. However, they will always be inferior to Him. If our focus on those other things distracts us from our focus on God, then that center of our attention has become an obstacle. In order to acknowledge God perfectly, we must learn to focus on Him, not on distractions. The best thing on Earth, even though it may be good, is not as good as God. Good things can become obstacles that distract our focus from God.

Everyone's life is a mixture of good and bad things. However, *the things* we choose to focus on make a great difference. If we focus on negative things, life fulfills negative expectations — bad things happen, and we become more negative. If we concentrate on positive things, our focus becomes a self-fulfilling prophecy — good things happen, and we become more positive. "Something good is going to happen" is not a trivial phrase; it is a powerful statement full of faith. Focus on the good and good happens. Acknowledge God's goodness in all your circumstances, and He will make your paths straight. That is not pop psychology — that is the Bible!

The person who acknowledges God with celebration is in tune with the reality that there is a good God. The person who ignores God disconnects with reality since a good God *is* a part of reality. Ignoring Him does not change either His existence or goodness. Disregarding Him only leads to unnecessary pessimism, hopelessness, and confusion because without Him, there is no hope. Though none of us is really without Him, *if we do not acknowledge Him*, we choose to live beneath our privileges *as though* He were not there.

> "Something good is going to happen" is not a trivial phrase; it is a powerful statement full of faith.

Not only is having faith in God more productive, it is also more consistent with the reality of God's ever-present and available (though hidden) goodness, power, and wisdom. Discounting these true and beautiful attributes is foolish. Knowing that good is available, praying for it, and eventually receiving answers to prayer are part of a good life. We live with less than we might have when we neither pray nor experience the available good — or only pray a little and experience only a little good — when so much is available.

You make your best decisions when you consider all available information. When you need to make one of life's decisions, put God's available help on the discussion table. The impossible is possible for Him. When you cannot, He can. If it will not work for you, He can make it work. You must give your best attention to nothing less than the best.

It is as simple as this: praying makes good sense. Being optimistic is reasonable since God answers prayers. That is not fiction; it is fact. Prayer makes a difference — a lot of difference.

Situation-Specific Responses

If we acknowledge God, how do we act upon it in specific situations? We never know when a particular type of situation will develop. Therefore, it is best to plan in advance how we will react to that kind of situation. For example, if I had known to prepare ahead for the sudden appearance of pornography, I could have turned the switch off immediately. We must respond to specific circumstances as they develop, one step at a time. I call them *situation-specific responses*. A God-acknowledging response is available in any situation; the right way is to involve God appropriately and meaningfully in any kind of moment.

A situation-specific response is the appropriate human response to what is happening at any given time. Recognizing God's involvement and working with the circumstances we are given is the appropriate response. If we are in the habit of acknowledging God, eventually we learn to recognize what He is doing and seek to work *with Him* even in difficult circumstances in order to accomplish His will. Having this positive attitude helps us to relax and enables us to flow along with the situation and the One who allowed it.

> A situation-specific response is the appropriate human response to what is happening at any given time. It means to recognize God's involvement and work with the circumstances we are given.

On the other hand, other situations exist in which God will lead us to pray, fight, or work *against* our circumstances. It all comes down to seeking God to know His mind and to do His will. In every circumstance, we should seek to submit to *God* whether it means we submit to or prayerfully resist *circumstances*; the point is we acknowledge God, find His purpose, and work with Him.

In Proverbs 3:6, we read, "... *in all your ways* acknowledge him, and he will make your paths straight" (emphasis mine). This passage does not tell us how to do this in every specific situation. Yet, Paul tells us God is involved in every situation. He says, "... *in all things* God works for the good of those who love him, who have been called according to his purpose" (Romans 8:28, emphasis mine). The writings of Solomon and Paul converge. Solomon says, "Acknowledge Him *in all your ways,"* and Paul says, "God is working *in all things.*" God is working for good, and we honor Him to acknowledge that.

God is working "for the good," He is doing it in ways consistent with His wisdom and power. God's motive is to bring good, His method of doing that is wise, and He is working powerfully to make it happen. Nevertheless, we still lack specific instruction for what we are to do even though Solomon and Paul instruct us to acknowledge God and to know that He is at work in every specific situation.

Following these steps will enhance your acknowledgement of God.

1. Thank Him.

When we see the good that God is doing, we should thank Him. Acknowledging God — from seeing open parking spaces to protecting us from burning logs — contributes to the healthy attitude of rejoicing when we see God at work. Thanking Him is easy because we see the good.

However, are we thankful about the times when we do not see Him at work? By faith, we should still be inclined to give thanks and resist the urge to complain. We know God is dependable and He will always do something good even when circumstances are evil. "Always giving thanks to God the Father for everything, in the name of our Lord Jesus Christ" (Ephesians 5:20). "And whatever you do, whether in word or deed, do it all in the name of the Lord Jesus, giving thanks to God the Father through him" (Colossians 3:17).

2. Glorify and Praise God.

When we acknowledge God, we try to see through the surface dust to the gold beneath. We search for and find reasons to glorify God whatever the circumstance. What we look for, we find. Paul and Silas, in the jail at Philippi, praised God even in a bad situation because they knew how to acknowledge God. Their praise was true praise; they saw the gold through the dust. We can read in the Book of Acts that Paul and Silas praised God and God opened the jail doors. Paul and Silas did not have that story to read, yet they praised God because they loved God and saw the value of praising Him. Praising God is what people who acknowledge God do.

3. Ask for Wisdom.

"If anyone of you lacks wisdom, he should ask God, who gives generously to all without finding fault, and it will be given to him" (James 1:5). There are times in our lives, when we need special wisdom to interpret what God is doing in our difficult circumstances, and He graciously urges us to ask for it. And, just in case we might not be certain, James kindly reminds us that God "gives generously to all without finding fault" (James 1:5). When you need wisdom, ask for it.

4. Pray, Sing, or Call for the Elders.

James mentions three situations — trouble, happiness, and sickness — while instructing his readers what to do in each situation. "Is any one of you in trouble? He should pray. Is anyone happy? Let him sing songs of praise. Is any one of you sick? He should call the elders of the church to pray over him." (James 5:13-14). This is simple advice: When you are in trouble, pray. When you are happy, give praise. When you are sick, call the elders and ask them to pray for you.

5. Obey God.

Obeying God may be a little more difficult to practice though not any harder to understand. If we acknowledge God, we will recognize both His authority and His wisdom and then obey Him. "Acknowledge and take to heart this day that the Lord is God in heaven above and on the earth below. There is no other. Keep his decrees and commands, which I am giving you today, *so that it may go well with you* and your children after you and that you may live long in the land the Lord your God gives you for all time" (Deuteronomy 4:30-31, emphasis mine). This passage emphasizes that acknowledgment and obedience have a positive result: *things will go well when we obey God.*

6. Surrender to God.

Acknowledging God means to surrender all areas of our lives to Him. Sometimes we are stubborn, self-willed, or resistant to God. Yet the Father desires acknowledgment in all aspects of our lives and He wants all aspects of our lives to go well.

7. Give to God.

We should give God our affections, time, talents, treasures, and self. Whatever I give to God is more mine after I give it to Him than when I cling to it for myself. What I cling to for myself here on Earth passes away. What I give to Him is what I take with me to the next life.

8. Trust God.

Some people may distrust Him because they have never opened themselves to experience His trustworthiness. Once, while suffering the physical consequences of a forty-day fast, I recall, in my weakness and pain, dancing before the Lord because of what I anticipated. I chanted in cadence, "This condition is temporary. My body will regain strength. God is going to do a great work!" It is proper to believe the believable, appreciate the beautiful, praise the praise-worthy, and enjoy the enjoyable, and so we trust Him Who is trustworthy.

9. Accept *God's* Answers.

We insult God when we refuse to accept His answers to prayer just because they are different from what we requested. If we acknowledge God in *all our ways*, we let Him be God and answer as He sees fit.

To review, the first part of this chapter highlights that the newer Bible translation uses "submit to" rather than "acknowledge." Accepting God's answers requires submission. By acknowledging God, we express the fact that we are conscious of Him *as He is*. When we admit that *our* objectives are different from *God's*, it is time for *us* to change *our* objectives and join *God*. Submissive praying produces the conditions for God to work in us, which allows Him to make our paths straight and establish His Kingdom.

As we spend more time in prayer and strive more earnestly *to pray what He wants*, our acknowledgement of Him increases even in the hours when we are not praying. A stronger prayer life places God at the center, and He becomes more consciously present to us. Then, and only then, we will learn to move with Him more perfectly.

Each situation-specific response listed above is done one step at a time. If we walk on the water, we have to deal with the water, one wave at a time. Even on dry ground, Christians who walk closely with their Lord still have to keep pace with Him, one step at a time.

Keep praying. Keep trusting. Keep taking the next step and God will keep doing "immeasurably more" in your life. Prayer is answered more because of Who God is rather than because you are so good at praying. Watch for the surprises — *and enjoy them.*

CHAPTER FOURTEEN

Full Circle Back to Africa

> *"Now to him who is able to do immeasurably more*
> *than all we ask or imagine, according to his*
> *power that is at work within us, to him be glory*
> *in the church and in Christ Jesus throughout*
> *all generations, for ever and ever! Amen."*
>
> *Ephesians 3:20-21*

I n the previous chapter, I reflected on reasons to pray, but in this final chapter, I will expand on something different. Jesus told stories as an effective way to teach. I will follow His example by sharing a few personal stories. I hope you can learn something from them.

A Six-Year-Old Invalid Prays a Big Prayer — and Receives an Even Bigger Answer

In June of 1950, I had just finished my kindergarten year. Within days, at the age of five, I was diagnosed with rheumatic fever. This disease affects the heart valves, which can sometimes lead to permanent damage. In order to give my heart time to normalize, I was required to lie flat on the bed all summer long. My doctor told me not to walk or even sit up.

Our old family radio was a good friend to me in those days. I still recall listening to the Wilson's radio program called *Sunshine Hour*. They sang Christian music and gave a brief teaching from the Bible. I remember listening to a beautiful, popular song about waking up in the morning on Mockingbird Hill. However, my favorite song was *Today's the Day the Teddy Bears have Their Picnic.*

> If you go out in the woods today,
> you're in for a big surprise.
> If you go out in the woods today,
> you'd better wear a disguise.
> For every bear that ever there was,
> is gathered there for certain because,
> today's the day the teddy bears have their picnic.

As the summer months passed, many visitors came to our house to pray for me. My dear, hard-working parents were starting a church. My mother was pregnant and later gave birth to my younger sister that summer, just three days after my sixth birthday. My dad dripped sweat and gobbled salt tablets as he moved from press to press in the rubber plant in order to make a living, all while he tried to do God's work. As the hours, days, and weeks slowly passed, my muscles grew weaker and weaker from not being used.

Toward the end of the summer, I received my second electrocardiogram. Eventually, my doctor told me that I could get up and start walking again. My first step was too long, and I can still remember tumbling right over. I had no control of my weak legs, and I had completely lost my sense of balance. My grandmother taught me to walk again by standing me against the brick wall on our front porch. She patiently instructed me how to maintain balance by simply standing still then slowly shifting my weight from one leg to the other and moving each foot forward only a few inches at a time. She taught me how to walk by teaching me to move slowly, taking one step at a time.

I started first grade one month late and was required to take a nap during the time the other children were enjoying recess. At that young age, I had no real understanding of how my physical condition was hindering my social and educational development. I only knew that I wanted to do what the other boys in class were doing.

During those months, I inwardly lamented my weakened, physical condition. After coming directly home from church one day, without stopping to play, I pulled a dining room chair out into the middle of the living room and knelt alone to pray. I prayed that after I turned seven years old — the qualifying age for boys to go on the YMCA hike — I would be able to go with them.

I do not remember how many weeks or months passed between the time I prayed that prayer and the day of my seventh birthday. However, as my birthday approached in the summer of 1951, I realized that the weekly YMCA hike was the same date as my birthday. I proceeded with the formalities of showing the YMCA leaders that I would be seven. On my seventh birthday, after breakfast, I took my lunch and walked to the YMCA, hiked with the other boys, and returned home tired but happy.

I went hiking with the other boys precisely the day I turned seven!

Even as a young boy, I was deeply impressed with the accuracy in the timing of God's answer to my prayer. I went hiking with the other boys precisely the day I turned seven! Two years later, I won a first-place ribbon in the first-, second-, and third-grade boys' 50-yard dash at the Garfield Elementary School Summer Playground Annual Contest. My father told me later that he had wept with joy. For me, though, the hike was the big event. It was my first experience of the power of prayer — my own prayer.

A College Sophomore Learns the Power and Influence of Regular Prayer

In August 1962, I left home and entered Mount Vernon Bible College in Mount Vernon, Ohio. I was a bit of a rascal my freshman year. However, during the summer of 1963, between my freshman and sophomore years, my dad wrote a letter to me suggesting that I begin the habit of praying one hour a day. This has always been a curious thing to me because, to my knowledge, Dad did not have a regular time of serious prayer. Furthermore, I am not aware that he made this suggestion to any of my siblings. Yet, God used that letter to start me on a life-impacting habit.

Also in the summer of 1963, I turned 19, and read Elizabeth Elliot's *Through Gates of Splendor*. In the book, she tells how her husband loved and read the Bible. I decided that I would follow

Dad's suggestion for prayer and Jim Elliot's example for Bible reading. I began to pray an hour each day and read the Bible for an additional hour. Within months, I doubled my prayer time. I, more or less, maintained that prayer pattern until I began to experiment with praying four hours a day on July 9, 2002.

As I began my new praying routine in 1963, I realized that I needed to think of things for which to pray to ensure I was doing something constructive during my hours in prayer. I prayed for each of the teachers in the Bible College. I prayed for each of the students. I spent particular time praying for each of the new students — especially that they would find employment since most of us were working our way through college. It was in the fall of that year that I met Char. I do not think she would have been interested in me if it were not for the changes that God had made in me because of my time alone with Him.

> My time alone with God affected the way I thought — He rubbed off on me.

My time alone with God affected the way I thought — He rubbed off on me. What concerned Him began to affect me. I have found, since then, that this healthy, wholesome process delights God. In prayer, we pray that the kingdom of God will come and that His will be done on Earth as it is in heaven, which ultimately serves him and benefits others. Therefore, another advantage of time spent alone with God is that we change in character by associating with such Good Company.

My natural intensity focused on something good, something that was worth being the center of my attention. I have always been intense, but now I was earnestly seeking God. I felt that my passion had a noble purpose. This passion still holds true for me today. It was God's blessing that in the summer of 1963, my daily time in the presence of God caused a significant change in me. I even heard through the grapevine that students who had returned to school that fall commented among themselves about the difference they saw in me. Prayer changes *things*. Prayer also changes *us*.

Financial Miracles Moving Us toward Africa

In my book, *Habits of Highly Effective Christians,* and in earlier chapters here, I told many personal stories of how God has used and answered the increased prayer in my life. Many miracles have occurred along the way. As I write in 2007, to our surprise, God is doing even greater things. These blessings, however, have developed through difficult twists and turns of events. In Chapter Four, I made a reference to how we walk on water. The following is how God responded to our earnest prayers.

In 2005, an organization for international missions offered Char and me positions that would have opened ministry doors to many parts of the world for both of us. We were excited about that and felt God was leading us to accept the offers. I resigned positions at ORU and the Tulsa Chinese Christian Church. We began to make relocation plans, along with everything else that goes with them. However, in February 2006, the organization withdrew our offers. We were heart-broken. Why was God placing us on another job-related roller coaster ride?

Several days later, we explained our tragic situation to a pastor friend. We also expressed to him our long-term buried desires to return to the mission field. And as we discussed the fact that we were without jobs, we realized we were now free to follow our hearts! We then told him about our relationship with the World Mission Centre (WMC) headquartered in Pretoria, South Africa. This fine networking organization had coordinated my two ministry trips to Madagascar for pastors' conferences. Our pastor friend understood that we did not want to go to Africa if we were only motivated by our disappointment. He comforted and encouraged us.

A frantic, hurried search for just anything that looks like a fruitful ministry opportunity is not a good method for carefully finding the will of God. We wanted *the* plan, not *a* plan. We kept praying.

Looking back, many miracles have occurred since the international missions offer was withdrawn and we decided not to reverse the process of resigning at ORU. These miracles have confirmed the rightness of our decision to go to Africa. Some of those miracles include such things like receiving sufficient long-term financial commitments to cover our room and board while abroad; receiving an offer to buy our house in Tulsa; and being offered storage for our furniture at no cost. All of these "gifts" are good for as long as we are in Africa.

More miracles continued. Within days, the WMC told us that they would be willing to coordinate travel and conferences in Africa if we wanted to do that full-time. Additionally, the mission that initially decided not to engage our services graciously gave us funds to bridge us through the time between the discontinuation of my salary at ORU and our arrival in Pretoria, South Africa. My website manager offered to waive the maintenance expense for my two websites for the duration of our years in Africa. A technically gifted friend offered to help us select laptop computers and set up our high-speed and wireless Internet connections. An anonymous donor gave a gift to our work, now called the African Pastors Training (APT) Project, which was large enough for us to purchase a vehicle and home furnishings in Pretoria. Lastly, a professional financial advisor recommended that, since I was qualified, I could retire early—three years before age 65—and could begin to receive Social Security benefits.

Network Miracles Also Moving Us toward Africa

Networking with groups of ministers, ministries, and organizations is extremely important to a foreign missionary. Our objective was not just to go to Africa, but to join hands and hearts with God's people, His laborers. In doing so, we will contribute to the development, education, and empowerment of thousands of pastors. We want to serve and help them become influential, effective, successful, and fruitful.

On five of the previous six annual ministry trips abroad, I had traveled to multiple nations in Africa. When I contacted the WMC to tell them of our desire to train pastors in Africa, I asked them if they would be willing to help coordinate our conferences and activities. The WMC told me that they receive more invitations to conduct pastors' conferences than they can accept, and they were happy to have us join them in this work.

To be someone new, you have to do something new.

In the weeks that followed, we met many fine people who were involved in ministry in Africa. Some of these were new contacts while others were friends of friends, missionaries, and nationals from across Africa. What is even more extraordinary is that I did not know that this network even existed until I started making trips to Africa in 2000. Char and I had no idea that our newly found relationships would eventually lead us to travel from nation to nation as we teach pastors full time. I only know that in July 2002, during my second trip to Africa, I opened myself to something new when I doubled my prayer time as an experiment to see what God would do. The experiment continues to this day. To be someone new, you have to do something new.

For the past 10 years, our home, cars, positions, and social networks in the United States have been very nice. However, the glory cloud is on the move again, and you just do not mess with glory! If it were my own, selfish decision, I would be tempted to remain at ORU and TCCC. When I think of our move to Tulsa from Beijing 10 years earlier, I remember tearfully leaving the mission field. However, I also recall how we modified our lifestyle to include cars, carpeted floors, and enjoyed a quiet place that was our own, and how we quickly adjusted! I also distinctly remember, however, that my level of personal happiness did not rise with these conveniences. We had been just as happy on our bicycles in the noisy, crowded, and exhaust-filled streets of Beijing while living in concrete apartments. Personal happiness does not depend on life's conveniences as much as on one's attitude toward God-given tasks. We are anxiously waiting to serve alongside our brothers and sisters in the nations of Africa's sub-Sahara region.

> **Personal happiness does not depend on life's conveniences as much as on one's attitude toward God-given tasks.**

Earlier, I shared a rapid succession of miracles. Char and I are "walking on water" and yet we are just getting started in Africa. The transition from Tulsa to Pretoria has forced us to look intently to Jesus. I do not dare focus on the impossible circumstances. I do not ever want to take my eyes off Jesus. I want to maintain my concentration on Him. In addition, I am eager to discover what else will happen if I stay serious about prayer.

Several Conclusions to Consider

In this book, I invite you to experiment with prayer. You may be wondering, "Where do I go from here?" If testing prayer seems like too big of a risk to you, I believe it is a risk that you cannot afford *not* to take. Take some steps. Move forward. The following thoughts may help you advance on your path of increased fruitfulness.

Ask God how much, when, and how He wants you to pray. He is the one you serve. He cares so much about the expansion of your influence through increased prayer that He is very happy to help. As you ask God, the Holy Spirit will show you how you should seek God earnestly. Do not feel any obligation to duplicate another's prayer pattern — get your instructions directly from God.

Experiment with prayer. God is not threatened by our attempts to learn something new through experimentation. He is happy when we care enough about our growth to try *doing* something new in order to *be* something new.

Keep growing. We do not intentionally level off as years pass; we want to keep growing. So, to avoid being lulled into complacency, consider the possibility of *doing* something different in order to *be* somebody different.

Seize the opportunities. The needs and opportunities of our generation are great. Prayer is a much more constructive and fruitful alternative to just wringing our hands and sighing about how bad things are getting.

Seek his blessings. God is good. He does not reluctantly grant the few blessings He must. Rather, He eagerly listens to our prayers and gives far more than we can imagine. God wants us to learn how to pray effectively and efficiently in order to bear much fruit.

Do more. God does more when we do more. Try it. Though the way God works will always involve the mysterious element, it does appear that when we do more, so does He. A link exists between our action and His; our prayer releases God to work.

Get tough. Be tenacious in prayer. Persistence, perseverance, patience, passion, self-control, and steadfastness are all good qualities that will help you on your way.

Open your heart and mind. Determine God's will and pray accordingly. God has an opinion about your prayer concern — let Him show you what to pray.

Prioritize God in your life. Make your relationship with God through prayer the central, most important aspect of your life. If you do, you will have no regrets when your earthly life is over and your accomplishments are measured by an eternal yardstick. Acknowledge God in all your ways, in every circumstance. Pray about anything and everything. If something is worth your involvement, it is worth your prayer.

See your own results. Do not compare your fruitfulness with that of others. Rather compare your present fruitfulness with your former fruitfulness. This is how to determine if your increased prayer is making you more fruitful.

A Few Final Thoughts

We can divide our time as humans into the two categories of decision and implementation: deciding and doing; dreaming and accomplishing. Great feats and marvelous projects are possible as long as we keep these two functions separate, make good decisions, and act accordingly. If we decide well, then we act well. Life, therefore, is a matter of implementing decisions.

Before you can do anything valuable, first you must make a good decision. The process of making good decisions involves careful investigation, evaluation, obtaining sufficient information, weighing the alternatives, and then making the correct choices. The prudent person will not become busy doing anything until he has first carefully thought his way through to an informed decision. Many problems develop when we rush into activities without making thoughtful decisions. The Bible commends the doer, but to *do* right, you must first *decide* right.

After the good decision has been made, it is time to implement the choice. Remember, decision and implementation are very different. If we confuse these two, our actions can become clumsy — we become unstable, impulsive, double-minded, and undependable. A good decision can be lost if we repeatedly review the situations too much and later remake the decisions influenced by the mood of another moment. Unless there is new information or the situation significantly changes, do not change the decision.

Both are important — decision and implementation. God commends the doer: "Do not merely listen to the word, and so deceive yourselves. Do what it says" (James 1:22). "Anyone, then, who knows the good he ought to do and doesn't do it, sins" (James 4:17). Jesus taught, "But everyone that hears these words of mine and does not put them into practice is like a foolish man who built his house on sand. (Matthew 7:26).

While I am running, is not the time to decide whether to run or not. This is true whether it is a training run or a race. When I ran marathons, the pain in the balls of my feet traveled to my calves and then to my thighs. My lungs gasped for air and the salty perspiration stung my eyes. My shoulders ached and my whole body longed to lie down and breathe. This process happened throughout the entire race. That, however, was not the time to decide whether to run a marathon. The person who makes a good decision but does not implement it is like the person who hears the Word but does not do it.

By the same token, when an enticing, pornographic picture appears unexpectedly on our monitor screen, it is not the time to decide whether to look at it. Make the decision ahead of time not to look at those types of pictures before they ever appear and determine to stay with that decision if the time comes.

Deciding, then doing, is the same with prayer. Throughout this book, we have talked about the results available with praying more. I hope this has not been just a series of interesting stories, but an encouragement for us to be doers together. Make a good decision about how much you will pray, and then do it.

Acknowledgements

I thank God for the opportunity to experiment in my attempts to know Him and His ways better. My friendship with Him has increased enormously throughout the prayer experiment documented in this book. He has helped me crystallize my opinions throughout the additional adventure of writing about it. Anything good in this book is due to Him. The flaws in it are due to my own inadequacies.

My wife, Char, and our two sons, Dan and Joel, have greatly encouraged me. I thank God for their friendship. Char also helped edit some of the chapters. Most of the ideas developed in this book have been discussed with her over the years of the prayer experiment. She has been a good sounding board, but more than that, she has been a partner with me in learning about prayer. By helping me understand what I was feeling, Char enabled me to better verbalize these ideas.

My friend Millard Parrish, missionary to Kenya and writer, has been a great help to me in the writing process. His understanding of the editing process and his firm grasp of Christian theology and thought make his contribution to this book of great significance. He is a great blessing to the body of Christ.

Matthew McDaniel, a part-time art student who served in the prayer tower at Oral Roberts University, created the drawings used throughout the book. The front cover designer, TJ Pike, captured the idea of rising above the world's problems to spend time with God in prayer. I am grateful to these two gifted men and the godly way in which they used their artistic talents to help the reader visualize some of the concepts developed in the book.

Barbara Wolfer, a friend and English professor, helped in the early stages of the editorial process. Jana Wegner and Michelle Crissup spent many hours editing manuscripts at a later phase. I am grateful for the help of these fine women.

This is my second book to publish with Carrie Perrien Smith and Soar with Eagles. They have been a great publisher to work with both times. Carrie is very patient and persistent in her pursuit of excellence. Her combination of warmth and professionalism makes writing and publishing a book a pleasant process.

Ron Meyers
Pretoria, South Africa

Ron Meyers, PhD

Ron Meyers was born in 1944 and raised in a pioneer pastor's home. In July 1965, he began pastoral ministry as a student pastor in a rural community seventy miles from the Bible College he attended in mid-Ohio.

From 1996 until 2006, he served as the Professor of Missions and Coordinator of the Master of Arts in Missions program in the School of Theology and Missions of Oral Roberts University. During those years, Ron traveled to African, Asian, European, and Middle Eastern nations during his summer breaks from university responsibilities.

He, with his wife, Char, have served more years outside the United States as pastors in Canada and missionaries in Korea, China, and Africa than their years in the U.S. Since January 2007, Ron and Char have lived in Africa and traveled full-time to African nations Conducting Empower Africa Christian Leadership Conferences. Ron has a PhD in Intercultural Studies and Char has an EdD. The Meyers have two adult sons, one daughter-in-law, and eight grandchildren.

ONLINE TOOLS FOR LEADERS

Leadership Empowerment Resources Website

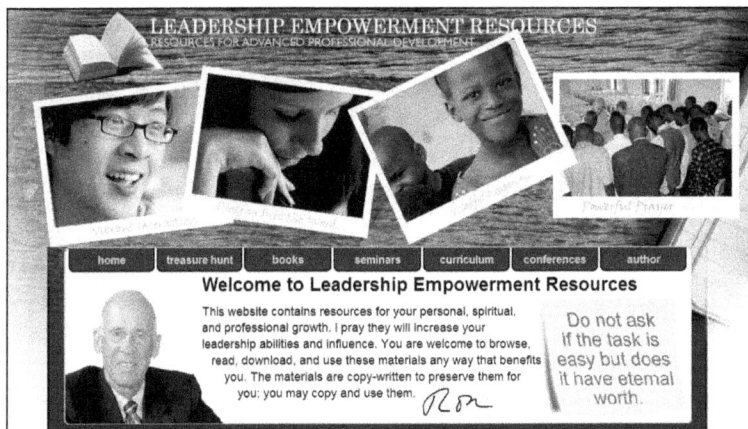

This website provides additional resources for Dr. Meyer's mission work abroad. It includes information on:

Books: Resources written by Ron Meyers for expanding your wisdom and knowledge to use in any way that serves your purpose in helping to enrich the lives of Christians you know

Leadership Empowerment Conferences: Ron and Char Meyers' Africa-based vehicle for strengthening His Church by training the leaders of churches

Treasure Hunt: A Christian conversational game intended to be a catalyst for drawing out practical wisdom and understanding — treasures — from the hearts of Christians who enjoy wholesome conversational fun

Visit the Website

To read the code, download the QR Reader app for your cell phone and scan it.

Habits of Highly Effective Christians Book and Study Guide

Habits of Highly Effective Christians Makes a Great Bible Study Program

When Ron Meyers followed his passion for international missions work forty years ago, he never imagined the rich educational curriculum God had in store for him. A lifetime of spiritual challenges groomed him for his role at the School of Theology and Missions at Oral Roberts University in Tulsa, Oklahoma. Then, after ten years educating Christian ministry candidates at ORU and serving as Coordinator of the Master of Arts in Missions program, he and his wife moved to Africa where they now train pastors and missionaries throughout the southern African nations.

Meyers wrote his book with life application in mind. He weaves his stories into each habit by providing real-life, insightful, and applicable examples. *Habits of Highly Effective Christians* guides you through biblical resources for creating a rich tapestry with the fibers of your own life.

A Great Tool for Growth and Discussion

Proven to create rich discussions, *Habits of Highly Effective Christians* is perfect for small-group Bible studies or college classroom discussions. Meyers has also written the *Habits of Highly Effective Christians Study Guide*. Together, this study combo will etch biblical principles on every aspect of the lives you encounter.

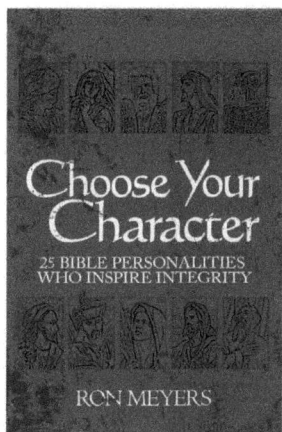

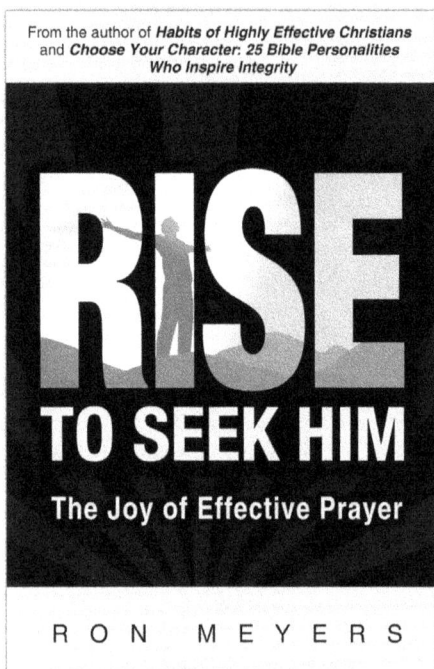

www.ingramcontent.com/pod-product-compliance
Lightning Source LLC
Chambersburg PA
CBHW051955090426
42741CB00008B/1399